The Public Life of
the Fetal Sonogram

Studies in Medical Anthropology

Edited by Mac Marshall

The Public Life of the Fetal Sonogram

Technology, Consumption, and the Politics of Reproduction

JANELLE S. TAYLOR

RUTGERS UNIVERSITY PRESS

NEW BRUNSWICK, NEW JERSEY, AND LONDON

LIBRARY OF CONGRESS CATALOGING-IN-PUBLICATION DATA

Taylor, Janelle S., 1965–
The public life of the fetal sonogram: technology, consumption, and the politics
of reproduction / Janelle S. Taylor.
    p.; cm.— (Studies in medical anthropology)
Includes bibliographical references and index.
ISBN 978–0-8135–4363–5 (hardcover : alk. paper)
ISBN 978–0-8135–4364–2 (pbk. : alk. paper)
  I. Fetus—Ultrasonic imaging—Social aspects. I. Title. II. Series.
    [DNLM: I. Ultrasonography, Prenatal—utilization. 2. Commodification.
  3. Marketing of Health Services. 4. Mothers—psychology.
  5. Ultrasonography, Prenatal—psychology. WQ 209 T243p 2008]
    RG628.3.U58T39 2008
    618.3′207543—dc22

                                               2007051732

A British Cataloging-in-Publication record for this book is available
from the British Library.

Visit our Web site: http://rutgerspress.rutgers.edu

Manufactured in the United States of America

For my parents,
Chuck and Charlene Taylor

CONTENTS

ACKNOWLEDGMENTS

Books share with sonograms the tendency to foster an illusion of independence, where the reality is one of profound reliance on the kindness, help, and active nurturance provided by others. Many people whose presence may not be readily visible in its pages have helped this project reach fruition, and I would like to thank them.

Though I cannot acknowledge them all individually by name, I am deeply grateful to the women, sonographers, and others who have shared with me their thoughts, views, experiences, and their own writings over the years that I have worked on this project. In the community of professionals who work with ultrasound, I would especially like to thank Joan P. Baker, Jeanette Burlbaw, Marveen Craig, Gary Loy, and Jean Lea Spitz. They will not agree with all of the arguments that I set forth and are not responsible for any errors or shortcomings, but any value this work contains owes much to the generosity and openness with which they responded to my many inquiries and requests. I hope that some of the many people who appear in this book will read it, and that they will accept my reflections on their words and their work, as the best form of tribute I know how to offer.

This book began as a dissertation project in sociocultural anthropology at the University of Chicago, and I remain indebted to the remarkable constellation of people I encountered there. In particular, I would like to thank Jean Comaroff, who served as my thesis adviser. As a scholar she is unfailingly incisive, creative, and brilliant; as a mentor and teacher she has also been unfailingly kind, generous, and responsive. I extend sincere thanks as well to other teachers and mentors I encountered at Chicago, especially Arjun Appadurai, Carol Breckenridge, Marilyn Ivy, Mary Mahowald, Marshall Sahlins, and Raymond T. Smith. No less indispensable has been the collegial camaraderie of scholars I first met as fellow students at

Chicago, especially Dan Cook, Ivan Ermakoff, Ilana Gershon, Esther Hamburger, Nancy Henry, Shao Jing, Rachana Kamtekar, Mary Scoggin, Florence Vatan, and my sister-in-law Michele Rosenthal. With gratitude and sadness, I acknowledge as well the late Daphne Berdahl and the late Sharon Stephens, two brilliant women and radiant human beings whom cancer took from us far too early.

In the loosely intersecting fields of medical anthropology, feminist science studies, and the anthropology of reproduction, I have found a vital and vibrant community of excellent scholars, many of whom have become indispensable interlocutors. I would especially like to thank Paul Brodwin, Monica Casper, Sarah Franklin, Linda Layne, Annemarie Mol, Christine Morton, Rayna Rapp, Liz Roberts, and Karen-Sue Taussig. And it is a special pleasure to acknowledge here my warm gratitude to Lynn Morgan and Lesley Sharp. Each has, in her own work, set an example of serious and engaged scholarship that I aspire to emulate, and each has also shown me warm generosity and friendship that have made all the difference.

The community of colleagues and friends closer to home (first in Iowa and then in Seattle) has been equally indispensable. In Grinnell I would especially like to thank Leslie Gregg-Jolly, Johanna Meehan, Minna Mahlab, Alan Schrift, Jill Schrift, and Maura Strassberg. Since moving back to my hometown of Seattle in 1999 I have found at the University of Washington a wonderful community of colleagues, both within and beyond the Department of Anthropology, in whose company it has been easy to thrive as a scholar and as a person. I gratefully acknowledge the collegiality and friendship of Ann Anagnost, Holly Barker, Laada Bilaniuk, Rachel Chapman, Kelly Fryer-Edwards, Sara Goering, Jim Green, Danny Hoffman, Biff Keyes, Celia Lowe, Linda Nash, Arzoo Osanloo, Bettina Shell-Duncan, Helene Starks, Kathleen Woodward, and Lisa Vig. It is a particular pleasure to thank Mimi Kahn and Lorna Rhodes, each of whom in her own way has been an especially vital presence—as scholars whom I respect and admire, as colleagues whom I value, and as dear friends whom I treasure.

I would like to thank series editor Mac Marshall and acquisitions editor Adi Hovav at Rutgers University Press for their wise and careful editorial attention. They have made the book better, and have made the process of improving it a pleasure. Rayna Rapp read the entire manuscript and offered detailed comments, for which I am very grateful. Thanks also to Lynette Miller for granting permission to feature her artwork on the cover.

Neither this book nor anything else in my life would be what it is without the love, humor, support, and intellectual companionship of my husband, Michael Rosenthal. He and those delightful creatures, our children Jacob and Lydia, have, in ways large and small, made possible the work out of which this book emerges. All along, however, not the book but our life together has been the main project. Thank you, my dearest ones.

One regret I have is that my parents will never read these words. My father died in 2005, and my mother is currently living with very advanced dementia. What my parents have given me is too much and too deep to name, much less repay. Such blessings, one must simply strive to deserve. I dedicate this book to them both, with love.

The Public Life of
the Fetal Sonogram

1

Introduction

This book has its origins in a personal encounter with a public fetus.

I was a young woman and aspiring anthropologist in my mid-twenties, concerned with reproductive rights but still far from having children myself and quite unfamiliar with reproductive medicine when, in 1991, I came across an advertisement in *Harper's* magazine that featured a large black-and-white sonogram image of a fetus, over the phrase: IS SOMETHING INSIDE TELLING YOU TO BUY A VOLVO?

What am I to make of *this*, I thought: a *fetus* is trying to sell me a *car*?!

On the most superficial level, of course, the sense of the ad did not take long to decipher: if you are expecting a child, you will want that child to be safe, and so you will want to buy a Volvo, because of its reputation for safety. Yet this equation of the image of the fetus with endangered childhood in need of parental protection was itself a highly political cultural artifact, emerging (as did my reaction to it) from antiabortion uses of the image of the fetus in the context of the U.S. abortion debate.

Coming across this Volvo ad was, for me, one of those small moments when public culture yields up something jarring. Most often, I let them pass with little more than a sarcastic snort, a roll of the eyes, and a bit of private grumbling. Yet such moments of dissonance are like tiny fissures in smooth surfaces of the everyday, through which one can, with effort, sometimes catch oblique glimpses of the human pain, dreams, and struggles that lie behind them. Each snort or grumble bespeaks an impulse toward critique—one that might, if pursued with seriousness and tenacity

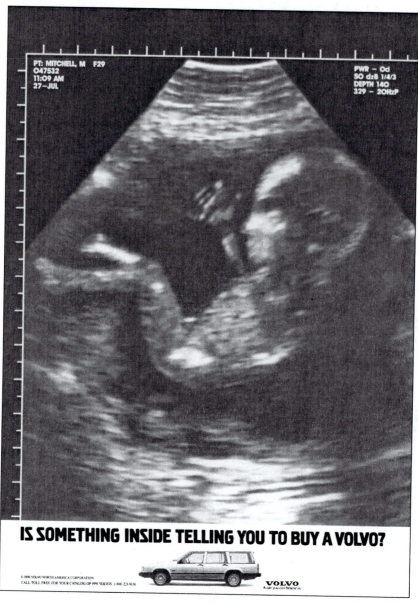

FIGURE 1-1. Advertisement for Volvo cars.

as part of a collective effort, develop into an articulate and compelling new perspective on the world. It is toward such an effort that the Marxist theorist Antonio Gramsci pointed when he wrote that "the healthy nucleus that exists in 'common sense,' the part of it which can be called 'good sense' . . . deserves to be made more unitary and coherent" (Forgacs 2000:329).

I found in medical anthropology both the conceptual and methodological tools and the community necessary to turn that momentary encounter with a piece of mass-cultural ephemera into the starting point for a sustained exploration into the conditions of possibility for its emergence. That meaning is embedded in collective social action is a fundamental insight and premise of sociocultural anthropology. From it follow two crucial corollaries. First, meaning is something that people *create* through social action, and they do so in ways that vary greatly. Second, the meanings that people make *shape* the actions they take, and thus have very real social and material consequences. Ethnography, as a disciplined mode of attending to the relationship between systems of meaning and systems of social action, can document and analyze how these twin processes work together in specific situations. I have put these basic disciplinary insights and commitments into practice to study how sonograms, as a particular kind of "text," are interpreted and used, with very real material and social consequences for people's bodies and lives.

This effort began with an essay reflecting on the Volvo advertisement, published in the then-new transnational cultural-studies journal *Public Culture* (Taylor 1992). In that essay, I argued that the Volvo ad, by employing the ultrasound image, drew upon public cultural deployments of fetal imagery in antiabortion materials, but in a manner designed to channel political passions into purchasing patterns. The Volvo ad, and that first attempt at puzzling it through, piqued my interest in the technology that had produced the imagery featured there, as well as the processes by which a medical imaging technology had become so embroiled with a product advertisement.

As I learned, diagnostic medical ultrasound devices generate information about the density and location of tissues of the body by exploiting the piezoelectric effect (from the Greek term *piezo,* meaning pressure), a very special property possessed by certain crystals. Piezoelectric crystals expand when they are subjected to an electrical field, and release an electrical charge when they are compressed; in other words, they can transform electrical energy into mechanical energy, and vice versa. When an electrical charge applied to a crystal causes a deformation in its surface, this deformation is transmitted into the surrounding substance in the form of a mechanical vibration—a very high frequency sound wave (beyond the range of human hearing, hence the term "ultrasound"). Sound waves propagate only through matter, and the velocity with which they pass through any substance (whether air, water, metal, or human flesh) depends upon its composition. When sound waves traveling through one substance meet the boundary with another substance, there is a change in velocity, and some of the sound energy is at the same time reflected back. The pattern of these returning echoes can thus provide information about the locations and relative densities of different substances encountered by the sound waves.

Ultrasound devices are complex machines specially designed to generate and process such information, which they present in the form of visual images. In the hands of a trained and skilled operator, ultrasound can be used to create visual images of internal bodily structures. Beginning in roughly 1970, ultrasound became an important diagnostic tool in many branches of medicine, but especially in obstetrics. Very quickly, the ability to visualize via ultrasound the fetus, placenta, umbilical cord, and other structures of the womb became central to medical knowledge and care of pregnancy. By the same token, an ultrasound examination became a regular part of the experience of medicalized pregnancy for most women in this country with access to medical care (including those who seek an abortion, as well as those who seek to carry to term). Ultrasound images of the fetus, meanwhile, came to be taken up and used outside the clinical setting, as expectant parents circulated "baby pictures" among networks of family and friends, antiabortion advocates incorporated ultrasound technology and imagery into their materials and tactics, and advertisers enlisted fetal ultrasound images to arouse viewers' hopes and fears and channel them toward consumption. More recently, some entrepreneurs have taken advantage of the increasingly lifelike images made possible by the advent of 3D and 4D imaging devices, opening nondiagnostic "entertainment" ultrasound enterprises that offer pregnant women fancy ultrasound images for a fee and without medical oversight, while antiabortion advocates have pushed to outfit "crisis pregnancy centers" with 3D and 4D ultrasound devices.

I was struck from the first by what seemed to me a curious paradox, of which the Volvo ad was but one manifestation: ultrasound imagery of the fetus was being used *outside* the medical context in ways that seemed to be potentially at odds with the ways ultrasound was being used *within* medical practice. In antiabortion materials, ultrasound imagery of the fetus has been used as evidence that the fetus is really a baby, a person (and that abortion is therefore murder). In medical practice, meanwhile, ultrasound is used as a prenatal diagnostic technology to diagnose a variety of problems with the fetus—for most of which medicine has no treatment to offer other than the option of selective abortion. This led me to ask, "How do the diagnostic functions of ultrasound technology relate to the meanings attached to ultrasound imagery in the broader culture?" And more generally, "How do the medicalized practices of reproduction relate to the politics of reproduction?"

I am, of course, hardly the first to ask what social consequences may follow from technologies designed to peer into or tinker with the body. This is a topic of perennial interest and much concern, in lay as well as scholarly discussions. Technologies that work in and upon the body—including genetic testing, assisted reproduction, cloning, psychopharmaceuticals, cosmetic surgery, and organ transfer, along with ultrasound and other devices that have already become commonplace—are taken by some as a harbinger of progress, and by others as the agent of troubling changes. Many more, meanwhile, regard new technologies with uncertainty and ambivalence, embracing them while also worrying a great deal about what they portend (Elliott 2003).

Such discussions tend often to revolve around the question of how best to predict, assess, or control the "impact" of technology upon society. Thus, some people (especially within the medical field) would argue that the impact of ultrasound has been positive, because it makes available so much more information about the fetus, which enhances physicians' ability to provide good medical care during pregnancy. Some people (especially within the antiabortion movement) regard ultrasound technology as having a positive impact on society, because they believe that the ability to see the fetus can enhance emotional connection with it and lead women contemplating abortion to reconsider. And some people (especially within the feminist health movement) hold that the impact of ultrasound has been negative or at least highly ambiguous because it has contributed to the medicalization of pregnancy and to the conceptualization of the fetus as if it were separate from the pregnant woman who bears it, with troubling implications for women's rights.

What anthropology stands to contribute to these discussions is an approach that proceeds from the insight that health, illness, healing, and medicine do not simply impact upon social life, but are part of it. This very simple insight, that medicine and medical technologies are part of social life, may—if we take it seriously—help us to better understand and more effectively engage ultrasound or the many other medical technologies and procedures that have so rapidly become woven into the fabric of our individual and collective lives. A commitment to pursuing the implications of this insight informs, in a very fundamental way, the ethnographic research that I undertook, seeking to answer my questions concerning the relationship between the diagnostic functions of ultrasound technology, the meanings attached to fetal sonograms in the broader culture, and the role played by ultrasound within the politics of reproduction. Before turning to the details of that research, therefore, I would like to address some of those implications in a bit more depth.

"Technology": Conceptual Hazards and Ethnographic Approaches

Historian Leo Marx in 1997 published an essay titled "Technology: The Emergence of a Hazardous Concept." In this essay, Marx asks when and how the word "technology" emerged in its modern meanings. While "technology" sounds very tangible and concrete, Marx shows that this concreteness is rather illusory and soon dissolves into a series of cultural and historical puzzles. Machines of various kinds have been around for a very long time, but the term "technology" is relatively young and emerged historically in tandem with new kinds of machines embedded within complex systems. Any specific machine or device to which we might point as an example of a "technology" can function only within the context of a large and complicated network that is as much social and economic as it is mechanical and material. A computer, for example, in order to actually work requires an elaborate network of people, institutions, and things: the knowledge of programmers and users, the labor of the workers who assemble and ship and stock and repair them, the legal and business infrastructure that mobilizes capital investment in computing, the infrastructure of electric grids and communications networks, and many other elements. A computer is, then, part of a complex system that includes social, economic, and legal as well as material components—and without them, it would be little more than an expensive paperweight.

So where exactly is the "technology" in all of this? As Leo Marx asks: "Where do we draw the boundary separating the solidly material, technical element of technology from the rest of society and culture" (1997:981)? His answer, of course, is that really there is no such boundary and indeed cannot be, because, as the example of the computer suggests, technology is *part* of social life. The problem with the term "technology," and its variants such as "biotechnology," is that it strongly encourages us to impute the concreteness of the mechanical device to the entire complex of social arrangements within which that device is embedded. Marx explains:

> [Technology] seems "thinglike" when we point to specific objects or techniques as its most visible manifestations, but the discursive power of technology as a term is in large measure attributable to its vague, intangible, indeterminate character—the fact that it does not refer to anything as specific or tangible as a tool or a machine. . . . A significant result of [the] history [of the concept of technology], with its unstable marriage of artifacts and socioeconomic structures, is that the concept of technology is particularly susceptible to reification. To borrow George Lukacs's lucid definition, reification occurs when "a relation between people takes on the character of a thing and thus acquires a 'phantom objectivity.' . . ." A distinctive result of reification observed by Karl Marx . . . is the power exerted by commodities over human beings; in that case social relations between people were mysteriously endowed with an objective, even autonomous character. I believe that something

similar has happened with technology, which has also taken on an objective character, as if it existed independent of its human creators, and is capable of controlling them. (1997:982)

The central problem with the concept of "technology," in other words, is that it encourages us to regard this whole complex system of social relations as being equally fixed and thinglike as the material device in question, and progressively changing along a trajectory quite independent of society. We implicitly adopt just such a framing whenever we ask what the "impact" of some new technology will be on society, or how society should "respond" to it: "To speak, as people often do, of the 'impact' of a major technology like the automobile upon society makes little more sense, by now, than to speak of the impact of the bone structure on the human body" (Marx 1997:981). The concept of technology may be hazardous, then, to cogent thought and effective political action if it leads us to imagine that technology is separate from social life, and in this way hinders our ability to engage with technologies as part of social life.

The first and perhaps the most important implication that follows from this is that that it is not only the tiny group of experts who specialize in producing and working with any particular technology who alone can have anything important to say about it. One can certainly acknowledge and respect the work that physicians and engineers do, and the specialized knowledge they have, without jumping to the unwarranted and troubling conclusion that this very small group of people alone should weigh in on decisions about technology that have broad social implications.

At what stage and in what capacities are other views and voices and values brought into the work of these experts? Too often, ordinary members of the public are presented with a particular device or procedure as a fait accompli and asked to "respond" to it. By that time, the device in question is already embedded within a particular configuration of material infrastructures, legal and social arrangements, and state, capital, and professional investments that is quite dense and not easily disrupted. Design decisions have already been taken that may have enormous consequences for the people who will eventually use it or upon whom it will be used. It becomes far more difficult, once a technology has already been developed to a certain stage, to meaningfully weigh in on the question of whether the purposes that a technology serves, the values embedded within its design, and the pattern of social power relations that it facilitates or upholds are the ones that we ought collectively to endorse. As the political scientist Langdon Winner writes:

> In a world in which human beings make and maintain artificial systems, nothing is "required" in an absolute sense. Nevertheless . . . once artifacts such as nuclear power plants have been built and put in operation, the kinds of reasoning that justify the adaptation of social life to technical requirements pop up as spontaneously as flowers in the spring. . . . In our times people are often willing to make drastic changes in the way they live to accommodate technological innovation while at the same time resisting similar kinds of changes justified on political grounds. (1986:38)

As is shown in the chapters that follow, many important social changes have already taken place around the advent of ultrasound technology. New industries, new forms of work, and new medical professions have sprung up. Physicians have changed how they practice. Whole new fields of medicine have been facilitated, such as fetal surgery (Casper 1998). Millions of fetuses have had their sex prenatally detected and been scanned for possible anomalies, and most of those who exhibited any have been aborted. Millions of women have come to regard prenatal testing and seeing their baby on an ultrasound screen as an integral part of the experience of pregnancy. Vast human, material, and economic resources have already been invested in devices and procedures aimed at detecting (and preventing the birth of) fetuses with disabilities. While all of these dramatic changes have taken place, social inequalities that demonstrably produce health problems have failed to change for the better (Farmer 1999, 2003; Krieger 2005; Navarro 2004). If a new technology can "require" social changes, why cannot change be demanded in the name of justice, for the sake of equality? Approaching technology as part of society invites us to ask such questions and to include the social relations of science, technology and medicine within broader visions of democracy and justice as well as health.

One way that ethnographic research can contribute to reclaiming technology as fully social is to enter the places in which these experts do their work, and show just how fully social and cultural it is. Anthropologists Sarah Franklin and Margaret Lock write:

> Given the importance of avoiding the "impact" model so frequently invoked to address developments in the life sciences—that is, in terms of their "effects upon society" or their "consequences for social life"—it is essential that attention remain focused on what is social about the production of scientific knowledge itself. To undertake this task, it is often necessary to work closely with scientists in the laboratory and the clinic, in order to create interpretations, descriptions, and analytical accounts that document emergent cultural forms. (2003:21)

Scholars in the relatively young field of science studies have by now produced a quite large and provocative body of writings along just these lines.

Part of what such research has documented is just how many other people besides the "experts" any given biotechnology involves. We may tend to associate biotechnology with laboratories, high-tech clinics, and highly educated men in white coats. But the work of any high-status researcher in any lab or clinic actually involves and relies upon many other people. Some of these people work within its walls: bench scientists and technicians, students, clerical and janitorial staff, and others. Playing equally important roles beyond the clinic or laboratory walls are the people who work to assemble, program, repair, sell, and maintain crucial items of equipment. Yet other people serve as the test subjects on whom new devices and procedures are tested, or provide (under varying degrees of coercion and consent) necessary bodily material: cells, tissues, or organs (Landecker 2003, 2007; Scheper-Hughes and Wacquant 2002; Sharp 2001, 2006; Taussig et al. 2003). Consumers or users at whom a particular technology is targeted are also critical (van Kammen 2003). And, last but not least, millions of people subsidize the development of biotechnologies through their taxes, investments, and purchases.

If technology is part of social life, then clearly all of these people are important. To arrive at an adequate understanding of technology requires that we recognize them all, listen to them, learn from them, and find ways of working with them. In my own research, as the following chapters will detail, I have come to recognize the critical role of sonographers, the technicians who work with ultrasound, most of whom are women (at least in the United States). These sonographers are the ones who actually perform ultrasound procedures, and more than this they have all along been actively involved in developing ultrasound equipment, finding new uses for it, and promoting ultrasound technology to physicians, many of whom were at first quite unconvinced they needed it. Sonographers are an important part of the social network of this particular technology. It matters a great deal who they are, what they do, and how they think about what they do. If people committed to feminist and other visions of social justice wish to include biotechnology within efforts toward social change, then a politics must be developed that includes as wide a segment as possible of the entire social network surrounding any particular biotechnology.

"The Body": Conceptual Hazards and Ethnographic Approaches

Since we are concerned here with a technology that is designed specifically to image the body, it is worth pointing out that not only may the concept of "technology" be hazardous in these ways, but so too may the concept of "the body." The concept of "the body" strongly encourages us to treat bodies as existing outside of social life, in nature. *The* body—the singular, universal, unchanging body depicted in anatomy atlases and biology classes—is a pure abstraction, albeit one that both shapes and constrains how we think about and deal with actual individual bodies. Just as with the concept of technology, so too with the concept of the body: our challenge is to resist the tendency toward reification, and instead insist upon framing bodies as *part of social life*. This takes us well beyond the claim that bodies are *shaped* or *conditioned* by social life, such that, for example, some bodies are intentionally marked and modified, some bodies are well nourished while others are stunted by hunger, some bodies are marked by hard labor while others are disciplined by exercise, and so forth. This relatively uncontroversial claim, while not exactly inaccurate, is incomplete in that it leaves intact the idea of "the body" as something upon which social life has an "impact"—which implies, of course, that "the body" is somehow outside social life to begin with.

The feminist theorist Judith Butler has suggested, famously, that "matter" may be understood as "not a site or surface, but a process of materialization that stabilizes over time to produce the effect of boundary, fixity, and surface we call matter" (Butler 1993:9). The important insight contained within this rather abstract pronouncement is that bodies may be understood not only as something that individuals *have* but as something that people collectively *do*—and do in multiple different ways (Mol 2002). The body, we might say, is not so much a thing as an –ing. Not simply the inert objects that mind and culture shape and transform, bodies actually take shape and take place through social practices of all sorts: feeding, legislating, training, cutting, explaining, beating, loving, diagnosing, buying, selling, dressing, and healing, among others.

If some of the practices through which bodies are materialized may fall on one side and some on the other of a magic line dividing representations from realities, this need not—indeed, should not—be construed, in the first instance, as a theoretical problem. Rather, it invites ethnographic inquiry. Such inquiry may, indeed, reveal representations to be not things unto themselves so much as moments in a dialectic linking forms of activity through which bodies are materialized. As scholars in science studies have argued (Pickering 1995), practices of representation do not only involve ideas; they also always entail working with, and on, bodily and other matter. By the same token, such practices not only creatively reorder ideas and meanings, but can reconfigure matter in very consequential ways. The interesting question—the very important question that any careful use of the term "discourse" should signal—is exactly how, in any given instance, representational, social, material and other practices may work together to materialize bodies in very particular ways and within specific kinds of relations.

Such questions cannot be addressed through textual readings of representations alone; they require historical and ethnographic investigation. Just how do particular ways of narrating or imaging bodies relate to particular ways of materially intervening in them? How do both of these, in turn, relate to social mechanisms? How do all of these forms of practice work together to stabilize or unsettle the fixity of bodily surfaces? Who, finally, is empowered to direct such processes, and who is not?[1] Once we conceptualize the body as materializing in and through social practices, new perspectives open up. It becomes possible to recognize bodies as having contours and boundaries that are not simply given by nature, but accomplished through histories of collective human activity and struggle. It becomes possible to *ask*, instead of simply *presuming*, what a body is in a given instance, where its significant surfaces are, and how those surfaces came to be fixed.

The public life of the fetal sonogram seems to demand of us that we ask precisely such questions about "surfacing the body interior" (Taylor 2005). How has ultrasound imaging surfaced the fetal body into public view? This is not simply a matter of technology, but a question of how, socially and culturally, fetuses become public. Fetal sonograms are representations that emerge out of particular, quite material, always very specifically located ways of working with bodily and other matter—including crystals, computers, electric current, and the hands, eyes, and aching shoulders of sonographers, as well as pregnant bodies and the fetuses within them (Barad 1998). Every fetal sonogram that circulates in the public sphere must at some point have been produced in an encounter between a specific someone holding an ultrasound transducer and another specific someone carrying a fetus. From where, and from whom, do the images that circulate in public contexts actually come? How do they get moved around? Who applies a transducer to whose pregnant body to make any one such fetal sonogram, and who then takes that sonogram and reproduces it, in what other contexts and for what reasons?

Telling Stories

Equally crucial is the question of how the fetal sonogram gets drawn into social and material circulation, acquiring new valences and entering into circuits of commodification. As these images circulate, so too do narratives that seek to "fix" and constrain their meanings (Taylor 1992). The stories that get told about fetal sonograms are themselves quite telling. Who takes what roles in shaping the discourse around such imagery? Who is involved in crafting the narratives that get produced and reproduced—and who is not?

The difficulty of answering such questions is instructive. The trajectory linking that which circulates and acquires value with its origins is, of course, precisely what is at issue in any understanding of commodification. Inquiring into the trajectories followed by the images and information generated by ultrasound technology is very difficult, but is one path toward the very general task of understanding how bodies are collectively made and remade and unmade, and how they are very differently valued, in the world that we inhabit. In the pages that follow, I have traced as much as I could of the trajectory of one particular fetal ultrasound image, named "George," from its origins into the public sphere of antiabortion television commercials, "educational" videotapes, and congressional testimony.

Every pregnant woman and every sonographer must have her own story to tell about any particular sonogram—one that will necessarily be situated within a life being lived in a particular time, place, and social position, and shaped by a specific constellation of resources and constraints, needs and capacities, aspirations and values. Once detached from the social context of their production, however, such images may come to be narrated by other voices, in other ways, and to other ends. Whose narratives get to travel, and whose do not? The medical anthropologists Charles Briggs and Clara Mantini-Briggs, in a powerful analysis of the devastating social and health consequences of the stories that circulated about a cholera epidemic in Venezuela in the early 1990s, write that "[d]iscourse is not a free-floating chain of signifiers: the signifiers produced by people who lack access to power and material resources seldom float beyond their own locality. This is not because they think or act locally . . . but because institutional and political-economic barriers prevent these signs from becoming global" (2003:325). One important contribution that ethnography can make is simply to document and present the words and views of ordinary people whose voices are usually not much heard in public discussions of technology—people besides the experts, the legislators, and the leaders. Which and whose narratives get to shape public discourse matters enormously, because they will also become embedded in the reasoning and actions (as well as inactions) of powerful institutions, with important consequences in many people's bodies and lives.

Nor can ultrasound technology itself be readily separated from the "hype" that surrounds it. As anthropologists Sarah Franklin and Margaret Lock argue, stories may themselves be understood as forms of animating technology:

> The speculative, imaginary, or promissory dimensions . . . [are] the
> most generative and lively components of the "lives themselves"

that populate the world of the new biologicals. . . . In addition to commercial futures, there is offered a host of speculative promises and hopes about improvements to human and animal health, more sustainable and reliable agricultural methods, the preservation or restoration of extinct species, and greater knowledge about the origins and interrelatedness of life forms. Although the usual position in social and cultural research on the new genetics and biotechnology is to remain critical of such promises, it is also clear that a danger exists in underestimating the imagined or promissory futures of these life forms. (2003:15)

The stories that circulate about ultrasound technology can themselves have very real material effects. If researchers tell a story about the wondrous benefits that a new generation of ultrasound equipment promises to bring, and if that story gets circulated publicly and leads stock prices to go up and investments to flow in, enabling the further development of new equipment and the undertaking of new projects, then that story is not simply a representation of ultrasound technology, but actually an important part of it.

Narratives that get circulated along with fetal sonograms—narratives about the fetus, "life," and abortion, about childhood, safety, and normalcy, about the powers of imagery and the mechanisms of human emotional life—also matter because they stand to influence what Monica Casper and Lynn Morgan (2004) call the "new bureaucratic technologies": laws, judicial rulings, public policies, administrative rules, and professional guidelines relating to reproduction. How the public life of the fetal sonogram takes shape is thus part of how the edges of the public sphere, the market, and the state come to extend into people's bodies—into women's bodies more and in different ways than into the bodies of men, and into the bodies of poor and racialized women more and in different ways than into the bodies of other women.

To have an individual body whose surfaces are inviolable is not something we can take for granted as being given in nature. Rather, in this world at this moment in history, to possess an individual body whose surfaces are solid, opaque, and inviolable is an accomplishment, and it is one that lies beyond reach of many. Stark asymmetries materialize some bodies with impressive solidity and others in ways far more contingent, fragile, and vulnerable. To inquire into the ordering of materializing practices is to ask how, in the same movement that bodies are enacted, relations of power are forged. At stake, then, in how even a humble technology like ultrasound gets incorporated into social life, is nothing less than what sort of bodies and what sort of social world get created.

Dismantling Technology

Even to speak of any one technology as if it is a homogeneous entity may be a mistake, however. If technologies are, as we have argued, part of social life, then like social life they must be locally variable, while also interconnected globally. The concept of technology itself, as a seemingly monolithic entity, must be dismantled. What is the relevant context for exploring differences within a particular biotechnology, in any given case? Should we look for differences between nation-states, or between class strata, or between the global North and the global South, or should we frame our inquiries in some other manner altogether? There can be no one answer, of course; working to understand technology as part of social life will necessarily present for us all the same conceptual choices and challenges as does the study of social life more generally.

This study, being based in the United States, is necessarily a study of how ultrasound technology has been made local in *this* country. The linkages I trace here between medicine, consumption, and abortion politics are not only peculiar, but they are also peculiar to the United States. This peculiarity is in part "cultural," in other words reflecting shared systems of thought about such questions as what holds kinship relationships together, what it means to be a person, and what it means to see a picture. It is at the same time also deeply "social structural," taking shape against the broader background of social and economic inequalities, as well as the specific legal, political, economic and professional structures that organize how health care is financed, how medical technologies and medical professions are regulated, and so forth. Ethnographic studies of obstetrical ultrasound carried out in such varied locations as Canada (Mitchell 2001), Denmark and Sweden (Adrian 2006, especially pp. 169–192), Ecuador (Morgan 2000), France (Gerber 2002), Greece (Georges 1996), Japan (Ivry 2006), the Netherlands (van Dijck 2005, chapter 6), Norway (Saetnan

1996, 2000), Syria (Bashour et al. 2005), and Vietnam (Gammeltoft 2007) document that this rapidly globalizing technology is used and understood in quite different ways as it is made local within different parts of the world (see also Mitchell and Georges 1997). Anthropologist Tine Gammeltoft is certainly right to call for more ethnographic attention to how these processes play out in poorer parts of the world:

> Given this proliferation of ultrasonography across the globe, it is unfortunate that nearly all ethnographic studies of women's uptake of this technology are located within Euro-American or Australian social worlds, investigating the experiences of people living in materially secure and politically stable consumer societies. Little is therefore known about the social processes through which ultrasonography is perceived and applied by pregnant women and health care providers in the developing world. (2007:134)

At the same time, precisely because the United States exerts a disproportionate influence within global circuits of economic and political power, the configurations of technology, knowledge, social relations, and practices that take shape around ultrasound in this country may ramify far beyond national boundaries.

By thus insisting on locating ultrasound technology within social life, with all the complications that this entails, an ethnographic approach directly takes on the conceptual hazard of which Leo Marx speaks—the hazard of treating "technology" and "the body" as if they lie outside of social life, and regarding them as both more unitary and thinglike than they really are. Another name for this hazard, of course, is "fetishism," the mistaken attribution to an object of powers that really reside elsewhere. The fetishism of commodities, according to Karl Marx, is the social magic of capitalism, through which "value" is attributed to objects as if it were a power mysteriously inhering in them. This is possible only when the object's connection to the true source of its value, that is, the human labor through which it was produced, has been obscured. The challenge, then, is to "decipher the hieroglyphic, to get behind the secret of our own social products" (Tucker 1978:322). To combat the fetishism of biotechnology and women's bodies and reclaim them as fully social requires that we craft new contexts. This involves two related forms of work. On the one hand, it calls for an intellectual work of documenting and identifying unrecognized connections, and revealing how social life actually animates technologies and bodies. On the other hand, it also involves a political work of mobilizing people to transform the social worlds that have created current configurations of technologies and bodies.

The Research

Talented and committed scholars working at the intersection of medical anthropology with the interdisciplinary fields of feminist studies and science studies are actively engaged in crafting new contexts, intellectual as well as political, for a number of technologies. Especially notable feminist ethnographic work has addressed the intersections of reproductive medicine, everyday life, and abortion politics (see, for example, Casper 1998; Davis-Floyd and Dumit, eds., 1998; Ginsburg and Rapp 1995; Kahn 2000; Morgan, in press; Morgan and Michaels, eds., 1998; Paxson 2004; Rapp 1999). Ethnographers have also recently turned their attention to other technologies that have become central to medical science, such as genetics and genomics (Taussig, forthcoming; Goodman, Heath, and Lindee 2003; Rabinow and Dan-Cohen 2005), as well as cell-tissue technologies (Landecker 2003, 2007) and more (Franklin and Lock, eds., 2003). Joseph Dumit's study of PET scans (2004) offers an ethnographic exploration of a specific form of medical imagery, based on research that spans a similar range of contexts as those considered here. The present study is informed and inspired by this body of scholarship, and brings it into dialogue also with critical and cultural perspectives on consumption, commodification, and fetishism (e.g., Kopytoff 1986; Pietz 1985, 1987; Miller 1998; Chin 2001), thus joining a small but growing literature that addresses intersections of commodification, personhood and kinship (some landmarks of which include Layne, ed., 1998; Sharp 2006; and Cook 2004). The work of many others thus provides the crucial intellectual context for the approach taken here and shows by example how it is possible to craft new contexts for the technologies that we would understand.

Because ultrasound technology and pregnant and fetal bodies alike are part of social life, we can use the methods and conceptual tools of critical and feminist social research, including ethnography, to achieve a fuller and more accurate understanding of them. By the same token, because they are part of social life, we can address ultrasound technology and pregnant and fetal bodies as part of collective efforts to achieve social change. These are the defining commitment and premise of the present study, from which all methodological and other specific choices have followed.

Given the range of settings in which ultrasound technology and imagery now figure, the question of how to approach it ethnographically presents interesting methodological choices and challenges. Ethnographers must always make choices about how and where to bound their sites, conceptually as well as practically, and thus field sites are always in some sense constructed. Often, however, field sites are framed in ways that resonate with shared commonsense understandings concerning what constitutes a "culture," a "community," a "people," or an "institution." Certainly, the setting of a medical clinic suggests itself as one very plausible kind of field site, within which to situate ethnographically a medical imaging technology such as ultrasound. Indeed, Lisa Meryn Mitchell takes such an approach in her 2001 book *Baby's First Picture: Ultrasound and the Politics of Fetal Subjects*, which is the only other book-length ethnographic study of obstetrical ultrasound yet produced, and which is based on research conducted in Canada, where the contexts of health-care financing, abortion controversies, and language politics are quite different.

In my own case, however, it was precisely the strikingly diverse and apparently incompatible meanings and agendas that this technology was being drafted to serve outside as well as inside the clinic that led me to want to pursue ethnographic research on obstetrical ultrasound in the first place. Seeking an approach that could help me situate this medical technology in relation to both public culture and social practice, I have come to frame ultrasound as an ethnographic site whose contours do not mirror so much as disrupt commonsense ways of dividing up the social world, by tracing this technology and the imagery that it generates across the variety of contexts in which it comes into play. While this study thus could be considered an example of multisited ethnography structured on the model of "follow the thing" (Marcus 1995), I have found the image of a technological trajectory useful for conceptualizing these different contexts as linked parts of a single (if untraditional) kind of field site that begins in the medical setting but extends out far beyond its putative boundaries.

I conducted one year of ethnographic fieldwork in a hospital-based obstetrics and gynecology ultrasound clinic in Chicago in 1994, involving observations of medical practice, interviews with over 100 patients, and numerous informal conversations with sonographers. Questions, interpretations, and insights emerging from this clinic-based ethnographic work have been further developed, deepened, and enriched in the years since then, through interviews with physicians, midwives, ultrasound engineers, women reflecting upon their ultrasound examinations, and many sonographers. Nearly all of the sonographers I have interviewed have worked in clinical practice at some point, and many still do; others teach in ultrasound-education programs, and work in industry and marketing or in nondiagnostic "entertainment" ultrasound enterprises. These interviews have helped me flesh out a historical perspective on the emergence of obstetrical ultrasound in the particular configuration in which we now know it in the United States.

Anthropology as a discipline has a tradition of protecting the personal identities of research participants by assuring them of anonymity, and I have followed this tradition by using pseudonyms for most people whose words I quote in this text. I do use individuals' real names when quoting from their published texts, including medical and scientific articles. A few people I interviewed also specifically told me that they preferred to be quoted by name, and I have respected this preference.

I have followed the movements of obstetrical ultrasound imagery out of the medical setting and into the domain of public culture. Specifically, I have sought to document and analyze the ways that ultrasound imagery has been taken up and incorporated within what I argue are the distinctive, yet related, rhetorics of vision characteristic of the promotional materials of the antiabortion movement, on the one hand, and product advertising, on the other. The methods that I have employed in approaching this end of the trajectory lean heavily toward those of literary criticism, though the interpretations that I offer of specific public cultural texts and artifacts (including readings of materials as diverse as pregnancy self-help manuals, medical articles, product advertisements, and Web sites of a variety of organizations) are informed by my ethnographic research in the clinic (including a few occasions on which women spontaneously mentioned some of the texts in question) and other interviews. And while it does not figure prominently in these pages, my own experience of two pregnancies, including several ultrasounds, naturally also informs my understanding.

This ethnographic focus on obstetrical ultrasound has led me to explore the traffic that takes place across cultural boundaries between medicine, media, and the politics of reproduction. Underlying several theoretical and empirical issues addressed in the study is an argument that identifies ultrasound as a site where cultural contradictions surrounding reproduction become visible in new ways, as an ethnographic approach reveals that the fetus is in fact "commodified" at the same time and through the same means that it is "personified." That obstetrical ultrasound partakes in both of these apparently contradictory processes challenges us to move beyond the well-established feminist analysis that likens reproduction to production, and take into account questions of commodification and consumption as these come to bear upon reproduction.

Plan of the Book

We need new images to guide our thinking about how to define an appropriate context to produce understanding. The images I discuss here are only the beginning. (Martin 1998:146)

I would like to take up Emily Martin's invitation and suggest that the work of producing ultrasound imagery may itself offer a "new image" for an ethnography of this new imaging technology. Much as the sonographer's work of "obtaining an image" (as it is often called) requires that one learn to appreciate human anatomy from a novel and unfamiliar perspective, in cross-sectional "slices," this study traces an unfamiliar path through a range of contexts usually understood to be distinct and separate. Just as ultrasound is responsive to differences in density and texture, which makes it especially useful for locating the edges where different types of tissue meet, so too this study attends especially to points of intersection—between medicine and public culture, between reproduction and consumption, between personification and commodification. And just as obtaining an ultrasound image requires intimate contact, between the sonographer and the pregnant woman to whose living body she must hold the transducer, so too ethnographic research requires direct engagement with social practice. Finally, this study shares with sonography the characteristic of being at once documentary, interpretive, and in some sense diagnostic. The plan of the book is, quite fittingly, somewhat akin to the series of views that a sonographer captures in the course of an exam. Each chapter takes a somewhat different "slice" through the social and cultural world within which ultrasound is embedded, and each can be read on its own. Yet each is also part of the whole series, the totality of which forms the basis for an overall assessment.

Chapter 2 provides a historical account of the emergence of the particular cultural form that the obstetrical examination has assumed within U.S. medical practice, which has encouraged women to approach pregnancy and prenatal care as matters of consumption, and has also helped establish conditions for the emergence of the fetishized and commodified public fetus of the contemporary abortion debate. Feminist scholars have addressed the manner in which ultrasound imaging "opens up" the pregnant body and "reveals" the fetus within, to the gaze of medicine and/or the public. Yet this technology is not only applied *to* women, but also operated primarily *by* women. Sonographers, most of whom are women, largely have been overlooked as active and innovative agents in the development of obstetrical ultrasound. In this chapter I argue that the emergence of the "routine" obstetrical ultrasound exam, with all its culturally, emotionally, and politically fraught rituals of showing and telling, must be understood in relation to sonographers' gendered formation of professional selves, characterized by a tension between an emphasis on technical "skill" and on "caring."

In chapter 3, I show how the uses of obstetrical ultrasound within medicine are linked to its uses outside the medical context. Beginning with the puzzle of why medical practice so far outstrips official policy with regard to ultrasound use during pregnancy, I then move on to consider in some detail the theory of "psychological benefits" of obstetrical ultrasound, which I argue may in some part account for this gap. "Psychological benefits" encompass both "reassurance" and "bonding," which embody two quite contradictory views of pregnancy, the fetus, and the function of ultrasound imagery. Indeed, I argue that the tension between these two forms of "psychological benefits" points to a deeper contradiction, namely, that the fetus is constructed more and more as a consumer commodity, and pregnancy as a "tentative" condition, *at the same time and through the same means* that pregnancy is also constructed more and more as an absolute and unconditional relationship, and the fetus as a person from the earliest stages of development.

The fourth chapter critically examines the claim that obstetrical ultrasound imagery can help pregnant women to "bond" emotionally with the fetuses that they carry, which I refer to here as the theory of ultrasound bonding. I trace the troubled history of largely discredited maternal-infant bonding research lying behind this theory, examine the processes by which it has gained an appearance of credibility within the medical literature, and explore the range of professional, political, and commercial projects that this claim is invoked to support. I show that considered as science, the theory of ultrasound bonding is highly dubious, but considered as a social and cultural phenomenon it is very real indeed. It is "real" in the same sense that the concept of race is "real"—"real," that is, because this set of ideas really does have a firm hold on shared common sense, and really does shape how people act and interact: how policies are decided, how medical technology gets used (by whom, on whom, at whose expense, and for what purposes), what sort of care women seek and what sort they receive, how health-care expenditures are distributed, and much more.

Chapter 5 critically engages feminist analyses of reproductive medicine and technology that proceed from an analogy between reproduction and (industrial) production. I draw upon my ethnographic research to show how, in the contemporary United States, reproduction has increasingly come to be constructed as a matter of consumption, and how in the process the fetus is constructed more and more as a "commodity" at the same time and through the same means that it is also constructed more and more as a "person." I argue that feminists must recognize and address the extent to which reproduction has come to be construed in terms of consumption.

The sixth chapter draws upon lengthy interviews with two sonographer entrepreneurs who operate keepsake ultrasound businesses, as well as news reports and discussions taking place in the medical literature, to present an analysis of "entertainment" ultrasound and the controversies that surround it. As I show, the categorical distinction between "medical" and "entertainment" scanning breaks down upon closer examination of social practice, and both of these also prove difficult to disentangle from efforts to incorporate ultrasound into antiabortion efforts.

This book, the culmination of over a decade of research and writing on obstetrical ultrasound, shows how ultrasound has entered into medical practice, everyday life, and public culture in contemporary U.S. society, in the process becoming implicated in complex and contradictory ways in the politics and practices of reproduction. As such, it is both a study of the social and cultural dimensions of a particular technology, and a study of American society and culture as revealed by a focus on this technology. It is also an extended argument for the value and the promise of ethnographic research as a project of situating systems of thought in relation to systems of social action, and attending to the relationship between ideas and practices.

Ethnographic research into the public life of the fetal sonogram reveals surprising and consequential linkages between what might at first glance seem to be unrelated phenomena—between, for example, women technological workers' efforts to build their fledgling profession; U.S. women's eager embrace of pregnancy-related consumption; and the rhetorical and political strategies employed by antiabortion activists. This peculiar configuration of elements takes its shape from the deeper paradox of a system in which persistent social and economic inequalities, in combination with a largely privatized and commodified system of health care, conspire to deny medical care to millions of women, men and children, while at the same time offering it up as one among many other consumer goods to others. The public fetus floats above the American social landscape, as awe-inspiring an image of the disembodied individual as the enormous Head that Dorothy confronts in the Throne Room of the Great Oz—equally awe inspiring, and equally misleading as well. In this case, what lies behind the curtain is not a single "little, old man with a bald head and a wrinkled face" (Baum 2003:183), but a vast and complex social world. By documenting and critically analyzing how the public life of the fetal sonogram arises out of social life, and shapes it in turn, this study seeks to facilitate greater awareness and understanding of some of the less easily recognized ways in which the technological is profoundly social and political. I hope in this manner to offer a scholarly contribution to broader efforts toward social justice and reproductive freedom.

2

Sonographers and the Making of the Public Fetus

The pan-European word whose English version is "fetish" derives linguistically from the Latin *facticius* or *factitius,* an adjective formed from the past participle of the verb *facere,* "to make."

—Pietz, 1987:24

In this chapter, I situate the ultrasound fetal images that make their way into public culture in relation to the emergence of sonography as a new "women's" medical-technical profession, and show how they bear the traces of the social and cultural context of their making.[1] First, I trace the emergence of the particular cultural form of the "routine" obstetrical ultrasound examination as we know it, which allows ultrasound to play the peculiar role that it does in contemporary U.S. society, in both the practices and the politics of reproduction (Taylor 1992, 1998, 2000), For reasons that will become clear, I place special emphasis on the active role that sonographers have played in this history, and on the dilemmas that it has bequeathed them. Having thus set the stage, I then indulge in a bit of "methodological fetishism" (Appadurai 1986:5), and pursue a version of what Igor Kopytoff (1986) has called a "biographical" approach to one particular commodified ultrasound fetal image, tracing its movements between different social domains and documenting the social processes through which it is both fetishized and commodified. The particular fetal ultrasound image whose "biography" I partially trace here is one that has been named (not by me!) "George," and has probably come as close to celebrity stardom as is possible for such an entity. It eventually made its way into a widely screened antiabortion television advertisement, into congressional hearings, and into pro-life "educational" videotapes. By thus tracing this "public" fetus back to the social conditions of its production, I attempt to do for fetal images what Karl Marx suggests we must do for all commodities—and I seek, in this way, to contribute to the larger feminist scholarly work of shifting the focus of discussions of reproduction away from disembodied fetal images and back toward the lives of women.

Feminists, Fetuses, and Fetishes

Both in the case of women's visual encounters in clinical settings with the fetuses they carry, and in the case of the broader viewing public's visual encounters with fetuses on television, bringing these fetuses onto the screen has arguably brought them "to life." Routine ultrasound imaging of the fetus during early pregnancy has made it possible to visualize the fetal form and document fetal heartbeats and movements long before the moment of "quickening." In this sense, ultrasound technology has brought the fetuses of today "to life" in a different way, and far earlier, than in decades past. The women who carry today's fetuses would, back when they were fetuses themselves, not have seemed "alive" to their own mothers at the same stage of pregnancy, nor in quite the same way. Even beyond these more narrowly "medical" diagnostic functions, however, the routine ultrasound examination itself has, in contemporary U.S. society, become a scene of commodification and consumption, bringing the fetus "to life" in part by inserting it in various ways into the mass circulation of goods and images (Taylor 2000). The "liveliness" that ultrasound helps impart to the fetuses women carry is related to the seeming "liveliness" of those other fetuses whose images circulate in public culture, though the latter are more obviously problematic for those concerned with reproductive rights, especially when fetal images enter our lives and our living rooms as the deputed representatives of "Life" (Boucher 2004a).

Rosalind Pollack Petchesky was the first to suggest, in her landmark essay "Foetal Images: The Power of Visual Culture in the Politics of Reproduction" (1987), that the public fetus is perhaps best understood as a fetish. Fetishism of the fetus consists in attributing to it value as "life," as if this were a property magically inhering in the fetus alone, in a manner that obscures the fact that the continued vitality of any actual fetus depends utterly and completely upon its continued sustenance by the woman who carries it. The task, for those who would contest the power of the fetishized fetus, is to reframe it in such a way as to make visible what has been rendered obscure, and reveal the hidden context of social production from which it draws its seeming "life."[2]

This task, to the extent that it necessarily involves making visible the invisible, revealing and unmasking what has been hidden and obscured, inevitably draws us into a rhetoric and a politics of vision. Indeed, if the Marxist concept of the fetish grants us critical leverage on "the absolute strangeness of the normal capitalist everyday" (Spyer 1997:10), it does so in large part by invoking a long cultural history of love and fear of images (Mitchell 1986), compounded by a particular fascination and revulsion with those images and objects that occupy a special place in the alien system of values of some cultural Other (Pietz 1985, 1987). It is thus perhaps overdetermined, by the theoretical apparatus we employ no less than by the phenomenon we address, that feminist scholars who have sought to critically engage the ideology of opponents of abortion in contemporary U.S. society have attributed considerable power to visual images of the fetus. In particular, Petchesky (1987), historian Barbara Duden (1993), and others have argued that obstetrical ultrasound technology enables the fetishism of the fetus by visually objectifying it in a manner that conceals the pregnant woman from view even as it "reveals" the fetus—to the medical gaze on the one hand, and to the gaze of the mass-mediated public on the other.

Unmasking fetishes is a slippery business, however. I fear that in our efforts to unmask the fetishism of the fetus, we risk being seduced into the error of fetishizing technology. Reframing the fetus-as-fetish requires that we bring into view not only the technology that generates the images that seemingly grant it "life," but also the *people* who operate the technology, without whose skilled labor the technological device would be capable of nothing at all. As historians of technology remind us: "[T]he history of technology is a history of human actions. To understand the origin of a particular kind of technological power, we must first learn about the actors. Who were they? What were their circumstances? . . . Why was the innovation made by these people and not others?" (Smith and Marx 1995:xiii). We would do well, I suggest, to revive the older meaning of "manufactured," lying dormant within the etymology of the term "fetish" (Pietz 1985:5, 1987:24). If in our discussion of obstetrical ultrasound we focus only on the formal visual qualities of the sonogram and fail to attend closely enough to ultrasound as social practice, then we end up casting women only as the embodied objects of the technological-medical gaze— or at best, as subjects whose relation to their own embodiment is rendered newly problematic by new technologies of visualization. In either case, we fail to recognize the full range of ways in which women have been positioned relative to this technology—and more importantly, we miss the opportunity to document the *making* of the fetishized public fetus.

Undeleting the Image Makers

If we wish instead to seize this opportunity, one good place to begin is by interrogating the cultural form that the ultrasound examination has assumed in this country. Nothing about the physics of high-velocity sound waves, nor the medical imaging devices constructed to exploit them, requires that a diagnostic ultrasound procedure be performed in just the way that it has come to be in this country. Nothing about the device itself dictates, for example, that women undergoing ultrasound examinations should want and be encouraged to bring along partners, spouses, loved ones, or other family members or friends; that they should be shown the fetus on the screen; that seeing it should be understood as a means of effecting maternal "bonding"; that the sonographer should provide a narrative of the baby's anatomy and activities and offer to determine its sex, or give the pregnant woman a videotape or "snapshot" image to take home. Noting that a recent study based on research in Sweden (Eurenius et al. 1997) indicated 87 percent of women show up for prenatal ultrasound appointments accompanied by their partners, radiologists Roy A. Filly and James P. Crane comment wryly that "that does not happen when they are reporting for flexible sigmoidoscopy [a visual examination of the lower bowel by means of a specially designed speculum], nor are mementos sought" (Filly and Crane 2002:714).

If these elements were not present in the practice of ultrasound—if, for example, an ultrasound exam really were a little more like a sigmoidoscopy and a little less like a visit to the hospital nursery—we would still have good reason to critically question the routinization of ultrasound in obstetrics in this country. And we would doubtless still see ultrasound used for sex determination leading to sex-selective abortion, both here and elsewhere in the world, in contexts where women are under great pressure to bear male children (Jha et al. 2006; Marquand 2004; Silliman 2003; Wertz and Fletcher 1989). Yet if these elements were absent, it is hard to imagine that ultrasound could occupy the peculiar position that it does in contemporary U.S. society on the porous and contested boundaries between medicine, media, and public culture. Indeed, if we follow Butler's insight that "matter" may be understood as "a process of materialization that stabilizes over time to produce the effect of boundary, fixity, and surface" (Butler 1993:9), then surely the practice of the routine ultrasound exam in the particular cultural form in which we know it—all these acts of showing, viewing, and explaining, repeated millions of times each year— must be one of the ways that the fetus has come to "matter" in the particular way it does in contemporary American society (Barad 1998, 2003).

How, why, and when did the ultrasound examination assume the particular cultural form that it presently takes in this country? Available historical accounts of obstetrical ultrasound, including specifically feminist accounts, have surprisingly little to say on this question. One reason for this is simply that most discussions of ultrasound that do address its history end their narrative in the early to mid-1970s, just at the beginning of what some people working in the field of ultrasound call "the sonic boom" (Blume 1992; Goldberg and Kimmelman 1988; Oakley 1984; Yoxen 1987. But see Kevles 1997; Mitchell 1993, 2001). In the early 1970s, ultrasound technology was just beginning to be produced commercially, ultrasound screening of pregnancy was just beginning to move from an experimental to a standard medical procedure, and people who worked with ultrasound were just beginning to organize themselves professionally. In other words, most of the complex, diffuse, interlocking series of transformations that led to the obstetrical ultrasound exam, in the particular form in which we now know it, becoming a taken-for-granted part of the cultural landscape of medicalized pregnancy in this country, took place after these narratives end.

To be sure, the difficulty of simply documenting these kinds of changes is considerable. Millions of ultrasound devices of all sorts have been sold over the past thirty years to hospitals, imaging centers or mobile imaging services, as well as doctors in private practices. These may be operated by obstetricians, by radiologists, by midwives, or, more commonly, by sonographers (persons specially trained in the use of ultrasound technology to produce diagnostic information), though no formal education or certification in ultrasound is at present legally required. Because it involves a nonionizing form of radiation, the government does not regulate and monitor ultrasound in the way that it does, for example, X-ray and other modalities, and little data are therefore available on ultrasound usage (Moore et al. 1990; Martin et al. 2005; see also note 3 in Chapter 3). To write the history of obstetrical ultrasound during the period between 1970 and 2000, it is not entirely obvious where and how one could or should locate (or more likely, construct) one's archive—though surely this cannot be any more daunting than many other topics that creative and resourceful historians have successfully taken on.

But my own research has made very clear to me at least one point: as reproduction increasingly becomes subject to medical and technological surveillance and intervention, one woman's labor has become another woman's work. The routinization of ultrasound within obstetrics has not only meant that millions of pregnant women each year undergo ultrasound examinations, it has also meant new forms of work for tens of thousands of other women. These include the clerical workers who type and file reports and schedule appointments, the women in developing countries who perform much of the work of assembling component parts of today's ultrasound equipment, and, in the United States, a new allied-health profession composed mostly of women who operate ultrasound equipment and perform diagnostic procedures (Baker 1995; Mitchell 1993, 2001). Approximately 40,000 people in the United States are currently formally registered as sonographers, of whom about three-quarters have passed a registry examination in the specialized field of ob/gyn, and approximately 85 percent of these are women (although the percentage of male sonographers tends to be higher in other subspecialties such as cardiac or vascular ultrasound).[3] More than simply carrying out purely technical procedures at the request of physicians, sonographers have all along actively worked with engineers and physicians and others to develop and modify equipment, develop new medical applications, and market and repair ultrasound equipment, as well as teaching others how to use the equipment and interpret the information it provides (Baker 1995).

To understand how the obstetrical ultrasound examination has assumed its present cultural form requires that we "undelete" these "image makers," to borrow Deborah Heath's phrase (Heath 1998), and work to "locate the [technological] system in the disciplinary and cultural worlds of its creators" (Forsythe 1996:553). As the historian Edward Yoxen writes:

> The job of the person performing the scan has a history. The tasks involved have been designed, negotiated and defined in relation to the work of others and depend on the exercise of specific skills. Who has these skills and how they are valued by others has changed through time. Thus the experience of having an ultrasound scan depends on how various individuals are able to work, how they are intended to work, and how their constantly shifting relations with doctors are managed. (1987:303)[4]

From the earliest days of obstetrical ultrasound, and straight through to the present day, obstetricians usually have relied upon other people to do the work of actually operating the equipment and performing the scans; and the contributions that these people have made to the development of the technology and its applications, though often overlooked, are hardly negligible. Indeed, although the Scottish obstetrician Ian Donald is widely acknowledged as the "father" of obstetrical ultrasound, having been the first to adapt industrial ultrasound equipment for use in detecting intrauterine tumors, the very idea of using ultrasound to visualize the fetus may fairly be credited to Marjorie Marr, a staff nurse in his employ. As Ann Oakley notes in her landmark history of prenatal care, Donald noticed with some puzzlement that Marr always seemed to know which way the fetuses were oriented in the womb—and learned that she had taken to using the ultrasound equipment that he had had installed in the ob/gyn department to locate the fetal head before Donald conducted his daily rounds. This gave Donald the idea of using ultrasound to measure the diameter of the fetal skull (biparietal diameter, or BPD), which was in fact one of the few anatomical features that early ultrasound devices could reliably measure, and which Donald believed could be useful in monitoring fetal growth through successive measurements, and in determining whether the head would fit through the pregnant woman's bony pelvis for birth (Oakley 1984:161; Mitchell 2001:27–28).

In the early days of obstetrical ultrasound, some of the people who did the work of scanning had started out as secretaries or file clerks. Others were people who had come to ultrasound through their prior training in allied-health fields such as radiology, nursing, or nuclear medicine (Baker 1995), or who were trained in the sciences and working as research assistants or in other positions within departments of obstetrics or cardiology.[5] During this period, ultrasound offered unusual opportunities for women to find employment that developed technological interests and skills. A common type of career path among this older generation of sonographers practicing today was described to me by Marveen Craig:

> I was living in Denver in 1966 and was bored silly once my son entered the first grade. I went looking for a part-time job to keep me occupied until school let out for the summer. Because I had both a nursing and secretarial background, I started job hunting at the University of Colorado Medical School. They offered me the job of being a "gofer" in a new research lab, the ultrasound lab. I was hired to answer phones, fetch patients, type reports and scientific papers, and so on. What began as a part-time job quickly became full-time after an unexpected divorce several months later. I was so fascinated by ultrasound . . . that I began sneaking back into the lab after hours trying to teach myself to scan. After about three months of this clandestine learning I was "caught" by one of our OB residents who kindly began teaching me what he knew. . . . Several months later when our workload began to pick up dramatically, he recommended that I be hired to scan patients as well as my "gofer" work.

Until the late 1960s, ultrasound devices were still quite ungainly and difficult to use; some required, for example, that the patient be placed under a heavy membrane full of water, others required that the patient actually sit immersed up to the neck in a tub of water for the duration of the procedure (Goldberg and Kimmelman 1988:11–13, 33; Yoxen 1987; Blume 1992:95). The information that these devices produced was also presented in ways that were far more difficult to interpret than the sort of visual images that we associate with ultrasound today (in the form of graphed lines, for example); and in those days before computed tomography (CT) scans and magnetic resonance imaging (MRI), the way that ultrasound imaged the body, in cross-sectional "slices," was completely unfamiliar. Thus, individuals who had gained hands-on experience in ultrasound, some of whom became quite expert at it, were in considerable demand by the late 1960s, when ultrasound entered its period of rapid growth. Physician-researchers needed people skilled in the use of ultrasound to help do clinical studies; hospitals needed them to set up departments of ultrasound; and manufacturing firms needed them to test and demonstrate commercial equipment and teach their customers how to use it (Baker, 1995).

Show and Sell

In his historical study of the ultrasound industry (written as a Ph.D. dissertation in executive management), Pierre Coste (1989) points out that selling ultrasound to physicians in the mid-1970s was a considerable challenge. The technology itself had not yet been standardized, meaning that different manufacturers were still producing equipment based on a number of different principles, which presented quite different sorts of visual information, including "A-mode," "B-mode," and "M-mode" scanners. They thus faced the challenge of trying to persuade physicians that they needed ultrasound, while also trying to make the case for a particular type of equipment. Because of the ways that their preexisting habits of practice and their perceived clinical needs intersected with the distinctive features of different models, physicians in specific specialties tended to prefer certain types of ultrasound equipment; "B-scanners remained dominant in the radiology market as did M-mode in cardiology" (Coste 1989). In this context, the advent of "gray-scale" imaging (which allowed much more nuanced images than earlier black-and-white imaging devices) and early "real-time" scanners (which made it possible to visualize movement for the first time) seemed to promise to appeal especially to obstetricians. ADR, a company that introduced early gray-scale and real-time imaging equipment, focused its efforts on promoting equipment sales to obstetricians and gynecologists.

Using ultrasound to "show the baby" to obstetricians' pregnant patients was an important part of their strategy:

> ADR . . . focused solely on understanding the imaging needs of OBG physicians. ADR had its sales representatives spend time in hospital OBG departments to learn how to perform the examination themselves. They would bring the equipment on sales calls to OBG private practices and assist the physician in conducting the examination. The patient was delighted to be able to see her baby moving inside her body and was co-opted into advancing the sale. (Coste 1989:154)

Partly because ultrasound developed on a "frontier" located at the interstices between established medical disciplines (including obstetrics and radiology), people working clinically as ultrasound technicians[6] during this period similarly felt the need to promote the technology to physicians who, for the most part, did not know much about what it was, how it imaged the body, how these images were to be interpreted, and how ultrasound might be useful to them in their own practice. Dave, a sonographer I interviewed who had worked clinically in ob/gyn ultrasound in the late 1960s, recalls:

> We started by taking over an unused storage room in a women's clinic, and moved in our $25,000 piece of compound scanning equipment and we were just begging people to send us patients. Doing all kinds of publicity with the different department heads, mostly the OB/GYN people, but other internal medicine areas in the hospital as well, and just wanted to try everything. And it took off from three patients a day to eventually maybe sixty or seventy patients a day, and four full-time techs and me as a chief tech, and hundreds of thousands of dollars worth of equipment. . . . There was stuff going on in Europe, so we could get our hands on a clinical article and say, "Look, we should be able to do this. Give us a chance." But in OB it was a little simpler, typically they would send us somebody down with a very wild-goose-chase diagnosis of "rule out twins" or "bleeding, question placenta praevia."[7]

Clearly, this account of the process by which ultrasound gained a foothold within obstetrics (which accords substantially with recollections of this period that I have heard from other sonographers as well) hardly conforms to the usual picture of scientific "research." Sonographers were "begging for patients" and "doing all kinds of publicity" with obstetricians, then taking advantage of obstetricians' "wild-goose-chase diagnoses" to "try everything" on the patients that came their way. For them as for ADR and other manufacturers, highlighting the capacity of this equipment to afford visual views of the fetus proved a useful way of generating interest in ultrasound among physicians and their women patients. What we might tend to think of as the "nonmedical" aspects of the obstetrical ultrasound examination emerged, in other words, *alongside* the more narrowly "medical" applications, and these were indeed an important *part* of the process by which the technology and the procedure became established within medicine. These conventions emerged in the first instance in response to the need to promote ultrasound itself; "show and tell" was really a matter of "show and sell." Again, I quote from my conversation with Dave:

DAVE: It was a tiny room, about a twelve by twelve room, had a stretcher in it and an ultrasound machine and a table and a desk and a telephone, and can you fit another body in to watch? Oh yes. And then grandmother wants to come in too, or my younger children, and I think it became not unusual to have three or four observers, even people that weren't family members, that were on the hospital staff that had heard about ultrasound and wanted to see. So, I mean, then it turned into a real show, and I'm a ham, I'd try to make people laugh and comfortable with the situation . . . you wanted good PR for the procedure anyway, because it was a fledgling, and the more people that knew about it, got a buzz going about it, the better it would be. And some places didn't allow to give away films, it was against their policy. But then eventually there was a cheaper technology, it was a thermal paper printer, each one of those costs about 8 cents. The videotape recorder didn't come along until much later. It just was natural with the obstetrical process: not sick patients, they were just here for—you know, getting the gestational age pinned down and ruling out twins or something, and not a lot of tension, not a lot of concern, nothing unsafe about the technology for them, so, give everybody a picture. . . .

JANELLE: Did the hospital or the clinic that you worked in have a policy on these things, the kind of not-strictly-medical part of it?

DAVE: Well, there were no policies. We were outsiders, because we belonged
to radiology but we were in the women's clinic, in a part of the women's
clinic where there were other X-ray procedures done, but ... I don't
know, it was all alien to me, I never got to know what they did. ... So
there wasn't policy. There might have been policy in the women's clinic,
but I didn't have to answer to it. And radiology didn't feel ownership for
me, we were like a satellite to them, I was off on my own. And we weren't
rigid enough to have our own policy.

Of course, as ultrasound became more established over the course of
the 1970s and into the 1980s, these conditions changed, and things became
more "rigid." Ultrasound became the focus of professional "turf battles,"
waged on many levels between radiologists, who laid claim to ultrasound as
one among many imaging modalities, and obstetricians, who claimed it as
one among many ways of examining the pregnant patient (Blume
1992:109–112). Clinics became larger, with more staff and tighter workloads,
and came under the more direct supervision of the departments that suc-
ceeded in laying claim to them. Conventions of practice that had been
improvised on-the-spot came to be more or less established social forms.

The pathways that led people into work in the field of ultrasound also
changed over time. Until the late 1960s, skilled people who specialized in
performing ultrasound procedures were a mixed lot, and in many
European countries they remain so today: midwives, nurses, radiology
technicians, and doctors of various specialties. In the United States, however, beginning in 1969, nonphysician specialists in ultrasound have
organized themselves as a separate profession. Within the first decade or
so, they had formed a professional society (now called the Society of
Diagnostic Medical Sonography, or SDMS) and established formalized educational standards and competency exams (which are by now widely recognized and accepted, though not legally required), as well as a national
registry board. They acquired other essential trappings of a profession,
such as a professional journal, and official recognition as a separate occupation by the Manpower Division of the American Medical Association. In
addition, formal education programs designed to train sonographers for
clinical practice were set up in different locations around the United States
beginning in the mid-1970s, and ultrasound began to attract people drawn

to it as a career, one among a number of different established allied-health fields (Baker 1995). Finally, in 2002, Diagnostic Medical Sonography gained recognition from the Department of Labor as a separate occupation (U.S. Department of Labor Bureau of Labor Statistics 2002).[8]

Skill and Caring in a "Women's" Technical Profession

As obstetrical ultrasound has become widespread, routine, and familiar to the general public, many women have also decided to pursue a career in ultrasound after first encountering it during the course of an examination of their own pregnancies. Joan Baker, one of the founders of the SDMS, who for years served as director of an ultrasound education program in the Seattle suburb of Bellevue, explained to me in 1995:

> I might lecture to about five hundred people a year, and I asked them, "How many of you have had ultrasounds on yourselves?" And now, it's at least three-quarters. "And how many of you have watched an ultrasound?" And now, almost one hundred percent of the hands are up. Whereas ten, fifteen years ago, they weren't sure whether they came to listen to you to find out what the word *meant!* . . . If you ask [students today what interested them in sonography], typically they will say they had an ultrasound done on themselves or they were with somebody when they had one done. More people, it would have been an obstetrical experience.

Jane, another sonographer who has worked in obstetrics since the early 1970s, concurs: "What interested me was the detail, the completeness of it all. . . . [But] a lot of sonographers are idealistic about obstetrics, they identify with the mother. They're women who love to be pregnant."

As a general statement, Jane's characterization of sonographers working in obstetrics as "women who love to be pregnant" is surely much too glib, and she said it half in jest. Certainly, not all sonographers working in obstetrics "love to be pregnant," and not all of them are women. Dave, quoted above, had moved into a marketing position in the ultrasound industry already by the late 1970s, but there remain approximately 4,500 male sonographers currently registered in the field of ob/gyn ultrasound.[9] There may nonetheless be a kernel of insight in the contrast that Jane draws between her own technical fascination with "the detail, the completeness of it all," and some other sonographers' "idealism" and tendency to "identify with the mother." We can read her statement as pointing toward tensions and debates within the community of sonographers in this country over the relationship between professional identity, gender identity, and the practice of obstetrical ultrasound. Particularly at issue in these debates are precisely those elements of the cultural form of the obstetrical ultrasound exam that we touched on above: "showing the baby," determination of fetal sex, giving a take-home picture, and so forth.

In speaking with sonographers and in reading their publications (such as the *Journal of Diagnostic Medical Sonography,* which is the official publication of the SDMS), I have been struck by the frequency and the passion with which they exhort themselves and each other to strive to be professional. At the core of this call for professionalism is an insistence upon the high level of technical skill that ultrasound demands. Many contend that ultrasound differs fundamentally from other modalities because the production of imagery requires entirely different skills, as well as a much higher level of knowledge. The division of labor between sonographers and physicians is significantly unlike that between X-ray technicians and physicians, in that a certain degree of interpretation, or arguably even diagnosis, is necessarily involved in the very production of ultrasound imagery. Ultrasound technology images soft tissue (rather than bone); gray-scale images provide information about the density and the texture, as well as simply the shape and location, of these tissues; the internal structures that one seeks to visualize may be situated somewhat differently in the bodies of different individuals, they may be in motion (as the fetus, for example, often is), and they must be located by moving the transducer around on the body's surface. The views thus obtained are cross sectional, moreover, and acquiring a standard view or measurement therefore requires that one know enough cross-sectional anatomy and physiology to determine when one has found the right location and the right angle. For all of these reasons, the production of an ultrasound image is not just an exercise in mechanically recording a transparently available empirical reality, and is in this respect quite unlike other medical imaging modalities such as X-rays—much less the visual technologies of television and photography with which most people are familiar. One sonographer quoted in a recent newspaper article discussing sonography as a career articulated a view held by many: "The level of responsibility for us is growing so much that I can see sonographers becoming like physician assistants. . . . We'll be making our own diagnoses" (Rivera 2002).

Yet despite this emphasis on technical skills, for many sonographers it is precisely the responsibility to "identify with the mother," as Jane phrased it, and more generally to provide compassionate care for the people who come to them, that distinguishes their occupation from those they regard as being more purely "technical." One of the ways in which ultrasound is unlike other medical imaging modalities, some argue, is that it requires much more direct contact with the patient. Because no ionizing radiation is involved, the person performing the exam is not required to leave the room as do X-ray technicians. Indeed, the sonographer must hold the transducer in physical contact with the patient's body throughout the exam, moving it about on the body to obtain different views, or in some cases inserting a specially shaped transducer into the anus or vagina. This contact is, of course, not simply physical, but also social, and is further complicated by the cultural form that the obstetrical exam has assumed.

Ann, a sonographer with whom I spoke at the annual SDMS convention in 1994, described some of the ways that her practice of ultrasound called upon her capacities beyond her merely technical skill:

> Sometimes you have girls who come from this rural area, from a real strongly fundamentalist religious community, and they just can't admit [they're pregnant]. They'll come to the doctor because of "belly pains" and get sent for an ultrasound and they're eight months pregnant. . . . Or women who thought they had an abortion, but then they're still gaining weight, so they come back and there's a twenty-week fetus in there and now it's too late. . . . I say to them, "How can I help you?" And sometimes we talk, or I've given them cab fare to get to the doctor or get home. Sometimes they just need to be held. And I'll do that.

In 1997, Sharon Durbin, a sonographer working in an obstetrical practice, published a piece in the "Career Symposium" section of the *JDMS* titled "Words Spoken in a Dimly Lit Room." In it, she describes a number of especially emotionally charged encounters that she remembers from more than fifteen years of working with obstetrical ultrasound, and frames these within a broad call to sonographers not to forget such moments in the rush of economic competition and technological change. Echoing Ann, she suggests that it is less her technical skill than her capacity to provide compassionate care that should be at the core of the sonographer's professional identity:

> I believe there is a need to take the time to reflect on the true humanity of our job, why we really went into this field to begin with. It is the people who come to us at a critical time in their lives. . . . It is the miracle and sacredness of life, not the revolution of technology or how we can become more cost effective. . . . It is our challenge to open our hearts and make a difference. It is in caring, it is in nurturing, it is by supporting, that we reach the very depth of our being, and give the best of ourselves to our profession. (Durbin 1997:177)

And if "caring" is what ought to be at the core of the sonographer's professional identity, this caring is manifested above all in "showing the baby," rather than in the taking of measurements or views ordered by the physician. Indeed, Durbin's essay begins thus:

> In this age of technology, let us not lose touch with the humanity of our job. Let us remember the tumbling fetus we image, with arms and legs fluttering in amniotic fluid, faces with big, dark eyes peering out at the excited parents. You hear the "oohs" and "ahs" at the commencement of life when the bondings of the strongest kind are initiated. This is truly what the core of our job is about . . . memories, faces, beginnings—images permanently etched in the corners of our minds. These emotions are enhanced in the ultrasound room, with its darkness and soft music; communication barriers are dissolved, thoughts are uninhibited, and feelings are demonstrated. (Durbin 1997:175)

There is a delicate balancing act involved in emphasizing the traditionally feminine skills of caring as properly central to the professional identity of sonographers, when at the same time it is their specialized technological skill that underwrites their claims to professionalism more generally.

Furthermore, sonographers may more readily "identify with" some mothers than with others. Some sonographers I observed at work in the

Chicago clinic where my own research was based seemed to dispense "nonmedical" extras (showing the baby, giving a picture, informing of fetal sex) most readily only to women whom they perceived as already having demonstrated a certain seriousness about the "medical" aspects of the procedure, and who more generally were seen as taking a responsible attitude toward their health and their pregnancy. Not surprisingly, perhaps, some also displayed cultural attitudes widely shared in this country (and deeply entrenched in public policy and social theory alike) in regarding the pregnancies of young, poor, unmarried African American women in their care as symptomatic of their failure to be "serious" and "responsible" about reproduction—and regarding these young women as therefore less deserving of such "extras" than mature, middle-class, married, white women (Taylor 2000:411–412; see also Mitchell 2001:135). Because ideologies of motherhood are enmeshed with ideologies of medicine, race, and class (Roberts 1997), sonographers' professional identity, to the extent that it is grounded in a particular kind of gender identity, is inevitably entangled with questions of racial and class identity as well.

Marjorie DeVault, writing about dietitians and community nutritionists, who like sonographers work as " 'intermediate' or 'subordinate' professionals in the health care system,' " has suggested that feminists ought to consider "questions about professional socialization in the 'women's' professions—about the selves that form during professional training" (DeVault 1999:167; see also Boyer 2006). It may be especially important to ask such questions concerning sonographers, if we wish to understand how it is that the fetishized "public" fetus of the antiabortion movement emerges out of social practice.

"George" and the Cruel Commercial

The DeMoss Foundation, an antiabortion organization with ties to Jesse Helms and Jerry Falwell, produced an antiabortion television advertisement that aired on commercial stations in the Chicago area where I lived in 1994.[10] In this advertisement, a split screen shows, on the left side, a white baby that looks to be several months of age, dressed in a white outfit and lying on a white crib sheet, gurgling and cooing—while on the right side it shows a real-time ultrasound image of a fetus moving around in the

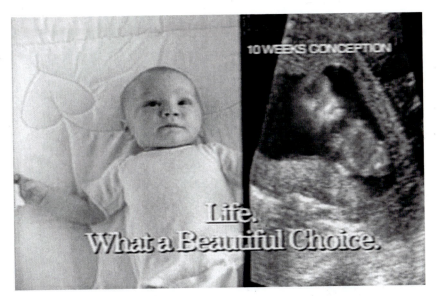

FIGURE 2-1 Still from "Left/Right," an antiabortion television advertisement produced by the DeMoss Foundation.

womb. Against a background of sentimental instrumental music, a male narrator's voice points out highly symbolic physical capabilities they share: "The baby on the left can feel pain, so can the baby on the right. . . . The baby on the left can suck its thumb, so can the baby on the right . . .," and so forth, then concludes: "The difference is, that the baby on the left has just been born, and the baby on the right would very much like to be." The screen then shows, in white script against a black background, the slogan "Life: What a Beautiful Choice."

For at least one woman with whom I spoke in the course of my ethnographic research in a hospital-based ob/gyn ultrasound clinic, it was this DeMoss ad that provided a reference point for her first personal experience with obstetrical ultrasound, seven months into her first pregnancy. In response to my question whether she had ever seen ultrasound pictures before she had an exam herself, Catherine, a twenty-seven-year-old African American elementary-school teacher from Chicago's Near North Side, replied:

> I saw it on TV, on the abortion commercial. That was really, really cruel of them, they put people under a lot of pressure. Ultrasound makes the pregnancy more real in the earlier stages. I think that was

cruel. Even though I am pro-life, I thought it was cruel, because people who are pregnant go through so many changes, so the ultrasound makes it real to you, seeing it move around makes it more difficult to decide, for someone who wants to decide to terminate. I'm pro-life pro-choice, if you can be that. It's not the decision *I* would make . . . [here, she looked down at her big belly and laughed] evidently!

The ultrasound image that was featured in this ad was supplied by Shari Richard, who is a registered sonographer in Michigan and since the early 1990s has combined her professional skills with her "pro-life" activism. Richard has made antiabortion videos using the same footage that is featured in the DeMoss ad, and also submitted this same footage as evidence in testimony before Congress in March 1990 when the National Right to Life Committee requested that she testify before the Senate subcommittee opposing the "Freedom of Choice Act." We might say that Richard is to ultrasound what Lennart Nilsson is to photography. Nilsson is the Swedish scientific photographer whose backlit color photographs of fetuses, first published in the mid-1960s, have circulated so widely in public culture that they have, to a considerable extent, come to define shared cultural imaginings of what "the fetus" looks like and what it is (Jain 1998; Lykke and Bryld 2002; Michaels 1999; Newman 1996; Nilsson 1966). The ultrasound fetal images that Richard has produced and publicized occupy a similar niche (Boucher 2004a, 2004b).

In 1990, Richard founded a company called "Sound Wave Images"; from this base she sells her videotapes and other materials, offers her services as a speaker to churches, schools, and pro-life organizations, and works to help Crisis Pregnancy Centers (what some of us know as "bogus abortion clinics") learn how they can incorporate ultrasound into their activities. On the company's Web site, http://unborn.com, Richard has posted, among other things, a narrative account of the production and circulation of an ultrasound image of a baby she calls "George." In that account, Richard describes performing an ultrasound examination in 1989 on a woman who was ten weeks pregnant and who (as she only learned later) had been considering abortion. As Richard tells it, this fetus was unusually active:

The baby I nicknamed "George" waved, jumped, turned somersaults, and was very active during the whole exam. I watched as the mother's sad, discouraged face suddenly changed to a glowing beam of delight. "Is that my baby moving? . . . Look how developed it is!" . . . She couldn't believe that all this activity was going on inside of her while she couldn't feel a thing. We both laughed as I warned her that she was going to be a very busy mother.

Later, writes Richard, she received a call from this woman on "George's" first birthday, thanking her. "George's" mother said that she had been intending to terminate the pregnancy, but that seeing the ultrasound images had changed her mind. "George" had been born a girl, who was still very active, just as she had been during that ultrasound examination. Richard writes that she was disappointed that she had nicknamed this baby "George": "Although I tried to change it to 'Georgette,' 'George' would always slip out." In other respects, however, "George" has not been in the least disappointing. According to Richard, it is "George" whose image is featured in her ultrasound videos entitled *Ultrasound: "A Window to the Womb"* and *Eyewitness to the Earliest Days of Life*. These videos, in her words, "act as a stage permitting the voiceless unborn babies to show off their inherent beauty and humanity."[11] According to Richard, "George" was then "selected by the DeMoss Foundation to be used in their national commercial campaign, 'Life, What a Beautiful Choice' which has now been viewed by millions and is the 'picture worth a thousand words'" (Richard 2007).

I know of no reason to doubt that Richard indeed provided the DeMoss Foundation with the ultrasound imagery used in this advertisement. The story of "George" as she tells it, however, would seem to have required a most extraordinary series of lucky coincidences. If a sonographer received a call such as the one Richard describes from "George's" mother, it would under most circumstances be highly unusual that she would happen to have saved a videotape record of that particular examination, a full year after it had taken place—especially when the exam had revealed no unusual medical conditions, and the sonographer was not aware until much later of its profound emotional consequences.[12] If such a videotape were available, one could hardly expect that the particular videotaped examination that had figured in this transformative bonding episode would also happen to exhibit all of the very specific visual features that make an obstetrical ultrasound image suitable for use in such an advertisement.

For a sonogram to be useful as a "baby picture" in antiabortion materials (or any other mass-media venue), the image must, in the first place, be very clear and distinct—clear enough to be easily recognizable as a "baby" by the general public. This level of visual clarity in a routine ultrasound examination performed in an ordinary clinic setting is perhaps not so unusual today, thanks to the development and diffusion in recent years of equipment capable of fully digital image processing, but it would have been far more unusual in 1989 (when Richard scanned "George").[13] In order for the ultrasound image to function as a "baby picture" in mass-mediated public settings, the fetus must also be small enough at the time of the ultrasound examination for all or most of its body to fit into the visual frame. At the same time, it must be developed enough that its form is easily recognizable, and must be positioned in the womb in such a way as to allow a profile view. An image of a small round gestational sac, or a cross-sectional "slice" through the fetal abdomen, would hardly be expected to hold the same visual and emotional appeal for the general public as a facial profile, a hand, a foot. Finally, it must exhibit the right level and kinds of movements to visually evoke those of a newborn baby.

Such details, although they may raise questions in the skeptic's mind about the veracity of Richard's account, only add to the rhetorical force of her narrative. The footage featured in this advertisement is necessarily an image of a particular woman's particular fetus; "George" is a specific somebody, and not a generic anybody. For the DeMoss ad to accomplish its aims, however, the fetus pictured must be both commodified (i.e., separated from the social conditions of its production and rendered "exchangeable" with other fetuses) and fetishized (i.e., falsely endowed with "life"). Some origin story for the fetus is needed to make the central antiabortion point that each fetus is a unique individual human life, but that origin story must hover somewhere between the pure abstraction of an idea and the concrete social specificity of a particular woman's particular pregnancy.

The uncertainty regarding the sex of "George"/"Georgette" is particularly telling, in this regard, given the role that sex determination plays in expectant mothers' and parents' construction of a social identity for the fetus. This deliberate obscurity, I suggest, points toward the practice of sonography as the social location at which two different kinds of commodification intersect. Reviewing anthropological approaches to the commodification of body parts, Lesley Sharp argues:

> [T]wo models of commodification may be at work simultaneously, one more akin to Mauss's understanding of the symbolically charged gift and reciprocity, the other to Marx's notion of commodities as goods produced under the alienating conditions of capitalism. Thus, different parties may offer competing readings of various goods of human origin. Whereas, for example, medical professionals may insist on the objectification of body parts, nonprofessionals may instead foreground understandings of kinship, body integrity, and selfhood, all of which may be embodied within an organ or other body fragment. Thus, Mauss and Marx can work in tandem. (Sharp 2001:293)

Sharp's analysis of organ donation illustrates how the two forms of commodification coincide and collide, as donor kin insist that the donated organ should not be severed from the context of its social production, that is, from the social identity of the donor, while organ procurement officials work hard to accomplish and enforce just this kind of detachment (Sharp 2001).

Thanks to its cultural form, the obstetrical ultrasound examination arguably commodifies their fetuses for pregnant women, who tend to approach pregnancy to a considerable extent as a matter of consumption (Taylor 2000). Yet this is, in Sharp's terms, a distinctly Maussian form of commodification; in the context of a diagnostic exam, or even in the context of a nondiagnostic screening at an "entertainment" ultrasound business, the social origins of the fetus (both the social context of a particular woman's pregnancy and the social context of production of ultrasound imagery) are always known.

By contrast, Richard enacts a form of commodification more akin to Marx's notion by deliberately obscuring (even while purporting to reveal) the social context of production of "George"/"Georgette," including the identity of the pregnant woman who carried this particular fetus. It is this act of erasure, an act performed by this particular person who took ultrasound imagery generated in the course of her work as a sonographer and made use of it in contexts far removed from (and in ways antipathetic to) the clinical medical setting, that in one movement commodified this particular fetus, fetishized it, and cast it in the role of "public" fetus.

Even thus detached from the specific social conditions of its production, however, the public fetus retains certain crucial markers of social difference. If ultrasound imagery presents the fetus as a white figure floating against a background of black nothingness, this may perhaps be explicable in terms of the technical features of the modality (though this merits investigation). Juxtaposing a specifically white baby to this ultrasound image cannot be similarly attributed to any sort of technological necessity. It is, rather, the result of a decision made by the advertisement's creators—a judgment that this is what a *valued* baby looks like. As Dorothy Roberts writes of public debates surrounding the new reproductive technologies:

> The images that mark these controversies appear to have little to do with Black people and issues of race. Think about the snapshots that promote the new reproduction. They always show white people. And the baby produced often has blond hair and blue eyes—as if to emphasize her racial purity. . . . Yet it is precisely their racial subtext that gives these images much of their emotional appeal. . . . The monumental effort, expense, and technological invention that goes into the new reproduction marks the children produced as especially valuable. It proclaims the unmistakable message that white children merit the spending of billions of dollars toward their creation. Black children, on the other hand, are the object of welfare reform measures designed to discourage poor women's reproduction. (1997:246, 269)

The visible, valued, white baby with which the fetus is equated in texts such as the DeMoss advertisement considered here takes its meaning at least in part from the implicit contrast drawn with babies (in the U.S. and elsewhere) who are neither visible nor valued in the same ways. It is to this contrast that Donna Haraway points when she writes of "the *missing* representations of fetuses and babies that must trouble anyone yearning for reproductive freedom. . . . [T]his nonimage is of 'human reproductive wastage,' that is, of the dead babies and fetuses, the missing offspring, who populate the earth's off-screen worlds in unimaginable numbers" (1998:203).

"George"/"Georgette" may be stripped of gender and all other markers of social identity, but remains—at least in terms of the racial categories of contemporary U.S. society—a specific kind of valued somebody. The DeMoss advertisement, in other words, racializes the fetus even while fetishizing and commodifying it—and this is, perhaps, part of what makes it so very "cruel."

"Pro-Life, Pro-Choice, and Pro-Fessional"

Richard has publicly narrated the path that led her to her present work (Doyle 1992:4). When she was young, she says, she decided to abort two pregnancies at a time when she felt unable to cope with the responsibilities of motherhood and viewed abortion as a "sensible solution" involving the removal of "blobs of tissue." When she later pursued a career in ultrasound, Richard was shaken by her encounter with fetal imaging. She regarded the fetuses she saw as "babies she could have had years before" and felt great remorse, guilt, and also anger that she had, as she now sees it, never been properly counseled about the realities of or alternatives to abortion. She became very religious and dedicated herself to sharing her newfound vision and knowledge with women contemplating abortion by showing them ultrasound images of the fetus. Her biography, posted on her agent's Web site, explains: "As a result of Shari's personal grief and trauma of abortion she has committed her gift of ultrasound to display the humanity of the unborn and to share God's grace and love that brought her complete healing" (Ambassador Speakers Bureau 2006).

Here again, it is the practice of "showing the baby" that is at issue. Prenatal care is not the only context in which obstetrical ultrasound is used; it is also routinely used to confirm pregnancy and estimate gestational age prior to an elective abortion. When it is known (from a notation on a woman's chart) that the purpose of an exam is dating prior to abortion, the generally accepted practice among sonographers is to allow the pregnant woman herself to decide whether she would like to see the screen or would like any other information about the fetus. Richard and her small cohort of "pro-life" sonographers, however, argue that all women considering abortion should be shown the screen for "educational" purposes before they make their decision.

In the way that she situates her antiabortion activism in relation to a difficult event in her own reproductive history, Richard is like most of the pro-life activists interviewed by Kristin Luker and by Faye Ginsburg in their respective studies of the American abortion debate (Luker 1984; Ginsburg 1989). One interesting aspect of Richard's story, however, is the way that her antiabortion activism also intersects with what DeVault refers to as the formation of professional selves in a "women's" profession (DeVault 1999). Shari Richard is certainly at the extreme of how sonographers understand their selves in relation to their work, and her activities have occasioned no small amount of consternation, as we shall see. Yet from another point of view, Richard is perhaps not so terribly unlike other sonographers, in that she places traditionally female skills of "caring" and what Sharon Durbin called "the miracle and sacredness of life," expressed especially in the "nonmedical" aspects of the ultrasound exam, at the center of her own sense of what her work means.

In 1993, Marveen Craig asked some twenty sonographers to respond to two questions: Do sonographers have the right to try to influence women considering abortion? And do sonographers have a duty to educate patients scheduled for an abortion? Twelve responses were collected and published an article in *JDMS* titled "Pro-Life/Pro-Choice: A New Dilemma for Sonographers" (Craig 1993). While the contributors varied in terms of their own stances regarding abortion, all alike emphatically condemned pro-life uses of ultrasound in the clinical setting on the grounds that they violate values of objectivity and neutrality central to the authors' under-standing of what it means to be "professional." In Marveen's words, "As individuals we have the option to choose to be pro-life or pro-choice, but acting as sonographers there is no choice: we must all be pro-fessional."

Being "pro-fessional" in this sense, however, seems to require beating a hasty retreat from all of those "nonmedical" aspects of the exam that Sharon Durbin emphasized in her own vision of sonography as a caring profession, and onto the seemingly safer ground of purely technical skills. As one contributor put it: "[T]he role of the sonographer is to collect and calculate data and to present it to the physician. It is simply not within the professional jurisdiction of sonographers to transfer their feelings to their patients" (Craig 1993:157). I doubt that most sonographers truly wish to envision themselves thus, as simple collectors and calculators of data—and even for those who do, this stance is one that the by now firmly entrenched cultural form of the obstetrical ultrasound exam, with all its emotionally and culturally fraught rituals of visual demonstration and explanation, makes it difficult to maintain in practice.

Where Fetuses Really Come From

There is a certain irony, perhaps, in the conclusion to which this exploration into the history of obstetrical ultrasound leads us. Feminists have long insisted we must recognize that fetuses come from women; what we've discovered is that this is true in more ways than one. Not only is it pregnant women who physically bear individual fetuses, but women technological workers have played critical roles in the *making* of the fetishized public fetus. Sonographers, like the pregnant women with whom they work, bring to the making of fetuses contexts that matter: their lives, their histories, their positioned perspectives—and indeed their own bodies as well, as their aching hands, wrists, necks, and backs often remind them (Magnavita et al. 1999).[14]

While this analysis complicates matters somewhat, it also has the advantage of allowing us to understand ultrasound technology, and indeed the fetishized public fetus that this technology has helped create, as *mediating relations among women*. Instead of locating their advent in relation to a grand narrative of the male medical and technological takeover of reproduction, we can locate them in relation to a narrative of the changing situations of women in this country. During the same period in which obstetrical ultrasound became routinized in medical practice and the fetishized fetus emerged as a new feature of the public cultural landscape, women in this country were also being "produced" as new sorts of subjects, positioned in new ways relative to work, family, and political life, as well as relative to their sexual and reproductive bodies. Women building careers in newly emerging professions such as sonography form one thread within this broader tapestry; women learning to approach pregnancy and reproduction largely as a matter of consumption (Taylor et al. 2004a; Taylor 2000; Layne 1999) form another. Obstetrical ultrasound is one site among others where the two come together—and one place, perhaps, to begin the work of reweaving a different future.

3

Obstetrical Ultrasound between Medical Practice and Public Culture

The more we explore the world of ultrasound, the more we learn of the world within. We gain fresh perspective on familiar territory. We rediscover ourselves.

—Siemens Quantum ultrasound equipment marketing brochure

In early December 1994, Paul Hill was sentenced to life in prison on federal charges stemming from his July 1994 murders of Dr. John Britton and Mr. John Barrett outside a Pensacola, Florida, abortion clinic. In response to his sentencing, Hill declared that in order to understand his motivations, the judge need only watch an ultrasound of an abortion being performed (West 1994). Few incidents could illustrate more starkly the paradoxical relationship between the medical uses of obstetrical ultrasound and the meanings it has acquired in the broader culture than this invocation of ultrasound technology to "justify" the murder of precisely those medical professionals who use it. How are we to understand the relationship between Paul Hill's use of ultrasound, and the ways in which Dr. Britton might have used it in his work? How do the polarized politics of reproduction relate to the everyday practices of reproduction more generally in contemporary American culture?

In chapter 2 we linked public cultural deployments of fetal imagery back to medical practice. We showed how the circulation of fetal images in and beyond the clinical setting is enabled by features of medical practice that have been shaped by the identities and aspirations of sonographers, an indispensable but often overlooked category of mostly female workers. In this chapter, we shall take a slightly different path toward the same goal of showing how the uses of obstetrical ultrasound within medicine are linked to its uses outside the medical context. Beginning with the puzzle of why medical practice so far outstrips official policy with regard to ultrasound use during pregnancy, we shall then move to consider in detail the theory of "psychological benefits" of obstetrical ultrasound, which I argue may in some part account for this gap. "Psychological benefits" encompass both "reassurance" and "bonding"—which, as we shall see, embody two quite contradictory views of pregnancy, the fetus, and the function of ultrasound imagery. Indeed, I argue that the tension between these two forms of "psychological benefits" points to a deeper contradiction—namely, that the fetus is constructed more and more as a consumer commodity, and pregnancy as a "tentative" condition (Rothman 1993), *at the same time and through the same means* that pregnancy is also constructed more and more as an absolute and unconditional relationship, and the fetus as a person from the earliest stages of development.

In the chapters that follow, we shall see how, when ultrasound is taken up and used outside the medical context—by patients and their families, by advertisers, and by antiabortion advocates—the promise of "reassurance," and ultrasound's function as prenatal diagnostic technique, largely drops out of view, in favor of a greatly expanded notion of "bonding." Here, we shall consider in some detail the manner in which this contradiction shapes the practice of the obstetrical ultrasound examination.[1]

Medical Applications: Policy versus Practice

The advent of ultrasound technology has had an enormous impact on medical knowledge and the treatment of pregnancy. As recently as the early 1970s, ultrasound remained a quite rare and experimental technique in obstetrics. Today, however, "practitioners under the age of 40 or 45 have difficulty imagining that pregnancy can be managed or gynecological disease dealt with unless high frequency sound waves have been caused to traverse a woman's body" (Pitkin 1991, cited in Gabbe 1994:67). From an obstetrician's perspective, it might seem that ultrasound has come to be so widely used because—well, because it is so useful.

Ultrasound provides a wealth of information, much of which could otherwise be obtained only through invasive procedures or would simply not be available at all. Today, an ultrasound exam performed by a competent individual can tell how many embryos or fetuses there are, how the fetus is positioned in the womb, whether its heart is beating, where the placenta is located, and how much amniotic fluid there is. Measurements of features of the fetus, such as the diameter of the head and the circumference of the abdomen, are also taken via ultrasound and then compared to standard charts that researchers have developed over the years. These measurements are used to estimate the "gestational age" of the fetus—in order to establish a "due date," to identify possible growth problems, or in preparation for elective abortion. By visually examining the anatomical structures of the fetus, many gross anatomical abnormalities may be detected—such as anencephaly (in which the skull and brain fail to develop), spina bifida (in which the spinal column is open), diaphragmatic hernia (when a deficiency in the diaphragm allows the contents of the abdomen to ride up into the chest), cleft lip and palate, and dwarfism. Equipment that indicates the direction and speed of flow allows for the detection of a variety of circulatory problems (notably of the heart and the kidneys) as well. Each new generation of equipment features new capabilities that quickly give rise to new applications, such that the range of conditions that can be diagnosed, with varying degrees of certainty, continues to expand. Since the mid-1990s, high-resolution ultrasound has facilitated detection of "soft markers," that is, features whose presence suggests a statistically higher likelihood of certain genetic disorders, though such findings remain highly ambiguous (Filly 2000; Getz and Kirkengen 2003). Ultrasound is also used in conjunction with invasive procedures, a common example being amniocentesis; the image on the screen shows exactly where the needle is, allowing the obstetrician to guide it to the right location in order to extract a sample of amniotic fluid for genetic testing without harming the fetus. Ultrasound examination of the ovaries, in order to monitor ovulation, is also important in the treatment of infertility. The strictly medical value of ultrasound is thus twofold: on the one hand, it is itself used as a technique for prenatal diagnosis and used in conjunction with other tests (though no treatment is available for many of the problems that can be detected). On the other hand, obstetricians also use ultrasound to make decisions about the medical management of abortion, pregnancy, and birth (for example, whether to induce labor, if the "gestational age" of the fetus as determined by ultrasound measurements is judged to be beyond accepted limits).

To say that ultrasound is used because it is useful, however, evades the question of how and why a whole generation of practitioners—and patients—have become convinced that they need, even for apparently unproblematic pregnancies, the kinds of information that ultrasound can offer. Clearly, practice has far outstripped policy in this regard. In the absence of any national health care system, the closest thing to a national policy that exists in the United States are the guidelines issued periodically by national organizations of medical professionals, such as the American College of Obstetricians and Gynecologists (ACOG 2004), and the American Institute of Ultrasound in Medicine (AIUM 2003). Though routine screening has long been instituted as national policy in various European countries, these U.S. guidelines have consistently recommended against the routine screening of all pregnancies by ultrasound, instead insisting that ultrasound should be ordered only on the basis of certain specified medical indications. Recent guidelines follow upon and generally are modeled after the first such list of approved indications, issued in 1984, in a statement developed by a consensus conference convened by the National Institutes of Health (see table 3-1). This list of approved indications might, if strictly observed in practice, be expected to significantly limit the usage of ultrasound in obstetrics. As radiologists Roy A. Filly and James P. Crane note, however:

> The list [of NIH approved indications for sonography] is so comprehensive that it is easier to state which pregnant women are not considered candidates for the test. Simply stated, if a pregnant woman is young (but not too young) and healthy; has a firm recollection of the dates of her last normal menstrual period; goes for examination by her obstetrician early in pregnancy; has completely unremarkable physical examination findings and medical, family, and obstetric histories; meets every milestone during her pregnancy; and has no unusual laboratory findings, then she is not a candidate for Sonography. Rather than argue about the need for "routine" Sonography in such a woman, one could argue whether she needs any medical professional overseeing the pregnancy for it to be successful. (2002:713)

TABLE 3-1

Indications for Obstetrical Ultrasound Approved by the NIH Consensus Conference

1. Estimation of gestational age for patients with uncertain clinical dates, or verification of dates for patients who are to undergo scheduled elective repeat cesarean delivery, indicated induction of labor, or other elective termination of pregnancy.

2. Evaluation of fetal growth (e.g., when the patient has an identified etiology for utero-placental insufficiency, such as severe pre-eclampsia, chronic hypertension, chronic renal disease, severe diabetes mellitus, or for other medical complications of pregnancy where fetal malnutrition, i.e., IUGR or macrosomia, is suspected).

3. Vaginal bleeding of undetermined etiology in pregnancy.

4. Determination of fetal presentation when the presenting part cannot be adequately determined in labor or the fetal presentation is variable in late pregnancy.

5. Suspected multiple gestation based upon detection of more than one fetal heartbeat pattern, or fundal height larger than expected for dates, and/or prior use of fertility drugs.

6. Adjunct to amniocentesis.

7. Significant uterine size/clinical dates discrepancy.

8. Pelvic mass detected clinically.

9. Suspected hydatidiform mole on the basis of clinical signs of hypertension, proteinuria, and/or the presence of ovarian cysts felt on pelvic examination or failure to detect fetal heart tones with a Doppler ultrasound device after 12 weeks.

10. Adjunct to cervical cerclage placement.

11. Suspected ectopic pregnancy or when pregnancy occurs after tuboplasty or prior ectopic gestation.

12. Adjunct to special procedures, such as fetoscopy, intrauterine transfusion, shunt placement, in vitro fertilization, embryo transfer, or chorionic villi sampling.

13. Suspected fetal death.

14. Suspected uterine abnormality (e.g., clinically significant leiomyomata, or congenital structural abnormalities, such as bicornate uterus or uterus didelphys, etc.).

15. Intrauterine contraceptive device localization.

16. Ovarian follicle development surveillance.

17. Biophysical evaluation for fetal well-being after 28 weeks of gestation.

(Continued)

TABLE 3-1 *(Continued)*

18. Observation of intrapartum events (e.g., version/extraction of second twin, manual removal of placenta, etc.).

19. Suspected polyhydramnios or oligohydramnios.

20. Suspected abruptio placentae.

21. Adjunct to external version from breech to vertex presentation.

22. Estimation of fetal weight and/or presentation in premature rupture of membranes and/or premature labor.

23. Abnormal serum alpha-fetoprotein value for clinical gestational age when drawn.

24. Followup observation of identified fetal anomaly.

25. Followup evaluation of placenta location for identified placenta previa.

26. History of previous congenital anomaly.

27. Serial evaluation of fetal growth in multiple gestation.

28. Evaluation of fetal condition in late registrants for prenatal care.

Source: U.S. Department of Health and Human Services, 1984.

Whether practitioners interpreted these guidelines in an expansive manner or ignored them altogether, ultrasound quickly moved from a technology reserved for use in pregnancies with known or suspected complications to one routinely prescribed even in apparently normal pregnancies. Few reliable national-level studies of ultrasound usage exist, but available data indicate that by far the majority of all pregnancies are scanned by ultrasound in the United States. A study published in 1990 (Moore et al. 1990) concluded that between 1980 and 1987 the percentage of all pregnancies scanned by ultrasound increased from 35.5 percent to 78.8 percent. Government figures published recently, based on quite different methods that likely significantly understate rates of usage, indicate that 67 percent of all women who had live births in 2003 had received ultrasound scans (Martin et al. 2005:13).[2] Neither study counted ultrasounds that were paid for out-of-pocket at physicians' offices or at "keepsake" ultrasound businesses. Although the upward trend has fluctuated somewhat, as HMOs and insurance companies have in recent years been reluctant to reimburse scans they deem unnecessary, it is probably reasonable to say that in the United States today, most pregnant women who have access to any form of health care will have at least one ultrasound scan during pregnancy.

Professional guidelines that recommend relatively limited usage of ultrasound in obstetrics balance the "usefulness" of the information that it provides against concerns about safety: "Fetal ultrasonography is considered safe when properly used and when medical information about a pregnancy is needed; however, ultrasound energy delivered to the fetus cannot be assumed to be completely innocuous" (ACOG 2004:1454). This cautious stance has been formalized as "ALARA," the acronym widely used within ultrasound professional circles to refer to the principle of keeping exposure "as low as reasonably achievable," though what counts as "reasonable" in this context continues to be debated. Popular perception of ultrasound remains haunted by vague concerns about the safety of the "radiation" involved. At the level of basic physics, "radiation" refers to all emission and propagation of energy. Ultrasonic waves clearly are a form of radiation, but they are a nonionizing form (that is, a form that does not convert atoms into ions by causing them to lose or gain electrons), and in that respect are more akin to relatively innocuous sunlight and radio waves than to harmful "radioactive" X-rays or gamma rays. The distinction between relatively benign (nonionizing) and relatively dangerous (ionizing) forms of radiation is, however, frequently lost in popular uses of the term. When I asked one woman in the course of my research if there was anything about ultrasound that worried her, she replied:

No, not really. At first, I kept thinking for a long time it's like an X-ray, asking the technician was any type of radiation involved, anything like that. That was when I first had one, that was eight, nine years ago. And I was like, "You can't have an x-ray while you're pregnant, *I* know *that!*" And they said, "Well, it's not really an x-ray." I said, "Well, is there any type of radiation involved?" I asked one ultrasound technician that and they're like, "No, not *much*." I'm like, "What do you mean like *not much?!*" Either you got some or you don't. But he said it's *not much* radiation, it's not the same as having an X-ray done or something like that. It's a certain amount of radiation, but not enough to affect the child, and that's all he said.

Or again, as expressed in this case by the twenty-year-old boyfriend of a nineteen-year-old woman pregnant with their first child: "I felt that ultrasound has a bad effect, really I didn't want no ultrasound for her. 'Cause maybe at this stage, they say it don't have no effect, but then later on down the line they'll find out." Such statements may reflect a certain confusion over the meaning of the term "radiation," but they are not unreasonable; nonionizing forms of radiation, too, can have biological effects. Of primary concern in the case of ultrasound is its capacity to raise the temperature of tissues and to cause cavitation, the formation of gas- and vapor-filled bubbles in liquids, which, when they collapse, produce high temperatures and pressures. Certain therapeutic applications of ultrasound (for example, in the treatment of kidney stones) exploit these bioeffects, while diagnostic applications, by contrast, seek to minimize them.

While ultrasound is widely believed to be very safe at levels used in diagnostic procedures, these levels of exposure have themselves shifted upward over the years as newer generations of equipment employ higher intensities of energy. A 2004 FDA bulletin cautioning against keepsake ultrasound quotes Danica Marinac-Dabic, M.D., an epidemiologist in the FDA's Office of Surveillance and Biometrics, as saying that "modern ultrasound equipment is capable of producing approximately eight times higher intensities than equipment used a decade ago" (Rados 2004:14). Ironically, because ultrasound was widely introduced into practice before large-scale controlled studies were conducted, the primary evidence for its safety is the apparent absence—thus far—of ill effects in the millions of women and their children who have already been exposed. Of course, any such effects could *only* be detected if the right kind of epidemiological research were carried out. X-rays were similarly considered safe during pregnancy until, in 1956, the physician Alice Stewart carried out the research that documented a link between exposure in-utero and a higher risk of early death from cancer (Greene 2001). As Anne Oakley observed: "As [ultrasound] begins to be used, and as it begins to be used more and more, and as no harmful effects emerge (which generally they do not because no mechanism for finding such effects has been set up), people become more and more certain in their claim that the technique is a safe one" (1993:195). Recent research suggests that ultrasound exposure affects fetal brain development in mice (Schmid 2006;

Caviness and Grant 2006). Further research may yet uncover other reasons for concern.

The routinization of obstetrical ultrasound, despite such uncertainties, has been shaped by many factors—including the growth of new industries and new professions associated with this new technology, the increasing cost and importance of insurance, the development of new applications, and, related to this, the gradual expansion of the category of medical indications. Perhaps most interesting, however, is the way that medical practice has been shaped by the theory that ultrasound has "psychological benefits." As we shall see, an examination of the relationship between "medical indications" and "psychological benefits" of ultrasound within medical practice provides an interesting angle into the relationship between reproductive medicine generally and the broader culture and politics of reproduction.

"Psychological Benefits": Behavior, Bonding, and Reassurance

Compared to its many clinical applications, the meanings that ultrasound may carry as an image for pregnant women and their partners are of strictly secondary significance from a medical point of view, and do not appear in any of the official guidelines. However, obstetricians and sonographers alike make frequent reference to ultrasound's "psychological benefits," both in informal conversation and in the medical literature—especially when seeking to persuade skeptical colleagues of the value of new technology. This has been especially striking in discussions surrounding new 3D and 4D equipment that has debuted since the late 1990s. The special capability of this equipment to image tissue surfaces (rather than cross-sectional slices) had no immediate medical application, at least initially. As we shall see in the chapters that follow, some physicians wishing to promote this new equipment have spoken passionately of its greater potential as a tool for promoting psychologically beneficial maternal bonding.

The concept of "psychological benefits" is worth considering in some detail, not only because it has shaped both medical practice and patient expectations of obstetrical ultrasound, but also because the logic of "psychological benefits" echoes that of Paul Hill's very different invocation of ultrasound. In both cases, the sight of the ultrasound image is expected to work an emotional transformation upon the viewer, which will in turn inspire the desired behavior.

Seeing Is Behaving

One reason that "psychological benefits" are considered important is because it is thought that if ultrasound increases a woman's awareness of the fetus—and if this awareness leads a woman to modify her behavior—then ultrasound's "psychological benefits" could potentially improve the physical health of the fetus.[3] For example, an often-cited study of "the short-term psychological effects of early real-time scans," which we shall examine more closely in the next chapter, concludes: "If [viewing the fetus via ultrasound] enhances awareness of the fetus and influences compliance with health-care recommendations such as stopping smoking and alcohol intake, then, as scanning accomplishes this at an earlier stage of pregnancy, there will be greater potential benefit to the fetus" (Campbell et al. 1982:60). Used in this sense, the term "psychological benefits" would probably be more accurately glossed as "behavioral benefits." Since the mind of a woman thus appears to provide one therapeutic route to the body of a fetus, and since images are apparently thought to make more of an impression upon women's minds than words (of explanation, advice, or persuasion), it has become possible to understand psychological benefits as a "medical side effect" of obstetrical ultrasound,[4] or indeed as sound medical grounds for ordering a scan. This is still not approved under official policy.

The "awareness of the fetus" that ultrasound is thought to facilitate encompasses two different ideas of how the sight of the fetus on the ultrasound screen affects a pregnant woman's state of mind—on the one hand, the notion that it promotes maternal bonding; and on the other hand, the notion that it provides reassurance. For example, a consumers' guide to prenatal testing (one of its two authors is an obstetrician who specializes in ultrasound) begins its response to the question "Why Is a Scan So Important?" by citing the importance of "reassurance" and "bonding":

Obstetricians are increasingly recommending that an ultrasound examination to check the structure of the baby be carried out during pregnancy. The advantages of doing so are as follows:
(i) It provides enormous reassurance to parents. Most parents worry a great deal about the normality of their baby during pregnancy. The reassurance of seeing normal structures, plus

the added bonding that a normal ultrasound examination provides, is reason enough for the examination for many people.
(de Crespigny and Dredge 1991:64)

Often, as in the passage above, "reassurance" and "bonding" are used
together, as more or less synonymous terms. The difference between them,
however, is crucial.

Reassurance versus Bonding

The word "reassurance" in this context evokes thoughts of health, happiness
and security—ultrasound, it would seem, dispels fear and doubt from the
mind of the happily pregnant woman by assuring her that her fetus is healthy
and normal. But the "reassurance" that ultrasound offers is always limited—
not all problems can be detected by ultrasound, and problems can also arise
later in pregnancy. Neither ultrasound nor any other technique is capable of
detecting all possible conditions. Faye Ginsburg and Rayna Rapp, in a coau-
thored article describing their joint encounter as friends and feminist ethnographers with the complexities of medicalized reproduction as research
topics and in their own lives, recount a conversation along these lines:

> Two-and-a-half weeks [after Faye's amniocentesis] the results were
> in and the news was good. Faye and Rayna had their usual rushed
> coffee date (Faye's was decaf) and Rayna popped the usual question:
> "What did you learn from this procedure and how do you feel about
> it now?" Faye, true to the pessimistic realism of her Eastern
> European Jewish background, shrugged her shoulders and replied,
> "Well, I learned that my fetus doesn't have three things. That does-
> n't tell me much about a whole lot of other things that might be
> wrong or that might happen before this is over" (1999:283)

An apparently normal exam offers no guarantee of a live birth or a healthy
baby. The "reassurance" that ultrasound may provide thus exists only in
relation to its repressed opposite, which is dread—of the loss of a pregnancy, of fetal abnormality or death, of agonizing dilemmas, of abortion.

When "reassurance" is invoked as one of the "psychological benefits"
of ultrasound, it is on the presumption that ultrasound will in most cases
not reveal fetal death or abnormalities. However, the only approved medical justification for ordering the examination in any individual case is the

reasonable suspicion that it *will* reveal problems, and one of the primary justifications for offering ultrasound screening to all women on a routine basis is the expectation that fetuses exhibiting anomalies will be aborted. Medical articles on ultrasound explicitly make this link between "reassurance" and selective abortion, especially in connection with cost-benefit assessments. For example, an article on "Routine versus Indicated Scans" concludes that "the short-term gains resulting from routine ultrasound would be reassurance that patients receive from the knowledge that the ultrasound study is normal. . . . Long-term gains would include identification of a major anomaly and termination of pregnancy, thus avoiding the birth of a child with an anomaly who is likely to survive but with a poor quality of life" (Gabbe 1994:72). Thus, if ultrasound offers women "reassurance" that their individual pregnancies are normal, it does so by granting tentative exemptions on a case-by-case basis from the broader conviction that pregnancy in general is inherently prone to go badly awry. Indeed, far from offering greater reassurance, advances in ultrasound technology and prenatal diagnosis have arguably only heightened the level of fear and worry that women experience. Getz and Kirkengen (2003) note that since the mid-1990s, the field of diagnostic ultrasound has seen an explosion of research and publications on "soft markers," that is, not structural abnormalities directly discernible in the fetus, but visible features known to be statistically associated with somewhat elevated risks.

If a pregnant woman has reason to feel reassured when problems are not detected, the obstetrician who provides care for her has some reason to feel reassured when they are. Given the realities of practicing medicine in the American context, another "long-term gain" from routine ultrasound is the protection that prenatal diagnosis can afford against possible "wrongful birth" or "wrongful life" lawsuits. In short, ultrasound as a prenatal diagnostic technique, in combination with selective abortion, is enlisted to attempt to minimize the possibility of a less than perfect child—while ultrasound for reassurance offers to dispel the dread that may attend the "tentative" pregnancy under these conditions.[5]

If the notion of "reassurance" contains repressed fears that the health of the embryo or fetus will not conform to expectations, the notion of "bonding" contains similar fears regarding the emotional disposition of the pregnant woman. As we shall see in the following chapter, the theory of bonding has undergone several transformations as it has migrated from the hospital labor-and-delivery room, to the ultrasound examination room, to the public cultural domain of mass media advertising and abortion polemics, with important implications. The notion of ultrasound bonding equates pregnancy with the relationship between a woman and her newborn child—in this regard, it presumes a view of pregnancy as absolute, a relationship of unconditional maternal love for the developing fetus. At the same time, however, the theory that ultrasound promotes bonding suggests that this relationship forms through technologically and professionally mediated spectatorship. Of course, the claim that ultrasound imagery can facilitate the formation of emotional bonds also implies, on some level, that without such technological and professional interventions, women might *not* in fact always feel the same maternal concern toward the embryo or early fetus, as they might feel for a fetus in the later stages of pregnancy or a newborn child.

Commodity, Person, Fetus

The contradiction between "reassurance" and "bonding" should be obvious. The notion of "reassurance" emerges from ultrasound's function as prenatal diagnostic technique. As we have seen, this enacts a view of pregnancy as a highly conditional matter, contingent upon the embryo or fetus successfully passing certain tests and measuring up to the scrutiny of a critical scientific gaze that evaluates its condition and its development in light of an ever more elaborate body of knowledge about what is normal. As Rothman, among others, has pointed out, the fetus appears in this context as a sort of consumer commodity:

> The commodification process has transformed pregnancy, as society encourages the development of prenatal testing. This process—genetic counseling, screening and testing of fetuses—serves the function of "quality control" on the assembly line of the products of conception, separating out those products we wish to develop from those we wish to discontinue. Once we see the products of conception as just that, as products, we begin to treat them as we do any other product, subject to similar scrutiny and standards. (Rothman 2000:8)

The notion of "bonding," by contrast, presumes that pregnancy should be a relationship of unconditional maternal love, the natural development of which ultrasound technology may speed up and enhance (or, if necessary, jumpstart). In this perspective the fetus, as object of a loving maternal regard, is construed as a person. The contradiction here is that ironically, pregnancy is constructed more and more as a "tentative" relationship, and the fetus as a "commodity," *at the same time and through the same means* that pregnancy is also constructed more and more as an absolute and unconditional relationship, and the fetus as a "person" from its earliest stages.

It often does happen that ultrasound in fact reveals no fetal abnormalities, and that a pregnant woman in fact does derive some pleasure from viewing her fetus on the screen. In such cases, this contradiction might never fully surface to consciousness—many women do indeed experience the ultrasound exam as a moment of both "reassurance" and "bonding." Yet the dominant narrative of ultrasound's "psychological effects," which tells of an intentionally pregnant woman happily reassured and bonded with her provisionally certified-normal fetus, always contains within itself repressed counternarratives of guilt and dread, in the possibility of a different ending. The ever-present possibility of a "positive" diagnosis threatens to force this contradiction to the surface, by putting the pregnant woman in the anguishing position of deciding whether to selectively abort, or knowingly carry a fetus that is in some way anomalous—demanding, in the terms set by the abortion debate, that she declare it either a "commodity" or a "person." It is this dreaded possibility that lends such drama to the routine ultrasound examination—the agonizing suspense of waiting and wondering, the climactic moment of diagnosis, the joy (or despair) that follows.[6]

A contradiction between opposing views of pregnancy and of the fetus may be discerned in the gap between policy and practice regarding ultrasound use during pregnancy, and in fissures within the concept of "psychological benefits." At the level of social practice, the same contradiction emerges in the form of tensions about the boundaries of the medical domain in the context of the obstetrical ultrasound examination.

The Ultrasound Examination: A Hybrid Practice

In the United States, the medical task of obtaining certain views and measurements of the fetus and placenta is carried out via an examination that has assumed a very particular cultural form that also encompasses a number of other elements. A pregnant woman usually is allowed to bring a companion (often her husband or boyfriend) into the examining room, and the sonographer typically shows them the screen, points out certain features of the fetus, offers the pregnant woman the option of learning fetal sex if it can be seen, and gives her an image to take home. While practice naturally varies and not all examinations include all of these elements, sonographers tend, at the very minimum, at some point to show the pregnant woman the screen. It is widely agreed that women generally want to see the image of the fetus, that they are entitled to, and that to do so is beneficial, for reasons we have explored. Sonographers themselves have their own reasons as well for wanting to meet these perceived needs and desires of their women patients. The ultrasound examination is thus a hybrid practice, in that assumptions about the nonmedical meanings and functions of ultrasound are incorporated into medical practice.

These conventions are not only enshrined in widely shared expectations, but indeed built into the very architecture of equipment and clinic. Many U.S. ultrasound companies, for example, have long built into their equipment a swivel monitor that facilitates turning the screen so that the pregnant woman can see it, as well as a special printer for producing "souvenir photos" to give to patients. Today's 3D and 4D devices come equipped to impart to fetal images a warm sepia tone reminiscent of old-fashioned photos. The dual aspects of obstetrical ultrasound, as high-tech medical device and as a form of consumer product, also enter into equipment design in more subtle ways, in the overall design of the visible exterior of the machine, as a design engineer at a major U.S. ultrasound company explains:

What feelings should this system convey, when you walk in the door? Is it a very ominous black box that magically produces an image, so are you in awe of this machine? Or are you a buddy with this machine? A lot of the forms that we play with in creating an overall aesthetic, how we use those forms and colors can really send a different signal. Like a very soft, curvaceous form may be something that's more consumerish, as opposed to sharp angles and hard edges, rectilinear shapes. But you have to strike a balance. . . . You may look at it and say, "Wow, that's fun. Let's have an ultrasound today." Or, "Wow, that's a serious product there, it looks lethal." . . . We will try to strive for *one* image with this product, a combination of "high-tech," because that still means a lot to people in a positive way, but at the same time "friendly."

Similarly, examination rooms in ob/gyn ultrasound clinics are often furnished with an extra chair for the woman's companion—typically the father of the expected child, but often a female friend or relative.

Professional practices, equipment features, and public expectations congealed around this particular ritualized form some years ago; by now it has become difficult to do things otherwise. As a hybrid practice, the ultrasound exam highlights the fact that medicine is *not* a completely distinct domain of knowledge and practice. Indeed, much of the cultural "work" that goes on around the practice of ultrasound involves struggles to establish clear boundaries between medicine and the broader consumer culture within which it is located—between medical indications and "psychological benefits," between medical professionals and patients-as-consumers, between medical procedures and visual entertainment.

Between Medical Indications and Psychological Benefits

Officially, ultrasound examinations may be ordered only on the basis of certain specified "medical indications," as we noted earlier. Some exams clearly are ordered because the practitioner has reason to suspect a problem, and there is reason to believe that others are actually ordered solely for "psychological benefits"—but most cases are in fact not clear-cut. At the clinic where I did research, sonographers usually began each scan by asking the patient why she was having an ultrasound. With remarkable regularity, women answered that: "The doctor ordered a scan just to check and make sure everything's okay."

What does this mean? Does it mean that the doctor has reason to think something is *not* okay but failed to communicate this clearly to the patient? Or does it mean that the scan was ordered to reassure the patient by "checking and making sure" that everything *is* okay? Both could be the case; ambiguity surrounding the distinction between medical indications and psychological benefits is inherent in the hybrid character of the ultrasound examination. According to sonographers, the majority of problems discovered via ultrasound are totally unsuspected—so that an exam ordered, in good faith, for "psychological benefit" may nonetheless unexpectedly reveal major or minor abnormalities or fetal death. Indeed, the ACOG's most recent guidelines on obstetrical ultrasound, published in December 2004, cite studies suggesting that "90% of infants with congenital anomalies are born to women with no risk factors" (ACOG 2004:1454). And unsuspected problems may turn up even with women who have had ultrasound scans previously in the same pregnancy; "in screened populations, the detection rate for congenital anomalies ranged from 16% to 85%" (ACOG 2004:1454).

Perhaps because they deal with the tension between medical applications and "psychological benefits" on a daily basis, sonographers I observed at work sometimes attempted to draw the line between them by exhorting women to demand from their doctors a *medical* reason for ordering an ultrasound. One exam started out this way:

S: Now tell me why she ordered the ultrasound.

P: I don't know.

S: You have to ask why. If somebody sticks a needle in your arm, don't you ask why? It's the same thing.

At the same time, however, sonographers could hardly help but conflate the two, since the convention of "showing the baby" for the "psychological benefit" of the patient is firmly entrenched in medical practice.

For a woman who is *already* focusing on medical indications, this may sometimes only heighten the intrusiveness of ultrasound as a medical procedure. Savita, a thirty-three-year-old administrator in a nonprofit organization, pregnant with her first child, described her experience:

We spoke to the genetic counselor, because there are some problems in my family and some in his family, and so we had an ultrasound just to look for any problems with the organs. And I must say I didn't enjoy that at all. First of all it took a very long time, they were looking at the heart, the four chambers of the heart, and the valves and the ventricles and the this and the that, and they looked at the kidneys, looked at them very closely. Just somehow ... I felt like the baby you know, until now, had been just fine and I could tell how it was doing by its kicking movements inside, and then. . . . Somehow

I just felt that I didn't want to know all this. It just felt like, too much. I got actually quite emotional, kind of crying a little bit, I didn't really want to look at the screen at all. . . . They were very willing to explain things, but I kind of didn't want to know.

Between Professional and Patient

Still, the incorporation of such practices may, in subtle ways, shape women's experience of the medical procedure itself, especially for those less well positioned to make demands as consumers in a medical setting. The convention of "showing the baby," for example, provides an opening for women to interrogate sonographers about the medical procedure in a way that might be unusual in the context of other diagnostic tests or in interactions with doctors. Consider this exchange between Linda (the sonographer) and Charlotte, a thirty-nine-year-old African American woman expecting her first child, previously employed as a nurse's aide, who was referred for an ultrasound scan from a prenatal care clinic operated by the Board of Health:

CHARLOTTE: You still lookin' at the head?

LINDA: Yeah . . . are you sure of your dates?

CHARLOTTE: Why, you think it's coming sooner?

LINDA: I'll have to do all the measurements. Here's baby's nose, and mouth.

CHARLOTTE: How can you tell? I mean, I expected to see like a human form. . . . So there's really a baby in there? This is the head and stuff up here, right? . . . Now what are we looking at?

LINDA: Baby's like all stretched out . . . there's the heartbeat, see it moving?

CHARLOTTE: Yeah. . . . Well, it's alive. What are those two holes there?

LINDA: Vessels.

CHARLOTTE [to screen]: Well, why don't you turn over so we can see what you are. . . . [then, to the sonographer]: Is he turned over?

LINDA: This is baby's belly. . . .

CHARLOTTE: Where at, right here? [She touches the screen.]

LINDA: This is baby's bladder, this is baby's thigh. . . .

CHARLOTTE: Gettin' close, huh?

LINDA: Sometimes when they're breach, butt down, we can't see . . . this is where the cord goes into the body. . . .

CHARLOTTE [looking at the machine]: Every time it hits a point it beeps, huh? What was that?

In practice, then, "showing the baby" often also means "showing the anatomy," "showing the procedure," and "showing the equipment." As we left the room after this particular exam, Linda whispered to me, "She's driving me nuts!!" In my observation, the sonographers at the clinic where I conducted research generally talked to women with respect and answered questions patiently and clearly, but Linda and other sonographers did sometimes express frustration when patients asked too many questions. And I most often heard such complaints about women who, like Charlotte, were "clinic" patients—those without private health insurance who must rely upon Medicare and Medicaid for coverage. Charlotte, perhaps emboldened by her experience working as a nurse's aide, took a rare degree of initiative—not only did she ask a great many questions during the exam, but when left alone for a few minutes afterward to dress herself, she seized the transducer and attempted to see for herself what she felt Linda had not shown her. "After she left I did it myself," she told me. "I put the gel on and I moved it around myself, and I could see things."

More than merely complicating the sonographer's task, the convention of "showing the baby" poses a subtle challenge to the hierarchy that separates the sonographer as medical professional from the patient. On the one hand, the sonographer's professional responsibilities require that she perform scans accurately and relatively quickly,[7] obtaining a series of specific anatomical views in a fixed sequence, looking for abnormalities and problems. If she sees any, according to most protocols she is *not* to communicate that information to the patient, but is instead to notify the attending physician, who will then arrange for the patient to be informed in a counseling session.[8] It is thus assumed that the sonographer commands specialized medical knowledge and skills, to which patients cannot have immediate access. On the other hand, however, the sonographer is also expected to show the patient the screen and give a play-by-play account of what she is seeing, both to "reassure" the patient and to facilitate "bonding." It is thus also expected that the sonographer can and will make ultrasound understandable to people with no medical training at all.

This tension surrounding the sonographer's professional status emerged particularly clearly on one occasion during my ethnographic research, when the friend of a young "clinic" patient, who had accompanied her into the examination room, pointed to the screen and gleefully declared, "It's a boy! I can tell, it *looks* like a boy!" Turning to me (as I sat in the back of the room taking notes), the sonographer said, with some irritation: "You know, it's amazing to me, we go through a very rigorous training to do this, and then patients come in and after one minute they think they know!" Those whose professional identity is bound up with their expertise in ultrasound may perceive that their own status as medical professionals is eroded when people appear to assume that this medical technology is comparable to television, photography, or other forms of imagery that require no special skills to interpret. As one obstetrician complained to me, "To us this is a deadly serious medical procedure, but to them it's just a form of entertainment!"

Between Medicine and Entertainment

Because women patients and others outside the medical profession do not necessarily distinguish between the somewhat medically acceptable pleasures of bonding or reassurance and the pleasures of entertainment, the notion that ultrasound has "psychological benefits" can in fact open the way for a serious challenge to both the integrity and the authority of the medical practice of ultrasound. Some sonographers get around this issue by separating the "medical" portion of the exam from the "entertainment" portion as distinct moments in time, with statements such as the following: "What I'm going to do is run through these pictures first, then I'll show you the baby in its entirety. So if I'm not talking much, that's because I'm trying to concentrate, okay?" In this way, the sonographer in effect divides the exam into two distinct parts. This allows her to first step into the role of medical professional, wordlessly performing a diagnostic procedure, and then step into the role of educator, providing a demonstration of fetal anatomy that often focuses on those features thought to be of interest to parents, such as the face, the hands, and the heart.

Dividing the ultrasound exam in this manner reestablishes the autonomy of the medical diagnostic procedure within the examination. At the same time, however, instituting a scan for "psychological" benefit alongside the medical procedure may tend to validate the performance of obstetrical ultrasound for nonmedical reasons, and this in turn poses a challenge to medical control. When the nonmedical exam is separated entirely in space and time from the medical procedure, then medical authorities may sometimes step in to put a stop to it. As early as 1994, an enterprise opened up in Texas offering ultrasound videos purely for entertainment purposes, and the Food and Drug Administration shut it down because, in the words of the FDA spokesperson, "It is an approved device, but an unapproved use. . . . The FDA only allows ultrasound to be used for specific conditions, and entertainment, or just the pleasure of knowing what's going on in the uterus, is not approved" (News Wave 1994). The FDA, however, has proven largely powerless to stop the many more such enterprises that have sprung up since, especially following the advent of 3D and 4D equipment in the late 1990s, as discussed in chapter 6.

One might argue, in any case, that the distinction between keepsake ultrasound and medical ultrasound is less clear-cut than such stern pronouncements would seem to suggest. Scanning for "entertainment, or just the pleasure of knowing what's going on in the uterus," is commonly incorporated into the practice of medically indicated scans. Even within the medical context, the "entertainment" portion of the exam may spin off to become quite separate from the medical procedure, as in this case described to me by a sonographer who worked in an obstetrical clinic for many years:

> At the clinic where I work, the doctors are very responsible, very conservative, but I guess they think that if it's safe at this level of exposure, it's just always safe no matter what. So, they will send a patient for an ultrasound exam, and if we can't see the sex that first time, then the patient herself can call back and schedule a second exam. At first it was just a matter of, you know, if we've done the exam and they want to know the sex, I could spend ten minutes just looking for the sex, but why not come back another time and do that ten minutes another time, when you'd have a better chance of seeing it? So it started out as a "sex check" for people who couldn't get the sex the first time, but it evolved into a situation where they'll schedule a "sex check" for a videotape, or so that grandma can come along, 'cause grandma didn't get to see it. . . . They bill the patient

directly for this, they charge $35, just for our time really, it doesn't go through the third-party system at all. So basically it's home entertainment video, but it's done in a doctor's office.

Cast in this light, allowing patients to schedule ultrasound scans on their own purely for viewing pleasure might sound like a case of questionable medical ethics—yet it is not, perhaps, so very different from ordering an exam for "psychological benefits," which appears to be a relatively widely accepted practice.

Indeed, just how tricky it is to separate medical from entertainment scanning is clear from the American Institute for Ultrasound in Medicine's recent official statement on keepsake ultrasound imaging:

> The AIUM understands the growing pressures from patients for the performance of ultrasound examinations for bonding and reassurance purposes largely driven by the improving image quality of 3D sonography and by more widely available information about these advances. Although there is only preliminary scientific evidence that 3D sonography has a positive impact on parental-fetal bonding, the AIUM recognizes that many parents may pursue scanning for this purpose. Such "keepsake imaging" currently occurs in a variety of settings, including the following:
>
> 1. Images or video clips given to parents during the course of a medically indicated ultrasound examination;
> 2. Freestanding commercial fetal imaging sites, usually without any physician review of acquired images and with no regulation of the training of the individuals obtaining the images; these images are sometimes called "entertainment videos"; and
> 3. As added cost visits to a medical facility (office or hospital) outside the coverage of contractual arrangements between the provider and the patient's insurance carrier. (AIUM 2005)

The AIUM then goes on to recommend that "only scenario 1 above is consistent with the ethical principles of our professional organizations." Because this statement, for the first time, acknowledges that keepsake scanning does in fact occur within the clinical setting and expresses disapproval of the practice, it has been described by some as a "toughening up" of policy. Yet this new tougher policy still "encourages the practice [of sharing diagnostic ultrasound images with patients] when a clinically indicated obstetric evaluation grants the opportunity" (Abella 2005). In conclusion, the AIUM statement on keepsake ultrasound notes that "the market for keepsake images is driven in part by past medical approaches that have used medicolegal concerns as a reason not to provide images to patients. . . . [W]e encourage sharing images with patients as appropriate when indicated obstetric ultrasound examinations are performed" (AIUM 2005).

Apparently, one consequence of the hybrid character of the practice of obstetrical ultrasound is that practitioners have to some extent ceded to women as consumers the authority to decide if and when to order an ultrasound scan. This is evident in the guidelines recently published by the American College of Obstetricians and Gynecologists. While sternly advising, as such guidelines have consistently done for more than twenty years, that "ultrasonography should be performed only when there is a valid medical indication," the same report states that "a physician is not obligated to perform ultrasonography in a patient who is at low risk and has no indications. However, if a patient requests ultrasonography, it is reasonable to honor the request" (ACOG 2004:1454).

Even some nurse-midwives with whom I have spoken routinely offer ultrasound, even though their clients are women already defined as "low-risk" and, by choosing to work with midwives, have already opted for a more "natural" pregnancy and childbirth.[9] Two nurse-midwives who work in a hospital-based practice explained:

> About a year and a half ago we began offering structural ultrasound to patients at twenty weeks, because so many of our patients were asking for ultrasound. You know, they see all their friends having two or three or even four ultrasounds during pregnancy, they get worried that something might be missed, medically. Also, they look forward to it. It's real reassuring, especially for women who've had a miscarriage in the past. . . . And they read about ultrasound in all the women's magazines, they expect it. . . . As midwives, we believe in less intervention, but we're also committed to the idea that women should be active participants in their own care. . . . And there is a big difference in the kinds of people that choose to work with midwives

now, compared to when we started out in the seventies—maybe it's because we're more accepted now? But it's much more technological. Women request ultrasound, they request induction. . . . So we offer them a structural scan, and about 80% choose to have one.

Some women, to be sure, resist having ultrasound during pregnancy, and many more simply agree to a scan because their prenatal care provider recommends it. Yet women themselves, as avid consumers of prenatal care, have also clearly been active agents in the routinization of ultrasound. In an environment where pregnancy is often experienced as a quest for scientific knowledge, and where medical wisdom and practices are constantly changing, women pass along to each other information about ultrasound along with other advice about pregnancy, birth and child care:[10]

> At our Lamaze class, you know, everyone was kind of comparing notes, and one woman said she hadn't had a sonogram yet and didn't think she was going to have one, and this other woman said to her, very sternly, "You go right back there and you tell that doctor you want a sonogram! You can get one!" (Debbie, a thirty-six-year-old white lawyer)

> I requested [an ultrasound]. I explained my fears, about me being over thirty-five years old, and [the doctor] said it's rare now a woman goes through a full pregnancy without one. . . . A woman in the waiting room showed me her ultrasound picture. And I got disappointed because I didn't have one. . . . People kept asking me, "What is it? What is it?" Everybody kept asking me, "Did you have your ultrasound yet?" I felt cheated. I wanted to see that it was normal, and also, I didn't want to miss out on that experience. (Charlotte, whom we encountered earlier in this chapter)

Between the two halves of that sentence—"I wanted to see that it was normal" and "I didn't want to miss out on that experience"—lies all of the contradiction that we have been tracing. On the one hand, Charlotte wanted to be "reassured" that the fetus she carried was normal—she wanted it to pass the test of prenatal diagnosis, to be assessed as a valuable commodity. On the other hand, she also didn't want to miss out on the experience of having an ultrasound examination as a valued part of the overall experience of pregnancy—she wanted the pleasure of seeing and "bonding" with her eagerly awaited baby. The contradiction is there in women's experience of pregnancy, and we have seen how it is built into medical practice itself.

It is here that we see most clearly the manner in which the notion of ultrasound as a tool for promoting maternal "bonding" may ironically work to undermine the integrity of the relationship between the pregnant woman and the fetus. We see, too, how the tensions inherent within the hybrid practice of obstetrical ultrasound may finally explode, as the theory of ultrasound "bonding" sets the stage for antiabortion advocates to use the authority, power, and tools of medical science *against* a medical procedure and the medical professionals who perform it.

Illogical Conclusions

Paul Hill's statement, which uses obstetrical ultrasound imagery to explain and justify his ideologically motivated murder of a physician who would have used obstetrical ultrasound technology in the course of his work, does not come out of nowhere—it is the logical (or rather, the very illogical) conclusion of the curious role that ultrasound plays in contributing to both of the two very different visions at stake in the U.S. abortion debate. Pregnancy is constructed as a highly tentative and conditional affair, subject to prenatal testing and quality control—and at the same time, the very technology that is used to perform the diagnostic test is also used to construct pregnancy as an experience of unconditional bonding. More generally, the fetus increasingly is construed as a consumer product, at the same time that it is construed more and more as a "person" from the earliest stages of development. Obstetrical ultrasound is involved intricately in many aspects of these contradictory processes, and the resulting tensions, which are implicit within medical practice itself, become glaring as ultrasound is taken up outside the medical context in the broader culture. An ethnographic focus on obstetrical ultrasound allows us to see, in part, how the black-and-white polarities of abortion politics emerge out of a level of practice that is, like ultrasound imagery itself, an ever-changing composition in many shades of gray, as ambiguous as it is emotionally charged.

4

Love Machine

The Theory of Ultrasound Bonding

[The Tin Man, to Dorothy]: "Do you suppose Oz could give me a heart?"
—L. Frank Baum, *The Wonderful Wizard of Oz*

When I met Pamela J., a thirty-eight-year-old child-care provider, she was pregnant with her fourth child and had come to the ultrasound clinic for a routine exam. Afterward, she reflected on her experience of pregnancy and how it differed from that of women in her mother's generation:

> Well, now we have all these new technologies. . . . I don't know what infant mortality was back then, I don't think there was so much emphasis on monitoring the baby—but now, you find out the health of the baby, you find out the sex, and that bonds you to the baby. When I found out it made me bond more with the baby instead of focusing on the negatives of pregnancy.

The idea Pamela voiced here, that ultrasound technology helps women to "bond" emotionally with the fetuses they carry, is one widely accepted and frequently articulated by ordinary laypersons and medical professionals alike. For brevity's sake, I shall refer to this idea (somewhat awkwardly) as "the theory of ultrasound bonding." This theory links the pleasure that many women take in the sight of ultrasound imagery to the social and emotional transformations that take place in the course of pregnancy, thereby suggesting that ultrasound technology accelerates and improves upon the natural process by which pregnant women enter into a specifically maternal relationship to the fetus.

Talk of "bonding" comes easily in the contemporary United States. We speak of bonding[1] not only between mothers and their infants, but between coworkers, acquaintances, siblings, lovers, strangers thrown together by circumstance, even large groups of people united by some common goal or experience. Indeed, the term's meaning as used in every-day parlance is broad enough to encompass a sentence such as this: "As part of a bonding ritual in their fledgling white supremacist group, the three men took [James] Byrd [Jr.] to a remote part of town, beat him, and chained his legs together before attaching them to the truck" (Sullivan 2000:182). Bonding thus can involve hate or fear as well as love, and can produce ties of criminal conspiracy as easily as those of kinship. It is a sort of catch-all term used to indicate that some process of social relationship formation is taking place, while telling us very little about exactly how that process works or exactly what sort of relationship results.

Currently, bonding is invoked in everyday speech to describe all kinds of relationships while explaining nothing about them precisely. The word is recent: the term "bonding" was coined only as recently as the early 1970s and initially referred quite exclusively to the relationship between a mother and her infant, about which it was thought to explain a great deal indeed. Webster's Collegiate Dictionary defines bonding as "the formation of a close personal relationship (as between a mother and child) esp. through frequent or constant association" and claims that this usage dates to just 1976. This new meaning emerged out of the research of scientists, including most notably the pediatricians John Kennell and Marshall Klaus, who (as will be discussed in more detail below) sought to document, understand, and strengthen the processes by which mothers form relationships with their children in the period immediately following birth. Previously, "bonding" as a verbal noun was hardly used at all, and the word "bond," used as a verb, had two principal senses. In one usage, "to bond" referred to physical processes of causing things to adhere closely to one another: the "bonding" together of surfaces by means of glue, for example, or the chemical "bonding" of atoms. In another usage, "to bond" referred to the legal and financial process of undertaking a debt or obligation: "to secure payment of duties and taxes (on goods) by giving a bond."

Echoes of these two older meanings persist in the idea of maternal-infant "bonding" as proposed by the researchers who pioneered the term.

On the one hand, the concept posits that mothers and their infants can be socially "glued" together in an almost physical manner, and on the other hand, it speaks of a universal obligation and duty of mothers to love and nurture their offspring. In an essay first published in 1986, the feminist sociologist Ann Oakley sharply questioned whether women and fetuses really needed scientists and high-tech medical devices to "glue" them together:

> It has been claimed that ultrasound in pregnancy now enables obstetricians to "introduce" mothers to their fetuses and facilitate a new phenomenon called prenatal bonding. In exactly the same way, the medical innovation of hospital delivery enabled paediatricians to discover the phenomenon of postnatal bonding. I would suggest that all this is rediscovering-the-wheel activity of a most primitive kind. Mothers and newborn babies bonded before hospitalized delivery disturbed the natural process. Mothers and fetuses were in a relationship with one another before they met on the ultrasound screen. (1993:196)

More than twenty years later, Oakley's criticisms remain unanswered. Even as ultrasound technology has advanced remarkably, the theory of ultrasound bonding remains both substantially unchanged and firmly entrenched. Pamela, like many others who speak casually of ultrasound and bonding, may not know the history of scientific research and debates that lies behind it. Leading figures in a variety of political and medical professional factions, however, draw upon the aura of scientific authority that lingers from this history, or in some cases explicitly claim that the theory of ultrasound bonding is scientifically proven, when they call upon it to support a variety of specific agendas. Some wish to promote wider use of new 3D and 4D ultrasound equipment within obstetrics; some are eager to enlist ultrasound in their activist efforts to stop women from having abortions; and some seek to sell fetal ultrasound imaging services directly to pregnant women consumers in a commercial setting.

All of these agendas have far-reaching implications, and anyone who cares about reproductive medicine, reproductive health, or reproductive rights therefore has good reason to pay close attention to the arguments marshaled in support of them. Because these arguments so often rely on the theory of ultrasound bonding and claim or imply for it scientific backing, the evidence behind such claims deserves to be investigated carefully. Upon closer scrutiny, this idea, which is so widely accepted as both reasonable and true, turns out to be rather more magical, and rather more troubling in its implications, than one might guess at first.

Questions of Evidence

Those who advocate a new technique are liable to suffer from a strange condition called certainty. (Ann Oakley 1993:193)

Claims regarding ultrasound's capacity to promote maternal bonding, and transform women's emotional disposition toward their pregnancies, make regular public appearances in the arguments put forth by people working to try to shape the ways ultrasound is used, inside and outside of the clinical setting. Some of these people also seek to enlist ultrasound in their struggles to end abortion. Is there evidence to support such claims?

The question is remarkably seldom raised. But perhaps we should not be surprised that efforts to promote and sell ultrasound services to the general public tend not to bother much about evidence. Thus, for example, the Fetal Fotos Web site explains that "what we offer is a bonding experience using this technology and the skills we have developed" (Fetal Fotos 2004), and the Web site for Elite Diagnostics states that "we are also offering 3D/4D scans to patients on a self-referral basis for the purpose of enhancing parental bonding. Acquiring views of the baby may provide reassurance to parents unparalleled by other methods. We are actively studying these reassurance exams for the potential psychological benefits they may provide" (Elite Diagnostics 2006). Neither company attempts to explain what bonding is, why it is important, or how ultrasound promotes it; neither includes any citations to other research, and neither text comes with a byline naming the person who wrote it. They simply assert that ultrasound promotes maternal bonding as if it is a settled matter of fact, and know that their audience may either buy it or not, but will not likely come back demanding specific citations to the scientific literature.

Even in the medical literature, where we might expect greater attention to questions of evidence, claims regarding maternal-infant bonding are often simply flatly asserted, with no reference to any controversy or uncertainty and no citations to supporting research. Often, the theory of ultrasound bonding appears as an offhand, by-the-way observation, in the context of an article whose main focus lies somewhere else entirely. Radiologist Dónal Downey and colleagues, for example, discuss the clinical advantages and disadvantages of three-dimensional as compared with two-dimensional ultrasound, focusing on quite technical matters of how the device generates the image, how it presents data, types of transducers, imaging artifacts, practical tips for obtaining optimal imaging, and so forth. The final section, on "Applications for 3D US," lists first of all "Fetal Imaging." The authors write:

> Three dimensional US has shown the most promise in obstetric imaging. Rendering techniques give a novel perspective on the fetal anatomy and have been reported to make anomalies easier to recognize. Three-dimensional US also improves maternal-fetal bonding and can help families better understand fetal abnormalities. (Downey et al. 2000:566)

As seen in the previous chapter, the promise that ultrasound will enable better detection of fetal abnormalities meshes rather uneasily with the promise that it will also promote maternal bonding. Here, we might merely note that although the authors of this article quite scrupulously follow scientific conventions of citation with regard to many other details of their article, the reference to maternal-infant bonding is simply dropped in passing, stated as fact, with no supporting evidence.

Of course, a certain appearance of solidity attaches even to otherwise unsupported statements, when these are published in an authoritative medical or scientific journal. The same is also true of words spoken by someone officially anointed as an expert, having been granted a doctoral degree. Many journalistic pieces on ultrasound present the theory of ultrasound bonding in the form of words spoken by a medical professional. Thus, for example, an article posted on Web MD (a very popular Web site to which many people turn seeking self-help information on a variety of health- and medicine-related topics) informs readers:

> One of the best ways you can bond with your baby, says Thomas Ivester, MD, clinical instructor in maternal-fetal medicine at the

University of Tennessee Health Science Center in Memphis, is by having an ultrasound. "Bonding during pregnancy gives a mom a better sense of responsibility in caring for herself, and by extension, the baby," he says. "When you can actually see the baby, that increases the feeling that the baby actually exists." (Sorgen 2006)

Does Dr. Ivester know of research that supports this claim? If so, he does not mention it—nor does he need to, as the MD degree attached to his name apparently provides sufficient guarantee that whatever he might say must be true.

Persuasive texts written for the already-persuaded—such as articles with an antiabortion emphasis that are directed at conservative Christian audiences—sometimes deal with questions of evidence in yet another manner, invoking "science," "studies," or "research" without actually naming or quoting any specific researchers, much less providing any citations to the scholarly literature. One example of such a text (to which the Fetal Fotos Web site provides a link) is the transcript of a July 2003 episode of *The 700 Club* Christian television show, in which Kristi Watts, who appears regularly on that show, recounts her own recent visit to a keepsake ultrasound studio. Watts quotes the franchise owner's vague reference to unspecified "studies":

Valerie explained how this technology has changed the way we view life. "Certain studies show the benefits of showing an ultrasound, and we've definitely seen it here," said Valerie. "To see the baby act like a baby, the little fetus is doing things in there—yawning, stretching, and rubbing the eyes—they get so excited when they see this little life. Also for fathers, they can see the baby. The reality is there. They're excited. You can see the way they treat their wives is changing. There's a real person in there, and we really need to take care of you. It's just kind of nice to see, and you hope that lasts through the whole pregnancy and after." (Watts 2003)

Similarly, an article about ultrasound and abortion in the conservative Catholic periodical *Crisis* mentions "new evidence" in support of the theory of ultrasound bonding, and concludes: "In fact, scientists no longer really dispute the phenomenon. Numerous studies in the United States,

Canada, and Europe have all found strong evidence for it" (Stricherz 2002). Which studies these are, exactly, and where they have been published, is not disclosed. Elsewhere in the same piece, Stricherz cites just one source, which is neither recent nor a study, but rather a 1983 letter to the editor of the *New England Journal of Medicine*—a document to be considered in more detail below. Stricherz also writes, however, that no studies of ultrasound and bonding have been conducted in the two decades since that piece appeared:

> In an oft-cited 1983 article in the *New England Journal of Medicine*, Drs. John C. Fletcher and Mark I. Evans found that the viewing of a sonogram image "in the late first or early mid-trimester of pregnancy, before movement is felt by the mother, may also influence the resolution of any ambivalence toward the pregnancy itself in favor of the fetus." . . . But in the nearly two decades since the appearance of this report, no researchers appear to have followed up on it. Neither Lawrence D. Platt, the past president of the American Institute for Ultrasound in Medicine, nor Delores H. Pretorius, a professor in the radiology department at the University of California at San Diego and a leading authority on 3-D ultrasound, could recall a single study on the topic. (Stricherz 2002)

How does this square with his references to "new evidence," "strong evidence," and "numerous studies"? Stricherz does not say.

If this kind of inconsistency regarding questions of evidence were unique to this author, we could perhaps dismiss it as the idiosyncrasy of a not-particularly-gifted writer, writing a not-particularly-rigorous article for a not-particularly-discerning audience. What makes it far more interesting, however, is that an inconsistency of a very similar kind, only submerged within the scholarly apparatus of quotes and citations, runs through much of the medical literature on ultrasound and bonding as well. This literature is by now quite sizable and growing all the time, but the trails of evidence supporting claims regarding ultrasound and bonding are rarely trodden, very short, and tend always to lead to the same two texts: a 1982 study published in the *Journal of Psychosomatic Obstetrics and Gynecology* (Campbell et al. 1982) and a 1983 letter to the editor of the *New England Journal of Medicine* (Fletcher and Evans 1983).

Upon closer inspection, both turn out to be far too flimsy to bear the weight of the grand claims and sweeping policy projects they have been enlisted to support.

The Study

Much rests upon the claim that there is, as obstetrician and tireless advocate of ultrasound Stuart Campbell puts it, "evidence from randomized studies that ultrasound examination enhances maternal-fetal bonding, at least in the short term" (Campbell 2004:2). Campbell himself regards this question as settled; in a recent editorial he states that "Many years ago, my colleagues and I showed that the conventional 2-D scan was helpful in promoting bonding before birth" (Campbell 2004:5).

The study that Campbell cites in support of this claim is an article on which Campbell himself was first author, published in the very first issue of the then-new *Journal of Psychosomatic Obstetrics & Gynecology*. The aim of the study was "to investigate the effects of early real-time ultrasound examination on maternal attitudes toward the fetus and the pregnancy" (Campbell et al. 1982:57).

Methods used in this study are described in detail. Reasoning that the specific effects of the ultrasound examination would most easily be detected in a "homogeneous, obstetrically normal group" (1982:57), Campbell and his colleagues included as subjects only women "of Caucasian origin, aged between 18 and 32, married or within a stable relationship" (1982:57) "having planned the pregnancy jointly with their partner . . . and all having attended [prenatal care] early in pregnancy" (1982:60), who furthermore had no history of infertility, no previous miscarriages, and no known risk of congenital malformations. This carefully selected sample was

> Assigned at random to one of two groups from the outset. A high feedback group (n = 67) were shown the monitor screen and provided with standardized visual and verbal feedback as to fetal size, shape, and movement. A low-feedback group (n = 62) received a comparable examination with the one exception that they were unable to see the monitor screen and so receive verbal feedback

linked to visual image. Instead, they received only a global evaluation of progress in the form "all is well." (Campbell et al. 1982:57)

The authors note as well that in the high-feedback group, "in all cases
scanning was prolonged to ensure that fetal movement was seen"
(1982:58).

In order to measure the effects of these two different types of scans,
women were asked before and after the scan "to rate separately their feelings about being pregnant and toward the fetus according to a number of
adjectives [such as: 'fulfilled,' 'stressed,' 'pleased,' 'worried,' 'confident,'
'ambivalent,' 'loving,' 'maternal,' and 'concerned,' among others] on
7-point numerical scales" (1982:58). These scores were then subjected to
various statistical analyses, which indicated "consistent changes in ratings
as a result of the scan" (1982:59) in both groups of women, with "women
becoming less 'concerned,' more 'attached, reassured, secure, and confident' as a result of receiving the scan" (1982:59). The researchers noted a
significant difference between the two groups, with the high-feedback
group showing a more pronounced change in the numbers they used to
rate their feelings in terms of the various adjectives supplied; these findings are presented in a table.

Having described their methods and findings, the authors then reiter-
ate the study's aims, but with one interesting difference: "In the present
study the short-term effects of real-time ultrasound on maternal attitudes
toward the pregnancy, the fetus, *and the ultrasound procedure itself,* were
investigated by manipulating the level of feedback supplied" (Campbell
et al. 1982:59, emphasis added). In other words, the original question of
how the ultrasound examination influences maternal attitudes *toward
pregnancy and the fetus* appears, in the "discussion" and "conclusions" sections of this article, to have been displaced by the question of how high-
feedback versus low-feedback modes of performing the examination may
influence maternal attitudes *toward the ultrasound examination itself.*
Consistent with this subtle shift in emphasis, the authors include not one
but three different tables presenting data documenting changes in
women's attitudes, as measured by their rating of various adjectives before
and after the scan, toward the ultrasound examination. "Women in the
high-feedback group showed uniformly more positive attitudes *toward*

the scan. . . . These results suggest that *scanning is informative as well as emotionally rewarding* when specific and detailed feedback is made available to the mother" (Campbell et al. 1982:59, emphasis added). Almost as an afterthought, the authors add that "the groups also differed as to attitudes toward the fetus after the scan, the high-feedback mothers evincing more positive attitudes" (1982:59), and speculate that the exclusion of "high-risk" women may account for the relatively small difference noted in scores on negative attitudes.

Although later references frequently cite this study in support of claims regarding the purported bonding effects of ultrasound, the word "bonding" never appears, and discussion linking the study to the earlier "maternal attachment" research of Kennell and Klaus actually occupies only a single paragraph. This paragraph is, furthermore, by far the most speculative and least well-supported passage in the entire article, as can be seen most clearly by quoting it in full:

> The impact of scanning on maternal attitudes having been demonstrated, it is necessary to consider the possible significance of these findings. Attitudes toward the pregnancy and fetus have been found to be related to adherence to antenatal health-care recommendations, the delivery experience, and the mother's initial reaction to the neonate. For a number of women pregnancy has been associated with ambivalent attitudes, which in turn have been related to a higher level of pain at delivery and complications during pregnancy and at delivery. In view of this situation, procedures facilitating positive changes in attitudes may confer a broad range of benefits. (Campbell et al. 1982:60)

Note that "ambivalent attitudes" appear here as inherent qualities of the individual woman, divorced from all of the broader contexts of her life and pregnancy. If we were to inquire who these women were, and what the reasons for their ambivalence might have been, it would be far more difficult to assume that the primary problem in these cases is the narrowly medical problem of increased likelihood of pain and complications at delivery. In that case it would also be more difficult, of course, to leap to the additional conclusions the authors draw, that the cause of women's "ambivalent attitudes" lies in their failure to form the maternal attachments of bonding, and that an ultrasound examination is the solution. Campbell et al. continue:

> Klaus and Kennell have identified a number of events as important in the development of maternal attachment to the neonate; amongst these is fetal movement perception, which they believe prepares the mother for the birth and the physical separation from the child and with it the prospect of motherhood, since it is through fetal movement that the mother becomes aware of the autonomous status of her fetus. With the advent of ultrasound, it is now possible for a mother to see her fetus in utero. This additional sensory information may have similar emotional and psychological significance to the process of quickening, and anticipate and augment the awareness brought on by the experience of fetal movement. (1982:60)

While it might make sense to *ask* whether visual perception of fetal movement on the ultrasound screen has "similar emotional and psychological significance to the process of quickening," this was not among this study's stated aims, and Campbell et al. have not in fact documented any such thing.

The real reason that this question interests the study's authors, of course, is that they are intrigued by the idea that ultrasound imagery might help them get pregnant women to better comply with doctors' orders: "If such feedback enhances awareness of the fetus and influences compliance with health-care recommendations such as stopping smoking and alcohol intake, then, as scanning accomplishes this at an earlier stage of pregnancy, there will be greater potential benefit to the fetus" (Campbell et al. 1982:60). Campbell and his colleagues are, in short, interested in the "seeing is behaving" notion and the "behavioral benefits" discussed in the previous chapter. As a tool for promoting bonding, ultrasound seems to promise to influence women's behavior in ways that might benefit the health of the fetuses they carry.

One might expect that practitioners would seek to use ultrasound to control behavior primarily with women who are judged likely to engage in harmful behaviors such as drinking, smoking, and drug use. Indeed, Campbell et al. suggest that they are especially hopeful that ultrasound will have such effects precisely upon women whose pregnancies are "high risk" even though, as noted above, they also specifically excluded all such women from participating in their study: "The intention was to study the reactions to ultrasound in a homogeneous, obstetrically normal group, before proceeding to investigate the effects in 'high risk' pregnancies, although it is with the latter that the psychological effects may have the greatest relevance" (Campbell et al. 1982:57). Recall that Campbell and his colleagues eliminated from the study women whose life situations might lead them to be more likely to consider aborting a particular pregnancy: those who were unmarried, whose pregnancies were unplanned, or who had a known risk of fetal malformations. Indeed, it is most unlikely that the women included in the study would ever be thought to *need* ultrasound in order to behave properly during pregnancy, because many of the very criteria that qualified them for the study (planned pregnancy in the context of a stable relationship, early prenatal care attendance, etc.) already exhibit the desired forms of behavior. In this paragraph, the authors then speculate that the responses of this carefully preselected sample of women is a direct reflection of a universal and biologically grounded phenomenon of maternal bonding—and suggest, on this basis, that ultrasound can and should be used to try to influence the behavior of precisely the categories of women that they deliberately excluded from the study. It is perhaps not so very surprising, then, that in the more than two decades that have passed since this piece was published, the authors apparently never did "proceed to investigate the effects in 'high risk' pregnancies." If Campbell and his colleagues never did get around to asking how women approaching pregnancy from quite different positions might respond differently to ultrasound, perhaps this is because telling women how they should respond seemed a more compelling task.

Having briefly conjectured about the possible effects of ultrasound on maternal attachment in the "discussion" section of the study, Campbell et al. retreat in their conclusion to more solid ground. Interestingly, their conclusion deemphasizes the study's original stated aim of investigating the ultrasound examination's effect on maternal attitudes *toward pregnancy and the fetus,* and highlights instead the positive effect of high-feedback modes of scanning on women's attitudes *toward ultrasound.* The article concludes:

> The results of this study . . . demonstrate an enhancement of positive attitudes toward the scan and the fetus, contingent upon receiving high feedback, which suggests that feedback should

become an integral part of scanning procedure if the full potential of ultrasound in antenatal care is to be realized. (1982:60)

What this study really documents, then, is simply that when the person conducting an ultrasound examination provides more information and feedback, pregnant women experience it as a more positive event. In other words, women appreciate it when the people who provide medical care to them also talk to them about it, and explain what is happening.

The Letter

The year after Campbell et al. published their study, authors of a letter to the editor of the *New England Journal of Medicine* suggested that ultrasound performed in the first trimester might facilitate earlier maternal bonding with the fetus, and that women who had bonded in this way might be less likely to choose to abort (Fletcher and Evans 1983). Note that a letter to the editor of a scientific journal is not subject to the same standards of proof as a scientific study, nor does it undergo the peer review process in which prominent scientists with expertise in the relevant area are asked to evaluate its significance. So claims made in such letters do not have the full weight of authority behind them of either the journal or the larger scientific community. Letters to the editor, *NEJM* instructs authors, "provide a forum for readers to comment about articles recently published in the *Journal*, and they are a place to publish concise articles, such as reports of novel cases" (*New England Journal of Medicine* 2006) They inhabit the realm of opinion and debate, rather than that of scientific knowledge accepted as true.

Fletcher and Evans certainly did not claim otherwise; they simply offered a tentative suggestion that perhaps ultrasound facilitates the process of maternal-infant bonding earlier in pregnancy. This suggestion was based on two cases they had observed in which women considering abortion in the first trimester had decided against it after seeing the fetal ultrasound image. They presented this suggestion not as an ironclad proven finding, but as a question they deemed interesting and important enough to deserve further investigation:

We were impressed with the potential importance of many other similar events. We report these cases and our reflections to encourage

more systematic study of two questions: Does parental viewing
of the early fetus (before "quickening") by means of ultrasound
imaging accelerate bonding with the fetus? If so, what are the
medical, emotional, and ethical implications of this phenomenon?
(Fletcher and Evans 1983:392)

Even in a letter to the editor, however, one would expect that the references cited should support, or at the very least bear some relevance to,
the points that the authors wish to make. Thus it is quite odd to find that
Fletcher and Evans support their key suggestion "that maternal viewing of
the fetus by means of ultrasound results in an earlier initiation of parental
bonding, the oldest form of human and animal loyalty," with a citation
to an article that has nothing whatever to say about bonding. The article
they cite is a 1978 review published in the journal *Radiology*, on "Biological
Effects of Diagnostic Ultrasound" (Baker and Dalrymple 1978) that discusses topics such as thermal effects, cavitation (the creation of small air-
bubbles), direct mechanical effects of sound waves on particles of the
matter through which they pass, and the evidence then available regarding
growth retardation and tissue damage at high levels of exposure. Nowhere
does this article about biological effects address Fletcher and Evans's
topic of parental bonding generally, nor the more specific question of
whether such bonding can be achieved through ultrasound. Why then did
they cite it?

One can only surmise that the citation was meant simply to point to
"biological effects of ultrasound," and by this to imply that maternal bonding also might be *among* those biological effects, though no previous studies suggested that this might be the case. As with later articles that would
mischaracterize this letter to the editor as a "study" providing "proof" of
maternal bonding via ultrasound, here too we find that the authoritative-
looking references cited do not in fact provide convincing support for the
claims that are made.

One need hardly follow the trail of their citations, however, to arrive
at some questions concerning Fletcher and Evans's letter. As mentioned,
the letter describes two cases in which women considering early abortions
were persuaded to continue their pregnancies after viewing their fetuses
via ultrasound. The details of those two cases are instructive. The first case

concerned a woman who was undergoing an obstetrical ultrasound examination because, the authors write,

> ten weeks earlier she had been beaten in the abdominal area by
> the father of the fetus. She had been brought to the emergency
> room, and x-ray films had been taken before she was treated for
> the injuries. Subsequently, it was discovered that the woman was
> pregnant. The ultrasound examination was being done to establish
> the date of conception and the size of the fetus and to gather infor-
> mation about possible fetal damage inflicted by the beating or the
> radiation or both. (Fletcher and Evans 1983:392)

The second case involved a woman considering elective termination of a
fetus that geneticists judged to be at very high risk of a congenital condition:

> A 32-year-old woman was referred to the genetics clinic at the
> National Institutes of Health, along with an affected 4-year-old
> daughter, whose ambiguous genitalia had been successfully treated
> with surgery. The mother, who was probably mildly affected by the
> adrenal disorder, was 10 weeks pregnant, according to the date of
> her last menstruation. The geneticists at the clinic calculated that
> the risks of recurrence were between one in four and one in eight if
> the fetus was female. While the physicians devised an approach to
> experimental fetal therapy by means of daily doses of desametha-
> sone, the mother had an ultrasound examination to establish the
> date of conception and the size of the fetus. Family members, the
> primary physicians, a genetics counselor, endocrinologists, a social
> worker, and an ethics consultant then met to discuss the medical
> and moral aspects of the choice to be made. The parents clearly
> preferred the early trial of innovative therapy to deferred action,
> mid-trimester amniocentesis, and possible abortion of an affected
> female fetus. (Fletcher and Evans 1983:392)

From today's vantage point, it seems questionable, at the very least,
whether infants born with ambiguous genitalia should always require cor-
rective surgical or other "treatment" (Dreger 1999; Fausto-Sterling 2000).
Since its founding in 1993, the Intersex Society of North America has advo-
cated energetically (and with some success) for an end to "shame, secrecy,

and unwanted genital surgeries for people born with an anatomy that someone decided is not standard for male or female" (Intersex Society of North America 2006). While acknowledging that ambiguous genitalia are sometimes accompanied by other conditions that pose serious health risks and require medical attention, ISNA argues that "intersexuality is primarily a problem of stigma and trauma, not gender," and that "parents' distress" at the birth of a child whose genitalia are atypical in appearance "must not be treated by surgery on the child" (Intersex Society of North America 2006).

That said, it is understandable that for a woman whose four-year-old daughter had already suffered through surgery to "correct" ambiguous genitalia, at a historical moment when medical practitioners widely considered this a defect requiring surgery and few other voices were audible on the subject, the prospect of giving birth to another similarly affected infant might well have been very daunting. Nor is it difficult to understand that a victim of domestic abuse might reasonably have doubts about bearing a child fathered by the man who was beating her. Given their situations, both of the women about whom Fletcher and Evans wrote clearly had very real and serious socially grounded reasons behind their reluctance to carry these particular pregnancies to term.

I do not know what happened to these two women, and the children they may have borne eventually; having made this brief, troubled, and anonymous appearance in the medical literature, they and their stories quickly disappeared from view. But I am left to wonder, why did Fletcher and Evans frame these women's decisions in terms of bonding? To describe these decisions as evidence of bonding eliminates from consideration all social context, silences these women's own narratives, and reduces complex decisions regarding pregnancy and abortion to nothing more than an expression of an individual woman's relative ability or inability to form certain emotional attitudes toward the fetus.

It also transforms the very idea of bonding itself in ways that we would do well to ponder. First of all, the bonding theories of Kennell and Klaus and their followers had focused on the period immediately *after* birth, whereas obstetrical ultrasound by definition takes place *before birth*, that is, during pregnancy. Earlier maternal-infant "bonding" theories attempted to account for why some women were apparently better than others at "mothering"—they presumed that women are instinctively disposed to love and care for their offspring, but that an alienating birth experience might upset the natural development of the mother-infant relationship. By the time Fletcher and Evans transferred this notion of bonding to ultrasound during pregnancy in 1983, a decade of increasingly heated public controversy over the legalization of abortion had shifted the terrain of public debate (and the locus of anxieties) about women and reproduction from issues of child rearing to issues of procreation, and the question of why women have abortions. It is thus not surprising that the ultrasound bonding theory was first put forth in the context of suggesting how women who feel ambivalent about their pregnancies might be persuaded not to abort.

A second way in which Fletcher and Evans's proposal differs from older maternal-infant bonding theories is that it emphasizes not *when* mothers would form an emotional bond with their babies but *how*. Discussions of maternal-infant bonding in the 1970s had tended to focus on the problem of establishing the time frame for the "sensitive period" during which women were primed to form emotional attachments to their newborns: was it the first few minutes, the first days, the first months or the first year? The proposal that ultrasound might facilitate bonding shifted this time frame from the period after birth to the period of pregnancy, as we have seen. In the process, it also made a more radical suggestion: that emotional and social ties between a mother and child might form in an altogether new manner—not through physical and social interaction, but through spectatorship. Klaus and Kennell's theory of maternal-infant bonding had at first been welcomed by advocates of natural childbirth, because it argued that medical professionals must step aside after birth and allow women themselves to establish direct relations with their newborns. Ironically, this newer version of the bonding theory implicitly suggested that women need both medical technology and the assistance of medical professionals in order to form the proper emotional attitude toward their fetuses. If in the era of legalized abortion modern women could no longer be trusted to naturally feel love toward their fetuses and carry them to term, then ultrasound stood ready to help make them.

It would be a grave mistake to paint Fletcher and Evans as antiabortion ideologues on the basis of their letter. For each of these men, both of whom have had extremely successful and accomplished careers, the letter that we are considering here represents just one very small piece of a much larger body of work. Dr. Fletcher, who by the time of the letter's publication was already a prominent bioethicist and a founding member of the Hastings Center, later went on to become the founding director of the Center for Biomedical Ethics at the University of Virginia, where he remained until his death in 2004. Dr. Evans, who in 1983 only recently had completed his residency in obstetrics and gynecology, has gone on to become a prominent and prolific researcher in the field of fetal diagnosis and therapy. Over the years, Evans has taken stands on issues such as "fetal reduction" (the termination of one or more fetuses in a multiple pregnancy) that often put him at odds with antiabortion forces (see, for example, Evans et al. 2004), and according to the Web site of his company, Comprehensive Genetics, he has won "awards for the protection of women's rights from the National Organization for Women and Planned Parenthood" (Comprehensive Genetics 2006).

Still, texts can ramify in ways and directions that go far beyond their authors' intentions. The effects of this one letter, which presented these two researchers' rather speculative musings on possible linkages between ultrasound and maternal bonding under the imprint of a prestigious medical journal, continue to the present day. Fletcher and Evans concluded their letter with questions concerning "the immediate or long-term social and ethical consequences of ultrasound," asking:

> Could ultrasound become a weapon in the moral struggle [over abortion]? Some communities and even one state have debated proposed legislation requiring that a picture of a human fetus be shown to a woman who requests an abortion. A court-ordered ultrasound viewing would be a potent (and unfair?) maneuver in the hands of those who represented the interests of the fetus in a dispute over proposed fetal therapy. Of course, ultrasound could be used to the same end by those who oppose abortion itself. (Fletcher and Evans 1983:393)

With the goal of encouraging public discussion, they may merely have been pointing out some of the potential uses and abuses of ultrasound already beginning to emerge. Yet their letter also helped to call such abuses of ultrasound into existence, by seeming to lend them the weight of scientific authority, with consequences that continue to be felt. As if obediently following instructions, members of the antiabortion movement immediately took up the suggestion that ultrasound might facilitate maternal bonding, and put it to work in their tactics and materials, beginning with the 1984 release of the videotape *The Silent Scream* (Nathanson 1984).

Fletcher and Evans closed their letter with an almost prophetic call to their colleagues to recognize that ultrasound technology had catapulted them into the vanguard of a new era. Ultrasound, they suggested, opened up entirely new vistas on pregnancy and the fetus; it brought the fetus into view, and neither medicine nor pregnancy would ever be the same again. Physicians must step up to the new role that awaited them and assume the responsibility for guiding both women and fetuses through this new reality that they have helped to create: "Physicians and their colleagues in obstetrics and reproductive and fetal medicine should not be surprised to find themselves attracting the most careful human scrutiny and imagination. Of such stuff are many human dreams made" (Fletcher and Evans 1983:393). More than twenty years later, those of us who take the effort to pay "careful human scrutiny" to the kind of claims they made, and whose "human dreams" include reproductive as well as other kinds of freedom, can hardly fail to see in these words a certain ironic truth.

The manner in which advocates of the theory of ultrasound bonding have dealt with questions of evidence resembles the "statistical mischief" that Jonathan Kahn (2003, 2004) has documented in the recently successful efforts to develop and market BiDil as an "ethnic" drug for heart disease. These efforts were premised on the claim that African Americans suffered twice the rate of heart disease of whites, a claim that was much repeated but seldom investigated and turns out to have been just plain wrong. Kahn suggests that "perhaps the statistic was so readily and unquestioningly accepted precisely because it comported well with the institutionalized biomedical perspective to look first and foremost for inherent biological . . . explanations" (2003:481). Writings that expound the theory of ultrasound bonding similarly fail to critically examine questions of evidence, perhaps because many are predisposed to seek inherent biological explanations first and foremost. In this respect, the theory of ultrasound bonding also faithfully reproduces the most serious flaws and weaknesses of the maternal-infant bonding literature that preceded it.

The Short Life and Troubled Times of
Mother-Infant Bonding Research

The story of the rise and (partial) demise of the concept of maternal-infant bonding has been ably told by Diane E. Eyer in *Mother-Infant Bonding: A Scientific Fiction* (Eyer 1992; see also Arney 1982, especially chapter 5). Eyer notes that the pediatricians Kennell and Klaus first proposed the concept of maternal-infant bonding in 1972 in a study published in the *New England Journal of Medicine*. The authors claimed to show that mothers who were allowed sixteen extra hours of direct contact with their infants immediately after birth demonstrated better mothering skills, and their infants performed better on developmental tests, than mothers and infants who were denied this extra contact. Kennell and Klaus attributed these results to the bonding that takes place between mother and infant during a sensitive period following birth, when women are hormonally primed to accept or reject their offspring. Their research had been inspired by other scientists' research with animals, especially rats and goats, which showed that hormones exerted an especially powerful effect upon maternal behavior in the period during and after birth (Eyer 1992:2). This research also built upon earlier studies that explored maternal deprivation and infant attachment as factors in infant development, including Harry Harlow's famous experiments raising rhesus monkeys in isolation (Eyer 1992; Slater 2004), and John Bowlby's research among very young institutionalized war orphans in England following World War II (Eyer 1992:59).

Throughout the 1970s, research on mother-infant bonding flourished. Researchers sought to explore a number of questions that emerged from the bonding paradigm first proposed by Kennell and Klaus. How long, for example, did the "sensitive period" after birth last—was it minutes, hours, days, or up to a year? During this sensitive period, was actual skin-to-skin contact necessary for bonding to be accomplished, or would mere proximity and social interaction suffice? Could interventions designed to facilitate bonding help alleviate some of the problems of low-income women and their children? Could postpartum bonding be shown to contribute to children's health and well-being later in life, as measured by outcomes such as child abuse or juvenile delinquency?

This flurry of bonding research later came in for sharp criticism. However, the concept of maternal-infant bonding was widely embraced throughout the 1970s and was instrumental in the progressive reform of hospital birthing practices. Up to that time, it had been standard practice in many hospitals to whisk newborn babies away from their mothers to a nursery immediately after birth, on the grounds that this protected the infants from possible infection. In the wake of the second-wave feminist and women's health movements, many women demanded more control over childbirth, and along with other changes, they wanted to see and hold their newborn babies immediately after birth. The bonding research provided a seemingly scientific rationale for doing just that. It thus provided authoritative backing for the changes that women sought in how medical professionals managed birth.

At the same time, ironically, research also enabled physicians and nurses to construe bonding as yet another aspect of the birthing process that required their professional management. Again, I quote Arney: "The doctor's job was no longer simply to deliver a laboring mother, it now included 'Helping Mothers to Love Their Babies,' as a leader in the *British Medical Journal* put it" (1982:168). Very quickly, the view took hold that for proper bonding to occur, very specific actions should be taken at very specific moments. Eyer quotes a 1978 article by British pediatrician Hugh Jolly, describing how bonding was to be carried out, and warning of deadly results awaiting those who failed to follow proper procedures:

A normal baby should be delivered straight into his mother's arms. . . . The infant should lie nude and unwashed in contact with his mother's breasts for some time, using an overhead heating pad if necessary. The parents and the new baby should then be left alone for the first hour. . . . Animal studies of the effects of short periods of separation of mother and offspring have shown disastrous consequences—rejection and even killing of the baby. (Jolly 1978:19–21, cited in Eyer 1992:43)

Women whose births were medically complicated, whose infants were premature or critically ill at birth, who adopted, or who for other reasons were unable to bond according to instructions in the period immediately after birth, were made to feel like failures and left to suffer guilt and worry over possible consequences for their children.

These consequences were predicted to be dire indeed; Selma Fraiburg warned of the "diseases of nonattachment" that could follow from lack of bonding in early infancy:

> These bondless men, women and children constitute one of the largest aberrant populations in the world today, contributing far beyond their numbers to social disease and disorder. These are people who are unable to fulfill the most ordinary human obligations in work, in friendship, in marriage, and in childrearing. . . . Where there are no human attachments there can be no conscience. As a consequence, the hollow men and women contribute very largely to the criminal population. . . . The potential for violence and destructive acts is far greater among these bondless men and women; the absence of human bonds leaves a free, "unbound" aggression to pursue its erratic course. (1977, cited in Arney 1982:168)

Such ideas continue to live on today. The anthropologist Lorna A. Rhodes, writing about contemporary U.S. prisons, describes how prison mental health workers attach the label "psychopath" to certain prisoners. "Psychopathy" as a diagnostic label, although no longer part of the classification system officially recognized in psychiatry, lives on in prisons, where the term gets applied to individuals who are thought to be conscienceless and evil predators, from whom any reasonable speech or normal behavior is read as only further evidence of a dangerous talent for manipulation. Such psychopaths are thought to *require* the extreme isolation, intensive control, and constant surveillance of "supermax" control units within prisons, and they are also thought to be uniquely impervious to the psychologically damaging effects of supermax confinement. All of this is understood as a consequence of a failed process of bonding. Rhodes writes:

> The question of how this predatory, conscience-less orientation comes about has intrigued generations of clinicians. . . . Many clinicians consider psychopathy the consequence of events in early childhood, when the "magic cycle" of bonding that should "give birth to the soul" is unhinged by abuse or abandonment, resulting

in a cold, morally inert personality. . . . But many accounts of origins suggest that the child himself is a "bad seed" and as much responsible as his caretakers. . . . From this perspective, early bonding is a kind of redemption and the unbonded child—almost as though carrying a kind of original sin—is damned. (2002:452)

As Rhodes notes, theories that link psychopathy to bonding "derive their authority from scientific research, yet suggest that a full explanation is somehow beyond science" (2002:462).

Given the dramatic harm that was thought to follow from a failure to bond, together with a persistent vagueness about exactly what kind of contact bonding really entailed or required and for how long, it is easy to see how the bonding research of the 1970s provided powerful ammunition for those who argued that women should stay at home, in an era when middle-class women had recently entered into the workforce in large numbers. Indeed, as Catherine Lutz points out, bonding theory "naturalizes the connection between women and affect through evolutionary theory and is continuous with earlier theorizing about the elevated moral status of women achieved through their divinely assigned and naturally embedded mothering skills" (1990:82).

Lutz regards bonding theory as exemplifying how "social science disciplines women and their psyches" (1990:82). Arney similarly points to bonding research as yet another manifestation of the common tendency to try to blame mothers for all kinds of problems that are in reality fundamentally social in origin:

Bonding is an ideology which, like so many other ideologies that pose as social theories, turns social issues into individuals' problems. All of the social ills which concern bonding theorists are reconstructed by bonding theory as problems of women not bonding to their babies. Attention is directed away from fundamental social problems and toward the individual. Women are singled out by calling attention to the possible biological bases of bonding and through the argument that it is only women who possess the biological constitution for solving our social problems. Social order can be maintained only, it seems, by acquiescing to our biological heritage. This argument is being advanced despite the impossibility of making the attributions bonding theory makes and despite the rather firm location of sex-role behavior in history and society. (1982:173)

In recounting the history of maternal-infant bonding research and the controversies surrounding it, Eyer (1992) argues that the history of the idea of bonding offers a case study in how ideological assumptions regarding women, children, and family can come to masquerade as science, and how they can come to shape social policy and public debate.

Bonding research eventually came under fire from critics within the scientific community who pointed to animal studies that contradic-ted bonding researchers' claims regarding the existence of a biologically based critical bonding period. Some also questioned the studies' validity. Bonding studies measured particular maternal behaviors, such as how often a woman picked up her child, whether she stood next to her child during an exam, or how often she was seen to hold the baby face-to-face during a given observation period. Critics expressed doubt that such measurements, taken with no regard for the subjective meaning or social and cultural context of the behaviors in question, could reliably indicate whether women had formed or could form warm and close relationships with their children. Furthermore, because so many different measures of bonding were used even within a single study, any claims to statistical significance were quite difficult to defend. Critics also pointed out that the studies failed to distinguish bonding from other confounding variables such as the mother's poverty, lack of social support, or indeed the extra attention that went along with additional postpartum contact for mothers involved in the studies. In studies with a more rigorous design, conclusive evidence for any long-term consequences of postpartum bonding failed to materialize (Eyer 1992:18–26).

Critiquing the idea of mother-infant bonding from a different angle, the anthropologist Nancy Scheper-Hughes drew upon her research among desperately poor women inhabiting a shantytown on the periphery of a city in northeast Brazil, to call into question claims regarding the univer-sality of mother-love made by some feminists, as well as by the bonding researchers (Scheper-Hughes 1985, 1992). In the shantytown, where child death was an overwhelming reality of daily life, Scheper-Hughes found that maternal love unfolded far more gradually, with the result that infants were sometimes mortally neglected as women awaited signs that any particular infant was likely to survive—that it had, as they put it, a "knack" for living. Ugly and upsetting as she found this, Scheper-Hughes also came to regard this watchful delay of maternal investment in any particular child as an understandable emotional and cultural consequence of life under conditions of severe poverty, plagued by constant hunger, chronic sickness, and early death. Attention to the lives (and deaths) of these extremely impoverished women and their children reveals that even mother-love, which might appear to be the most biologically determined, most natural, and most universal of all emotions, is in fact "shaped by political and economic context as well as by culture" (Scheper-Hughes 1992:341).

In the heyday of the 1970s, the concept of maternal-infant bonding appeared dazzling and resplendent in the garb of science. Then, in the early 1980s, when researchers in the fields of psychology and child development began to take serious notice of the flaws in that garment, the concept of maternal-infant bonding simply moved on into another specialized discourse, where others with interests in ultrasound and pregnancy welcomed it with open arms.

Maternal Impressions Revisited

> Where has the wonder gone? What has happened to the fantastic dimension, to the horror and the fascination of difference? What images were created of the bodily marks of difference, after they became locked up in the electronic laboratories of the modern alchemists? (Rosi Braidotti 1994:91)

Fletcher and Evans wrote their 1983 letter in a future-oriented tone, and with a conscious sense that they stood on the very brink of a brand-new age of human relationships ushered in by advances in medical technology. Certainly, ultrasound technology was then still quite new, was rapidly changing and improving, and had become incorporated only relatively recently into obstetrical practice on a large scale. The maternal-infant bonding research of Kennell and Klaus was then also less than a decade old. But was the theory of ultrasound bonding really so new?

Let us approach this question by way of considering the intention behind Fletcher and Evans's oddly inapposite reference to bonding as possibly one of the "biological effects of ultrasound." If the authors really wished to argue that ultrasound has a capacity to promote bonding, and that this bonding process is grounded in human biology, then it seems not only fair but necessary to ask: What exactly *are* the biological mechanisms at work? Do the bonding effects of ultrasound have to do with levels of hormones circulating in the mother's bloodstream at and shortly after birth, as some of the first wave of maternal bonding researchers proposed? Even bracketing for a moment the rather inconvenient fact that no such connection between bonding and hormone levels has ever been conclusively demonstrated, it is not clear exactly how one would extend this argument from the period after birth with which the original bonding research was concerned, to encompass the entire period of pregnancy. Levels of various hormones in the maternal bloodstream change constantly throughout the period of gestation, and continue to change after birth and during the period of lactation. Given that ultrasound scans can be and are performed at any point during pregnancy, from the first moments after conception to the last moments before birth, what possible connection to hormone levels could we expect to find?

Or perhaps the theory of ultrasound bonding involves some other biological mechanism altogether—one that concerns not hormones but vision. If so, then how might *that* work? How would we chart out the linkages between image, brain, emotion, behavior, and relationship? If bonding via ultrasound has primarily to do with vision, then does this work differently in women than in men, in pregnant women than in women generally, in pregnant women viewing their own fetuses than in pregnant women viewing pictures of other people's fetuses? Does it work differently with ultrasound than with other imaging technologies, such as X-ray or photography? Indeed, it is not clear why mechanically produced images should necessarily be visually and emotionally processed in a manner completely unlike other kinds of images; what effect might we expect from paintings, or statues, or even visions seen in dreams?

If we thus push it just a little way toward its logical conclusions, the theory of ultrasound bonding resembles nothing so much as a somewhat reconfigured version of the "doctrine of maternal impressions." This is the name that historians give to a congeries of ideas, ranging from simple superstitions to quite fully worked-out theories once considered unimpeachably true, that for centuries explained children's physical appearance (especially when anomalous) as the result of impressions made by the maternal imagination upon the soft, still-forming flesh of the developing fetus during pregnancy. (This doctrine itself, we should note, represented an enlightened innovation over older ideas that ascribed anomalous births to demons.) The sophisticated medical imaging technologies of today are new, of course, but contemporary arguments share with their historical predecessors two key assumptions: (I) that the well-being of their fetuses calls for careful surveillance of the thoughts, emotions, and actions of pregnant women; and (2) that visual images powerfully influence the maternal imagination and therefore offer an important means of intervention on behalf of the fetus.

The doctrine of maternal impressions, as formulated between the sixteenth and early eighteenth centuries, explained that a fetus might be imprinted with the likeness of any object, image, person, or idea that impressed itself strongly upon the imagination of a pregnant woman, especially in connection with emotions of fear or desire.

> The concept of embryonic imprinting as a result of a mother's irrational fears or desires (naevi materni, voglie, envies, Muttermahler) originated with Hippocrates and was perpetuated by Pliny. The feminine imagination, so the argument ran, was the mistress of errors and behaved even more capriciously than normal during pregnancy. During this altered state, it was credited with the physical ability to materialize, by simulation, objects either wishfully or fearfully perceived. These external entities were believed to exert an internal repercussive pressure on the delicate fibers of the fetus. (Stafford 1993:308)

Thus, for example, a woman who desired strawberries or grapes might give birth to a child with a red birthmark, while one who gazed upon a painting of Saint John the Baptist wearing animal skins might bear a child covered with a thick pelt of hair. A woman who laid eyes upon a person with a frightening deformity might, as a result, bear a child with a similar deformity.

Violent emotions experienced by a pregnant woman—such as those prompted by the view of a large wound or the beating, gashing, and execution of a criminal—rained pathological and teratological horrors upon the tender fibers of the developing infant. Thus it was . . . the mother alone who was susceptible to the natural or artificial environment. She was responsive to, and responsible for, the impact of frightful ulcers or beautiful works of art. . . . The infant took on the literal shape of the trauma, or the experience that had left a profound negative or positive groove in her psyche. Hence offspring visibilized concealed or surrogate passions on their surfaces. Like a blank sheet of paper, the skin became marbled by pathos, mottled by an alien pattern of interiority. (Stafford 1993:313)

The influence of the maternal imagination was not necessarily always harmful, according to this doctrine. A woman who gazed with passionate admiration upon a beautiful statue could, as a consequence, give birth to a particularly beautiful child. As Lynn Morgan notes, this set of ideas could sometimes work to women's advantage:

The theory of maternal impressions functioned to give women a justification for controlling their activities and those of the people around them. In addition, it located responsibility for good reproductive outcomes within the social arena, where people could influence those outcomes through their actions, rather than in the scientific arena, where they were removed from social reach. (2003:291n5)

In general, however, this set of beliefs worked to affix blame to women, as an infant's unusual or surprising appearance could serve as evidence of either unwise exposure to frightful sights, or hidden and illicit sexual unions or desires:

Whenever a monster was born with a certain similarity to a different animal species, the honesty of the mother was straight away taken into consideration. . . . There was no way women could free themselves from generalized suspicion. . . . Even a boy who resembled his father was not necessarily legitimate: his mother could have produced that resemblance by the force of her imagination during her illicit sexual contacts. (Pinto-Correia 1997:159)

Antique as such theories may appear, they were only quite recently definitively banished from the realm of serious scientific debate: "Until well into the nineteenth century, the question for most medical men who contended with this matter was not *whether* maternal impressions could cause deformed fetuses, but *how* they did so" (Oakley 1984:23–24, cited in Mazzoni 2002:23).

In 1880, Dr. Ernest Martin, a leading figure in the emerging science of "teratogeny," or the study of monstrous embryology, summarized contemporary scientific thought on this question as follows:

1. The imagination plays an undeniable role in the procreation of monstrous beings.
2. Its role is mechanical and the uterus is its agent. When excited by some nervous agitation, the uterus' contractility exerts a pressure that the embryo cannot bear with impunity.
3. Outside these cases, the imagination can also affect the embryo after a period of prolonged agitation, without, however, producing an actual monstrosity. It affects the embryo's general state, sometimes its intelligence, but it possesses nothing teratogenic.
4. In that imagination's main function consists in calling up images of objects and beings, it in no way has the power to reproduce these images: facts to the contrary are meaningless, they are purely coincidental, when not dictated by passion or superstition. (Martin 1880, quoted in Huet 1993:109–110)

While Martin and his contemporary scientists rejected the notion that specific irregularities in a child's appearance could be linked causally through resemblance to their origins in specific sights or visions beheld by the mother, they accepted fully that maternal impressions could cause monstrous births and proposed what seemed to them plausible scientific explanations for how this worked.

Even as late as the 1920s, scientists working to establish the new field of embryology had to expend considerable energy to refute the doctrine of maternal impressions:

Well into the twentieth century, many people, including doctors, believed that the unborn child was subject to prenatal influence (also called "maternal impressions").... Prenatal influence was blamed for birthmarks and birth defects such as cleft palate and clubfoot, behavioral idiosyncrasies, food likes and dislikes, personality characteristics, and so on. (Morgan 2003:273; see also Morgan, in press)

While the doctrine of maternal impressions has by now been definitively banished from the domain of respectable science, many people continue to hold similar views up to the present day, even as they also fully embrace high-tech modern medicine and all that it has to offer. For example, in the course of my own research in the 1990s, one woman in her forties who had accompanied her niece to an ultrasound examination explained her own granddaughter's physical appearance as an effect of maternal passions: "My granddaughter looks just like me, because my daughter-in-law was so mad at me during her pregnancy." Similarly, a twenty-year-old college student named Monique, speaking with me as she waited for an ultrasound examination, listed a number of what she called "old wives' tales" with which she was familiar from her own extended family: "Oh, they say don't drink soda, because it'll make the baby's skin wrinkled. Or if you cry a lot during the pregnancy, it'll give the baby rickets, make it nervous and shake. Also, they say the mother's mood will be the baby's attitude when it comes out—I believe that one is true." Nor is it only in the form of "old wives' tales" that belief in such linkages persists; a wide variety of music CDs, aromatherapy oils, and other products are now (quite successfully) marketed to pregnant women on the rationale that by calming the pregnant woman they will benefit the health of the fetus.

To be sure, it is both reasonable and important to ask whether and how emotional states have physical and health consequences in pregnancy, and researchers in a variety of scientific disciplines are actively inquiring into the complexities of maternal-fetal health. Today's theory of ultrasound bonding is persuasive, however, not because it is grounded in sound science, but because it both emerges out of and contributes to a discourse that links visual images, via the maternal imagination, to the physical form and health of the fetus, in a manner that radically decontextualizes women's emotions and authorizes efforts to control women's behavior.

Consumer Impressions

An obvious example of a contemporary discourse that similarly deploys visual images in efforts to control people's behavior is, of course, advertising. It is thus not surprising that advertisers have picked up on this idea that ultrasound promotes bonding among family members and have used it to try to sell products. In particular, the notion that ultrasound helps strengthen kinship bonds can, by analogy, be used to suggest that other technologies have similar effects. This approach has been exploited most visibly in advertisements for telephone services (not coincidentally, perhaps, the very networks along which a faxed sonogram travels). A notable early example of this was an AT&T television spot that aired frequently on national networks for a number of months in 1994.

This advertisement centers around the narrative of a pregnant woman who has come for an obstetrical ultrasound examination, but whose husband couldn't be with her. Slightly eerie, space-age sounding music accompanies our first glimpse of a pretty blonde woman in her thirties, lying on the examination table with her pregnant belly exposed for the examination.

> "Excited about your sonogram?," asks the sonographer, standing by her side [strangely enough, on the side *opposite* the ultrasound machine].
>
> "Yeah."
>
> "Not even a little nervous?"
>
> "Well . . . ," she confesses, "Sam was supposed to call. I guess he's going to miss it." [Is he not in any case "missing it" by not being there?] The sonographer applies the transducer to the belly, and the fetus appears on the screen. Then the phone rings, and the sonographer hands it over to the woman patient. As she talks to her husband, we see alternating shots of her in the examination room—touching the image of the fetus on the ultrasound screen, twisting the phone cord around her finger, putting her finger in her mouth—and Sam, briefcase in hand, speaking to her from a phone booth on a busy city street. Sam asks, "How's our kicker?"
>
> "He's almost as gorgeous as you! Same long legs . . . big head . . . . Hey," we see her mouth ask, "wanna say hi?" We see the sonographer's

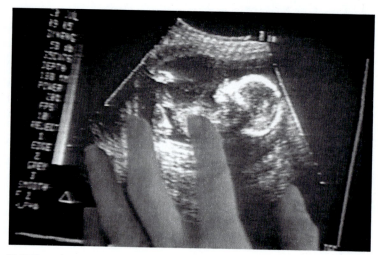

FIGURE 4-1 Hand caressing the fetal image on the ultrasound screen; still image from AT&T television advertisement.

FIGURE 4-2 Finger tangled in telephone cord; still image from AT&T television advertisement.

hand putting the receiver to her pregnant belly in place of the transducer.

Sam speaks to the fetus, "Hey big boy, wanna come out and play?"

A rapid series of close-up shots show the woman's mouth opening, her eye blinking, the image on the screen jumping. "Oh Sam, he kicked!"

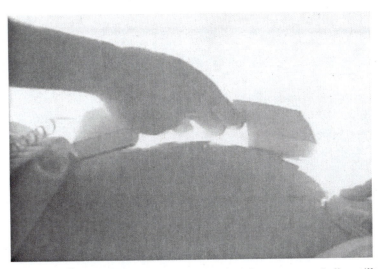

FIGURE 4-3 Telephone receiver applied to the pregnant belly; still image from AT&T television advertisement.

FIGURE 4-4 Sam speaks to the fetus from a public phone booth; still image from AT&T television advertisement.

We see Sam's smiling mouth at the receiver, "Really?"

"Yeah!" she responds, laughing happily, her hair spread out around her face on the pillow.

A male narrator speaks. "With AT&T True Voice Long Distance, the clearest, truest sound ever will soon be coming your way. So everyone you call will hear everything you feel."

Sam asks, "Do you think he heard me?"

"Yes," the woman laughs, "he did!"

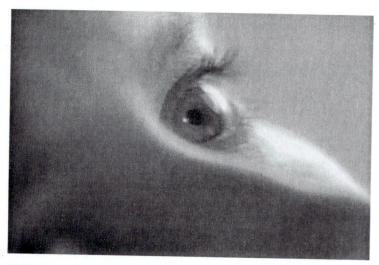

FIGURE 4-5 Woman's eye blinks as the fetus kicks in response to Sam's voice; still image from AT&T television advertisement.

FIGURE 4-6 "1-800-BE-CLOSE"; still image from AT&T television advertisement.

Sam closes his eyes and smiles, leaning his head against the phone booth, weak with happiness. A female voice sings, "The real you/coming through/your True Voice," as the screen fades to black and an AT&T logo appears, over a phone number: 1-800-BE-CLOSE.

This advertisement clearly plays upon the idea that ultrasound technology facilitates bonding between members of the family, but attempts to transfer the emotional significance from ultrasound technology to tele-phone technology. A number of details in the advertisement are rather unrealistic as a portrayal of an actual ultrasound exam. For one thing, the sonographer is pretty much absent from the picture, standing on the oppo-site side of the woman from the ultrasound equipment—it is as if the woman is there alone, watching the ultrasound as she might watch TV. The image of the fetus, furthermore, remains on the screen even when the telephone receiver is put there in place of the transducer—implying, of course, that the telephone itself acts as a sort of transducer. The advertisement implies, moreover, that the telephone is even more powerful than ultrasound as a technology for promoting bonding, because the bonding that takes place via ultrasound is all one-way—the mother sees the fetus and feels love, while the fetus just sits there passively. The telephone, on the other hand, seems to make the fetus bond actively with its father, kicking in response to the sound of his voice—perhaps an early form of Oedipal response to the distant father's inevitable intrusion into the mother-child relationship.

Even the camera style in this AT&T advertisement is deliberately odd—in an attempt, it would seem, to mimic the visual style of ultrasound imagery. Thus, when we are looking at the woman, we see her in the same way that one sees the fetus on the ultrasound screen, focusing on a series of distinct anatomical features in turn—the eyes, the fingers tangling in the cord, the fingers in the mouth, etc. The implication here, of course, is that through the television we bond with the pregnant woman, while through the ultrasound screen she bonds with the fetus, and the fetus in turn bonds with the father through the telephone. Not only the product being adver-tised here, but even the medium of television itself can, it would seem, like obstetrical ultrasound, forge bonds between viewer and viewed.

The ultrasound device as love machine seems to promise so much, one could almost wish that those promises were not grounded in such a lot of humbug.

Against Humbug

[Oz, to Dorothy]: "How can I help being a humbug, when all these people make me do things that everybody knows can't be done?" (L. F. Baum 2003:199)

The love that women feel for their children, and for the fetuses they carry, is very real indeed. This does not mean, however, that it is any more automatic or mechanical than any other form of love. The emotions of pregnant women are without doubt grounded in bodily processes, as are the emotions of nonpregnant women, men, and indeed any living, breathing, feeling, conscious person. But like other aspects of human life they are radically undetermined by biology, being at the same time fully embedded in history, biography, and social life. As Marshall Sahlins has argued with regard to color perception, so too with emotions, the parameters set by biology "appear not as the imperatives of culture but as its implements. They constitute a set of organizational means and possibilities at the disposition of the human cultural enterprise" (2000:160). Roger Lancaster writes:

> Even if it could be convincingly demonstrated that human bodies come equipped with only so many basic emotional responses, such a finding would not really amount to much in the way of positive knowledge about social life, for everything significant about *human* emotions relates to their institutional context, their symbolic valuation, and to the jostling of interests within modes of cultural organization. That is to say, people the world over might very well understand feelings of pride and shame, joy and sadness, and we might clearly recognize pieces of our own selves, our own feelings, in the emotional responses of other people, other cultures. But all of the pertinent questions remain: How are such dispositions symbolically organized, what social occasions give rise to such feelings, and how are these feelings mobilized for institutional purposes? (2003:208)

While all but the most severely impaired human beings share an ability to feel emotions and to form attachments with others, the love that any particular mother feels for her own child(ren) realizes these potentialities in a form that is always socially, culturally, and historically specific, and is never the only one possible. Love, as a structure of feeling and as a relationship, is not simply a command issued by nature, but a complex accomplishment, one that calls upon the full range of human capacities—the social, the cultural, the intellectual, the linguistic, and the aesthetic, no less than the biological.

Indeed, if maternal love really were so simple and automatic as proponents of bonding would have us believe, then one might reasonably wonder why people would need ultrasound, or any other sort of intervention, to make sure that it actually develops. If bonding really were biologically determined, then it should hardly require the help of medical professionals and elaborate technologies. If, on the other hand, women's feelings toward their fetuses are not dictated by nature, then we must acknowledge that they are bound to be as complex and as situated as any other human relationship, in which case there surely can be no technological shortcut.

To be sure, the promise of a quick fix for emotions holds obvious appeal, in a society much given to narratives that describe technology as the driving force behind all forms of change. In this regard, historians Merritt Roe Smith and Leo Marx note:

> The structure of such popular narratives conveys a vivid sense of the efficacy of technology as a driving force of history: a technical innovation suddenly appears and causes important things to happen. . . . Unlike other, more abstract forces to which historians often assign determinative power (for example, socio-economic, political, cultural and ideological formations) the thingness or tangibility of mechanical devices—their accessibility via sense perception—helps to create a sense of causal efficacy made visible . . . [such that] a complex event is made to seem the inescapable yet strikingly plausible result of a technological innovation. (Marx and Smith 1994:xi)

If technological determinism seems a compelling explanation for large-scale historical changes, "enhancement technologies" also appear to many as a compelling means to effect desired changes at the level of their individual lives. Enormous numbers of ordinary people in the United States regularly turn to elective surgery and pharmaceuticals (not to mention other legal and illegal drugs) to help them feel less shy, less socially awkward, less depressed, more "themselves," in the hope of becoming more loved, more sexually satisfied, more persuasive, more successful in dealing with people (Elliott 2003). We should hardly wonder, perhaps, that so many might also welcome the promise of a technological enhancement of the relationships most central to their lives, and the emotional dispositions that ground them.

Of course, what makes good on that promise (to the extent that anything does) is not so much the ultrasound device itself as the social and cultural work that goes on around it. Although it may *look* like a technological shortcut, ultrasound in the service of maternal bonding is perhaps better understood as a ritual, in Victor Turner's sense: "a mechanism that periodically converts the obligatory into the desirable" (Turner 1967:30). Turner, of course, regarded ritual as serving the function of transforming individuals in such a manner that they would come to know, assume, and *want* to assume their assigned places within a social order, thus allowing that order to reproduce itself. More recent approaches to ritual expand the concept to embrace not only traditional and highly marked "Rituals" intended to preserve and reproduce the existing order, such as the initiation rites considered by Turner, but also "more mundane meaningful practice, practice meant to transform, not reproduce, the environment in which it occurs" (Comaroff and Comaroff 1993:xvi). In this perspective, ritual can be found at many sites and "is less about giving voice to shared values than about opening fields of argument; about providing the terms and tropes, that is, through which people caught up in changing worlds may vex each other, question definitions of value, form alliances, and mobilize oppositions" (Comaroff and Comaroff 1993:xxiii). Ritual, in other words, can also be a site of politics. As such, one may recognize the power of a ritual, and still—if one has a stake in those politics—also contest it.

As a form of ritual, then, practices of bonding through ultrasound may obey a logic and achieve effects quite independent of any claims to scientific evidence offered on their behalf. Recognizing this possibility need not, however, stop me—or you!—from critically questioning the evidence offered, the claims made, the effects achieved, or the ritual itself. Ultrasound bonding is "real" in the same sense that the concept of race is "real"—"real," that is, not because it offers an objectively true description of the role of biology in human life, but because this set of ideas really does have a firm hold on shared common sense, and really does shape how people act and interact: how policies are decided, how medical technology gets used (by whom, on whom, at whose expense, and for what purposes), what sort of care women seek and what sort they receive, how health-care expenditures are distributed, and much more.

To acknowledge that the theory of ultrasound bonding, though false as science, is nonetheless "real" in this sense is, of course, quite humbling. Much as I might enjoy playing the all-powerful scholar-heroine who dashes false theories to smithereens in a single chapter, like others I must acknowledge the powerful wizardry of the social. If a single good argument alone could have dislodged the theory of ultrasound bonding, the much more impressive scholar-heroines who have preceded me surely would have accomplished this long ago.

The lesson to take from this is that to really challenge the theory of ultrasound bonding—and, more importantly, the ideologies and relations of power that it legitimates—will require the work of many minds, and the sound of many voices. It will require that scholars and journalists actively seek out and follow the trails of evidence supporting claims made in the name of science, and actively challenge people who dress up humbug as science—even (or perhaps especially) when they speak on the authority of advanced degrees and in the pages of respected scientific journals. It will require that many people actively question any theory that purports to reduce emotions, relationships, and other complex human realities to purely biological or technological phenomena. It will require that people gain an awareness of the many strings that come attached to the seemingly innocuous term "bonding" and choose no longer to use it—as many have chosen no longer to use a number of other problematic terms once made aware of the harm they can do. Terminology aside, challenging the theory of ultrasound bonding will require that Pamela J. and other ordinary people navigating times of great uncertainty in their lives resist the allure of too-simple responses to the very complex questions that pregnancy raises.

5

Prenatal Diagnosis, Pregnancy, and Consumption

> The transformation of any society should be revealed by the changing
> relations of persons to objects within it.
>
> —J. Comaroff and J. L. Comaroff 1990:196

In previous chapters, we have reviewed many of the ways in which the emergence of ultrasound technology in the United States has been shaped by processes of commodification and consumption—for the simple reason that the social order of which this technology has become part is one that is organized along consumer-capitalist lines. I am, of course, far from the first to point this out. In the context of ongoing conflicts over abortion, the routinization of prenatal diagnostic technologies has aroused concern from many quarters that embryos and fetuses are being reduced to the status of commodities. Feminists have voiced the further concern that women are, in the process, being reduced to the status of unskilled reproductive workers, who produce these valued commodities through their alienated labor. In these responses to prenatal diagnostic technology, we may discern a number of related anxieties about perceived threats to boundaries between persons and things—the intrusion of technology into the body; the incorporation of biological reproduction (of people) into the structures of industrial production (of things); and the specter of treating human beings as if they were mere commodities. These discussions are structured by two key assumptions:(1) that reproduction is best understood by analogy to production; and (2) that we can and should clearly distinguish persons from commodities.

Part of what makes anthropology so interesting, however, is the way that ethnographic research can allow social life—in all its richness, its complexity, and its capacity to surprise—to "speak back" to the very frameworks of ideas that inform it. In this chapter I draw upon what I have learned through ethnographic inquiry into obstetrical ultrasound, to propose a new angle of vision on prenatal diagnostic technologies. The case of obstetrical ultrasound shows, I argue, that in the contemporary United States (1) reproduction increasingly has come to be constructed as a matter of consumption; and (2) in the process the fetus is constructed more and more at the same time and through the same means, both as a "commodity" and as a "person." I shall first sketch out the argument by analogy to production, which is a compelling and influential strand within the feminist critique of reproductive medicine, and show how this line of analysis explains the advent of obstetrical ultrasound. I shall then discuss a number of other aspects of ultrasound that do not easily fit into this framework, and which I believe are better understood in terms of consumption.[1] I suggest that there are at least four different (if interrelated and overlapping) ways in which reproduction has come to be construed in terms of consumption in the American context: (1) consuming on behalf of the fetus, (2) pregnancy as consumption, (3) consuming pregnancy as a commodified experience, and (4) consuming the fetus.

Reproduction and the Analogy to Production

The same timespan that has witnessed a proliferation of prenatal diagnostic tests and other new reproductive technologies also has seen the rise of compelling and influential feminist critiques of reproductive medicine. One important position staked out within these critiques turns on the analogy between reproduction and production, specifically identifying ways that the analogy to industrial factory production operates within medical discourse and shapes medical practice. Scholars such as Emily Martin, Ann Oakley, Dorothy Wertz and Richard Wertz, and Barbara Katz Rothman, among others, have argued that as pregnancy and childbirth have come under the aegis of the male-dominated medical profession, these natural processes have come to be represented and understood in terms of analogies drawn from the world of industrial production. Doctors have come to be positioned as "managers" relative to reproduction, fetuses appear as valuable "products," and women are like reproductive "workers." These metaphors operate within medical discourse and structure the medical treatment of reproduction—with negative consequences for women. In this view, the routinization of ultrasound and other prenatal diagnostic technologies appears to further this process on every front: bolstering the power of doctors as managers, enhancing the value of fetuses as products, and further alienating the woman as reproductive laborer.

Doctors as Managers

Let's first consider the claim that doctors are like managers. In *The Woman in the Body*, Emily Martin shows how medical textbooks use imagery that likens labor to factory production:

> Medical imagery juxtaposes two pictures: the uterus as a machine that produces the baby and the woman as laborer who produces the baby. Perhaps at times the two come together in a consistent form as the woman-laborer whose uterus-machine produces the baby. What role is the doctor given? I think it is clear that he is predominantly seen as the supervisor or foreman of the labor process. (1987:63)

She argues that such texts, by teaching doctors to view themselves as managers, encourage caesarean sections and other surgical and technological interventions—which are often alienating, dangerous, and unnecessary—whenever pregnancy or labor appear to deviate from a fixed, abstract schedule of production. From this perspective, the rapid routinization of prenatal diagnostic technologies appears as merely the latest step in a long historical process by which doctors, via the culture of Fordist capitalist production, have established their power and authority over pregnant women.

And indeed, ultrasound technology as used in prenatal care can be seen as having this effect. Obstetricians have embraced ultrasound eagerly as a relatively inexpensive, noninvasive, and presumed safe means of obtaining a great deal of information not otherwise available about the position, appearance, and activity of the fetus. However, the availability of such information does not explain in and of itself why the information is considered valuable or useful. Ann Oakley (1984, 1993) has argued convincingly that a large part of ultrasound's appeal for doctors is that it allows them technologically to bypass pregnant women themselves as a source of knowledge about pregnancy. For example, instead of asking a woman for the date of her last menstrual period (and having to rely upon her word), a doctor may seek an ultrasound estimation of "gestational age." In this regard, it seems plausible to interpret the routinization of ultrasound as a strategic move by doctors to solidify their position as "managers" of reproduction construed as analogous to industrial production.

Fetuses as Products

A second comparison through which the feminist argument by analogy to production proceeds is the claim that fetuses are like products. In this light, prenatal diagnostic testing represents a way in which doctor/managers try to make sure that fetuses, whose production they oversee, are of consistently high quality. Recall Barbara Katz Rothman's description of how prenatal diagnosis turns fetuses into commodities, which we encountered in chapter 3:

> [G]enetic counseling, screening and testing of fetuses—[serve] the function of "quality control" on the assembly line of the products of conception, separating out those products we wish to develop from those we wish to discontinue. Once we see the products of conception as just that, as products, we begin to treat them as we do any other product, subject to similar scrutiny and standards. (2000:8)

Again, obstetrical ultrasound seems to fit quite readily into this argument. An ultrasound exam can provide information about a variety of major and minor problems in the development and health of the fetus. However, with ultrasound as with other prenatal diagnostic tests, medicine at present has no treatment to offer for the majority of problems that can be detected, other than abortion—and indeed, one of the primary justifications given in the medical literature for offering ultrasound screening to all women on a routine basis is the expectation that fetuses exhibiting anomalies will be aborted. Diagnosis of fetal anomaly followed by abortion is sometimes described as a "gain" (Gabbe 1994:72; see also discussion in chapter 3), a term that reflects a managerial view of the fetus as a product that must be subjected to "quality control," rather than any appreciation of the tenor of this experience for women who go through it. [2]

As this view of the fetus as a product takes hold among pregnant women themselves and in society at large, it is argued, respect for persons necessarily diminishes. In Rothman's words, the routinization of prenatal diagnostic testing is symptomatic of "the expansion of a way of thinking that treats people as objects, as commodities" (2000:5). This assumes, of course, that commodification is directly corrosive of personhood, and can only mean devaluation—so that, to the extent that we think of fetuses as commodities, we fail to regard children fully as persons. I shall return to this point below, to show how an ethnographic approach to obstetrical ultrasound may challenge this view.

Women as Workers

For the moment, however, let us turn to the third crucial step in the feminist argument by analogy to production—the claim that women are like workers. When doctors act as managers, and fetuses appear as products, then women come to be regarded as unskilled workers, alienated from their own reproductive labor. "As babies and children become products, mothers become producers, pregnant women the unskilled workers on a reproductive assembly line. . . . What are the causes of prematurity, fetal defects, damaged newborns—flawed products? Bad mothers, of course—inept workers" (Rothman 2000:6). In a similar vein, Emily Martin argues that with new reproductive technologies, "the possibility exists that the woman, the 'laborer' will increasingly drop out of sight as doctor-managers focus on 'producing' perfect 'products'" (Martin 1987:145).

As deployed in medical practice, then, the analogy between reproduction and production appears clearly to work to women's detriment. However, the same analogy may also be used analytically to ground feminist demands for change and calls to action—on the logic that "women have control over the means of reproduction (at least for the present . . .) in the form of their own bodies"(Martin 1987:143). Or, in Carol Stabile's words, "only women can carry out the work that is pregnancy"(1994:94).

From Production to Consumption

But is pregnancy really all work and no play, so to speak? My own ethnographic study of obstetrical ultrasound leads me to think not.

The argument by analogy to production represents an important strand within the broader feminist critique of medicine. This argument does have considerable merit, and as I've tried to show, it can help to account for the routinization of ultrasound within obstetrics. But perhaps this analysis takes doctors a bit too much at their word, by assuming that obstetrical ultrasound really is about just what they say it is about—prenatal diagnosis and medical management. Indeed, the fact that obstetrical ultrasound has been so completely routinized for all pregnancies in this country, despite medical professional guidelines that have recommended consistently against routine screening of all pregnancies, should suggest to us that in reality matters are a bit more complicated. As with any technology, its use in social practice does not correspond exactly to any one set of intentions. Indeed, as discussed in chapter 1, it was precisely the strikingly diverse and apparently incompatible meanings and agendas that this technology was being drafted to serve that led me to pursue ethnographic research on obstetrical ultrasound. An ethnographic approach reveals that in the United States, the medical practice of obstetrical ultrasound assumes a particular cultural form that has been shaped significantly by the ways that ultrasound imagery of the fetus has been valued and appropriated *outside* the clinical context. And while it is true that the exam is often fraught with anxiety over the possibility of a "positive" diagnosis of fetal anomaly or death, it is also true that many women look forward to and enjoy ultrasound, and even actively seek it out.

What are we to make of women's acceptance, or even embrace, of ultrasound? In terms of the analogy to production, we might ask: If prenatal diagnostic technologies help reduce women to the position of unskilled laborers in the reproductive process and expand the power exercised over them by doctor/managers, then why do more women not actively resist? This, of course, is a version of the old question: Why don't the workers revolt?

I suggest that perhaps part of the reason is because the same transformations that have positioned women as "workers" relative to reproduction have also offered up to them the pleasures of reproduction construed as consumption. The seeds of this approach already lie within the feminist critique by analogy to production. For if women are the unskilled workers on the reproductive assembly line, and doctors are the managers supervising their work, and the fetus is the valuable commodity being produced, then it seems only natural to ask: Who are the consumers? What do they consume, and how? In the discussion to follow, I shall suggest several ways in which reproduction has come to be construed in terms of consumption.

An All-Consuming Experience

Consuming on Behalf of the Fetus

It began to dawn on me that ultrasound has a lot to do with consumption, only after many months of listening to women tell me so. Among the questions that I asked women about ultrasound was whether they were interested in finding out the sex of the fetus if it could be visualized—and if so, why. Time and time again, women told me that they looked forward to the ultrasound exam because they hoped to learn the sex, so that they could start buying things for the baby.

> "I'm just curious, and I want to shop."
> "I hope it's a girl, I'll get dresses."
> "I'd rather know, to see what type of clothes to buy."

This type of response seemed so banal that I kept looking for deeper or more interesting answers. It was only after some time that I began to recognize that there were deeper and more interesting issues at stake in the relationship between ultrasound technology and women's desire to purchase pink or blue baby clothes—namely, the whole question of how reproduction has come to be constructed as a matter of consumption.

The notion that knowledge of fetal sex is important primarily as providing information that is useful for purposes of shopping is, of course, quite culturally peculiar. Such information is very differently weighted in contexts where dowry practices and other social forces place women under pressure to bear male children, and the use of ultrasound for sex determination leading to selective abortion of female fetuses has already resulted in millions of "missing women" and skewed sex ratios in India, China, and elsewhere (Chung 2007; Hesketh and Xing 2006; Miller 2001; Sen 2003). Ironically, the view that knowledge of fetal sex is a harmless and generally enjoyable "extra" (which, as discussed in chapter 2, is enshrined within the cultural form of the ultrasound examination in the United States) opens a space for this technology to be used for sex selection in this country as well. Chris C. Fair, in an unpublished manuscript, discusses the case of Dr. John D. Stephens, who has patented a method for determining fetal sex via ultrasound in the first weeks of pregnancy (U.S. Patent #4,986,274), and operates clinics in several U.S. cities that advertise ultrasound for sex determination in Punjabi language newspapers, a practice protested by local Punjabi women's organizations. It is widely assumed that within the United States, sex-selective abortion would only ever be practiced in communities of recent immigrants, but I know of no data that could confirm this. Anecdotally, one sonographer I have spoken with told me that she knew personally of a case in which a nonimmigrant U.S. woman acted on information about fetal sex, provided in the course of an ultrasound examination, to selectively terminate a pregnancy. Available data concerning preimplantation genetic diagnosis, a far more expensive and invasive prenatal diagnostic technology than ultrasound, suggests that as many as 10 percent of all procedures carried out each year are for purposes of nonmedical sex selection (Knoppers et al. 2006).

While the linkages between ultrasound, sex determination, and shopping are thus quite peculiar to the U.S. context, the whole phenomenon of prenatal shopping for gendered baby items is also one that emerged historically only relatively recently. The purchase, during pregnancy, of mass-produced consumer goods intended for the anticipated child is, on one level, simply a rather unremarkable extension to the period before birth of the phenomenon of parents buying stuff for their kids. In the early part of the twentieth century, attempts to target children's needs as a potential marketing opportunity seemed to threaten an intrusion of the profane world of business into the sacred space of the home, as Daniel Thomas Cook has demonstrated in his historical study of the children's apparel industry. This potential conflict was resolved, according to Cook, "by recasting the expression of motherhood as consumer practice" (1995:519; see also Cook 2004). By now, a century later, Americans take for granted that consuming on behalf of one's children is an important parental responsibility. Indeed, shopping for one's children is arguably a ritual of parenthood that itself is vested with profound significance (Anagnost 2004, Layne 1999, 2003, 2004; Miller 1998, 2004; Wozniak 2004), and to at least some women the challenge of becoming a competent consumer of the ever-increasing array of goods aimed at children appears as a (rather daunting) test of their capabilities as a parent in general. As one woman expecting her first child said to me:

> We went to these childbirth classes, and they were telling us all about all these different things you have to buy, and it just seemed really intimidating. I mean, there's the baby carrier and the breast pump and the stroller and two different kinds of car seats, and I don't know how to even use them. It makes you start to wonder, am I really going to be able to take care of a child?

The material trappings of middle-class childhood in contemporary America are legion, indeed, including not only baby carriers and breast pumps and strollers and car seats, but much else besides. Just *how much* else is perhaps best illustrated by reference to one of the many self-help sources to which women may turn for advice and information about pregnancy. One feature of BabyCenter, a popular Web site aimed at pregnant women, offers expectant parents a collection of checklists of "essential" items (BabyCenter 2006a). The nursery and newborn checklists designate as "essential" no less than thirty-six mass-produced, commercially available items that new mothers will "need" upon their return from the hospital.[3] Of course, not all women are equally well positioned to meet all of these "needs," nor to command the forms of knowledge and the resources involved in this kind of consumption (including those required to surf the Internet in search of such information). Women may be painfully aware of their inability to provide these things, however; indeed, the inability to engage in such consumption on behalf of the fetus may now figure as one part of the experience of poverty as relative deprivation in contemporary U.S. society.

Many women who might be able to engage in consumption of baby goods during pregnancy resist doing so out of a sense of caution that something might go wrong, preferring instead to wait until just before the birth and then to buy only what are considered basic necessities. In the context of American society, where ubiquitous advertisements endlessly promise sex, happiness, and success through the purchase of goods, the notion that consumption during pregnancy could be seen as unwise or even dangerous ("tempting fate") might seem a curious superstition, a holdover from pre-modern systems of religious beliefs. Certainly, religious reasons do come into play for some women. For example, Susanna, a thirty-three-year-old marketing consultant who had two children and had previously lost a pregnancy at four months, attributed her reluctance to learn fetal sex via ultrasound or to buy things before the birth to her religion:

> I guess I kind of feel like some things are meant to be veiled from you until their time to be revealed has come. . . . Part of it is religious, I guess. I'm Jewish. I'm not Orthodox, but—you always think, "Well, it's great having a baby," but you never know if it's gonna work out or not. And in my case, in one case it did not work out.

This sort of ambivalence toward consumption on behalf of the fetus is perhaps best understood, however, as (also) a tacit recognition of the extent to which consumption of commodities functions to construct identity in contemporary American society. Buying things for the fetus on some level amounts to recognizing it as an individual consumer, a baby, a person. A woman might not wish to grant such recognition, or she might wish to embrace and proclaim it, depending on a number of factors, including how far along she is in her pregnancy (see also Layne 1999, 2004). Thus Susanna, elaborating further, segued from religious reasons to her sense that consumption serves to construct the fetus as a "baby" inappropriately early on in pregnancy:

> So I think sometimes it's better not to make too many preparations and get too involved until the baby's really there, because the baby might not come, and then the parents have to face all of these material things they don't have any use for, and it brings that much more pain. . . . Before the baby's born, it's hidden, maybe it's not completed yet, maybe the deal isn't done yet, and I guess that gave me a sense of—you know, *slow down*.

Most women who carry their pregnancies to term usually do end up engaging in some consumption of goods "on behalf of the fetus," if only passively, thanks to the American rite of the baby shower. The baby shower—which has evolved over time from a ritual passing on of knowledge among women (though it remains that too) to become more an example of what Leigh Eric Schmidt has called "consumer rites" in American culture (Schmidt 1995; see also Clarke 2004)—conventionally takes place in the last month or two of pregnancy. One item that family and friends often like to buy as a shower gift (and that prospective parents like to buy, too) is clothing for the baby, and convention dictates that girls should wear pink clothes and boys should wear blue.[4] To state what should be obvious, objects are used to construct identities and relationships, in contemporary U.S. society no less than in the Melanesian gift-exchange systems long familiar to anthropologists, though in somewhat novel and distinctive ways. In this context, given the fact that women undergoing prenatal diagnostic tests in this country are commonly offered the option of finding out fetal sex, it is easy to see that women's attitudes toward, and experience of, ultrasound and other prenatal diagnostic technologies might be shaped by cultural imperatives of consumption.

Pregnancy as Consumption

Not only do women engage in consumption during pregnancy, however, but consumption itself to a significant degree *constitutes* the experience of pregnancy, especially in its early stages. Arjun Appadurai has suggested that "consumption creates time and does not simply respond to it. . . . Where repetition in consumption seems to be determined by natural or universal seasonalities of passage, always consider the reverse causal chain, in which consumption seasonalities might determine the style and significance of 'natural' passages" (1996:70). Building upon this insight, I consider here the ways in which transformations in consumption serve to create the "time" of early pregnancy, and determine the significance of the "natural" passage into pregnancy. Specifically, consumption constitutes the chief avenue of control for middle-class women who are just beginning to view themselves as mothers, and also the chief performative arena where they may exemplify their mothering skills for others.

In her ethnographic study of the American abortion debate, Ginsburg (1989) has pointed out that women's relationship to reproduction has been transformed in recent decades, such that even conservative defenders of traditional values now frame motherhood not as women's biological destiny but rather as the result of a conscious decision to embrace their reproductive potential. For a great many middle-class women of all political persuasions, the decision to embrace their reproductive potential, and to enter a state of being possibly-pregnant, follows a long period of engaging in sexual activity while using birth control. This transition is often both marked and effected by a transformation in the meaning and practice of consumption. Long before it becomes possible to feel the fetus moving or to see the belly bulging, often before pregnancy is confirmed or even attempted, the transition to hoped-for motherhood may be experienced as a transition to a new, more highly disciplined regime of consumption—it is the movement from being an individual consumer to a mother-as-consumer.

This change concerns, in the first place, consumption in its most literal meaning—eating and drinking. Indeed, for many women, a change in patterns of consuming food, drink, and drugs both precedes pregnancy and in some sense "causes" it. The daily ritual of swallowing a birth control pill, for example, gives way to the swallowing of special vitamins high in folic acid, special foods full of nutrients, and special waters labeled and sold as free of contaminants. Many women temporarily forswear (or try to) some of the daily pleasures of consumption, giving up alcohol, tobacco, caffeine, and other substances thought to be harmful, as well as avoiding over-the-counter drugs. For many, the knowledge that one is pregnant comes as early as several days after a missed period, in the form of a mass-produced, disposable, over-the-counter device a woman can buy in her local drugstore: the home pregnancy test. And she watches for early symptoms of pregnancy to manifest themselves as disturbances in normal patterns of consumption of food: nausea and cravings.

Not only do *patterns* of consumption change when it begins to be "on behalf of" the fetus, but so too does the *meaning* of consumption itself. Suddenly, consumption is invested with new levels of moral significance—it is cast as an act of maternal love and an expression of a woman's strength of character and powers of self-discipline, even as it is also seen literally to create the fetal body. As a popular book on diet during pregnancy advises women, "Not only are you what you eat, but your baby is, too" (Eisenberg et al. 1986:16). Do you love your future child enough to give up coffee? Are you dedicated enough to resist sweets? How diligent are you in reading the labels of everything you eat and drink? A woman's first maternal duty, it would seem, is to act as an intelligent and effective filter between the fetus within her and the world outside, letting in the good and keeping out the bad, and the primary locus of this responsibility is her choice of what substances to consume (see also Markens et al. 1997).

To transform one's consumption patterns in this way is difficult, of course, demanding constant vigilance and self-denial. It is perhaps not surprising, therefore, that many women whose experience of early pregnancy is defined in large part by the burdens of newly significant consumption might welcome the prospect of an ultrasound examination as providing tangible evidence that (as so many women put it), "there really is a baby in there"—a baby whose existence gives meaning to the sacrifice of all those passed-up (or thrown-up!) desserts, cigarettes, cups of coffee, and glasses of wine.[5] By the same token, however, if any problems are detected or questions raised during the ultrasound examination, women all too readily attribute them to their own failure to consume properly.

Just such linkages between consumption of food, consumption of goods, and maternal responsibility can be discerned in a recent television ad for Carl's Jr. Hamburgers that premiered in April 2005 (Levins 2005). This ad features an animated fetus, clearly a cartoon but carefully designed to suggest a 3D ultrasound image, with bluish tints, a visual frame the shape of a slice of pie, rows of small white letters, and an audible whoosh suggestive of fetal heartbeats. The fetus wipes his brow dramatically and speaks in the voice of a young man, with a hip-hop inflection:

"Whew! It is *really* hot down here."

[The fetus puts his thumb and index finger into his mouth and whistles loudly]

"Mom. . . ."

[He yanks on the umbilical cord]

"*Mom!* You're not wolfin' down jalapeños again, are you?!" [He kicks, hard]

"Yeah, 'cause let me tell ya about my friend Ned. His Mama ate nothin' but spicy foods? Homeboy came out *red,* Ma. *Bright red.* So if you keep on crammin' those peppers down your neck, I might just bust outta here early, grab somethin' on my way out [he picks up a handful of placenta], take it with me!"

The cartoon-ultrasound disappears, and a large hamburger loaded with garnishes lands with a thunk on a white surface. The voice of a male narrator, who sounds like he might specialize in ads for horror films, growls: "The new Carl's Jr. spicy six-dollar burger, with crispy jalapeños. It *ain't* for *babies!*"

The humor in this ad plays off shared expectations and sensibilities that are taken very seriously indeed. Clearly, a pregnant woman has no business eating what "ain't for babies," and she had better make sure she knows how to consume carefully or she will be to blame for whatever might follow, whether fetal anomaly ("*Bright red*") or miscarriage ("I might just bust outta here early"). In the United States, women who engage in forms of consumption deemed harmful to fetuses are increasingly subject not only to social censure but to criminal prosecution (Oaks 2001; Daniels 1993). When the state invokes the need to protect fetal health to criminalize unwise consumption and prosecute women for smoking, drinking, or using drugs while pregnant, it places blame exclusively on individual women for problems that are arguably better understood in social and historical perspective. As Laury Oaks writes:

> Pregnancy advice books and public health campaigns portray [pregnant women who smoke, drink, or do drugs] as aggressively self-indulgent or as helpless victims of addiction. They are "bad mothers" because they do not put their baby-to-be's health first. But such labeling disregards the factors that may lead pregnant women to substance use—factors such as stress, poverty, nicotine addiction, or a network of family and friends who are substance users. Moreover, it fails to take into account that until recently, moderate smoking and drinking during pregnancy were accepted by the medical profession as well as the general public. (2001:2)

Such efforts are also highly racialized, in how laws get written as well as how they get enforced, as the legal scholar Dorothy Roberts has detailed. She writes:

> Poor Black women nationwide bear the brunt of prosecutors' punitive approach. According to a 1990 memorandum prepared by the

ACLU Reproductive Freedom Project, 70 percent of the fifty-two cases documented at that time involved Black defendants. . . . The racial disparity has not diminished in subsequent years. The reason Black women are the primary targets of prosecutors is not because they are more guilty of fetal abuse. . . . Rather, this discriminatory enforcement is a result of a combination of racism and poverty. Poor women, who are disproportionately Black, are in closer contact with government agencies, and their drug use is therefore more likely to be detected. Black women are also more likely to be reported to government authorities, in part because of the racist attitudes of health care professionals. In the end, it is these women's failure to meet society's image of the ideal mother that makes their prosecution acceptable. (1997:172)

The push to criminalize pregnant women's consumption of harmful substances flies in the face of both scientific evidence and medical professional opinion (Daniels 1993; Roberts 1997). Such efforts also overlook male contributions to fetal health, as well as collective responsibility for harms caused by environmental and occupational toxins (Daniels 1999).

But perfectly conscientious and careful consumption of food, even if difficult to achieve, appears to many to promise a means by which the individual woman (and her fetus) may transcend the effects of environmental damage—damage wrought, in large part, as a by-product of existing societal and global patterns of consumption. *What to Eat When You're Expecting* advises women that "even with so much in our environment out of our control . . . today, having a healthy baby is, most of the time, more up to us than up to chance. . . . Eating . . . is an area in which there are enormous possibilities for control" (Eisenberg et al. 1986:12). Consumption of food, in other words, is presented as a way to deal with the problems caused by consumption of energy and goods. Women engaged in reproducing the next generation are thus encouraged to regard their scope of effective action as limited to the realm of consumer choices, which do not challenge broader social and economic structures—indeed, which, if anything, serve only to reproduce them.

This may be an example of how "reproduction, in its biological and social senses, is inextricably bound up with the production of culture"

(Ginsburg and Rapp 1995:2). It may also show how consuming "on behalf of" the fetus reprises long-standing cultural associations between consumption and gender. The idea that consumption generally, and consumption of food in particular, is an avenue through which middle-class women may exercise "control" has, of course, a long history in American society; the conscientious pregnant woman of today treads a path already well worn by women shoppers and dieters through the years.

Consuming Pregnancy as a Commodified Experience

The sense that consumption carries heightened significance during pregnancy is not limited to the physical consumption of food and other substances. The experience of pregnancy itself has come to be a more or less standardized product, available (to those who command the resources) in a range of different varieties to suit individual consumer preferences. This is despite the fact that untold numbers of women, in this country and elsewhere in the world, still go through pregnancy and bear children without reliable access to food, shelter, or basic medical care.

Women in the United States who enjoy good medical coverage may now choose from among a range of options in the kind of care they seek during pregnancy and from whom, the kind of education or preparation they want, and where and how they plan to give birth. Robbie Davis-Floyd points out that "at present in our society, the culturally recognized spectrum of possible beliefs about pregnancy and birth is encompassed by two basic opposing models, or paradigms, which are available to pregnant women for the perception and interpretation of their pregnancy and birth experiences—the technocratic and wholistic models" (2003:155). Most women still seek care from physicians, and 99 percent of births in the United States take place in hospitals, but the less than 1 percent of women who do give birth at home under the care of lay midwives tend to be very committed and articulate (Martin et al. 2005:18). More and more women do give birth under the care of midwives, the vast majority of them certified nurse-midwives; in 2004, midwives attended 11.1 percent of all vaginal births in the U.S., almost double the 1991 rate of 5.7 percent (Martin et al. 2005:19). Most midwife-attended births occur in hospitals, however (Martin et al. 2005:19), and their presence there does not necessarily represent a triumph of the "wholistic" model; midwives are also cheap labor when supervised by obstetrical doctors who bring in the money through control of deliveries but rarely oversee a long labor, leaving that instead to midwives or obstetrical nurses.[6] Still, it is notable that many U.S. women now approach pregnancy and birth with some awareness that there *are* competing models or paradigms of birth, and with the expectation that they can (and must) select from among a range of different kinds of practitioners, approaches, and settings.

As with the choice of the provider and setting for prenatal care and birth, educational classes for pregnant women may also range widely along the ideological spectrum, from those that hew closer to the "technocratic" model of birth, to those that reflect more "wholistic" models. In addition to childbirth-education classes, women may attend a variety of other classes and groups on topics ranging from exercise during pregnancy, to breast-feeding, to infant massage, and many more. Pregnant or trying-to-become-pregnant women also have been discovered as a large and very lucrative market for educational or "self-help" books offering information and advice on conception, pregnancy, childbirth, and infant care, again written from many different positions between the "technocratic" and "wholistic" ideological poles. A glance at the "Pregnancy" section of most any branch of any large national bookstore chain will turn up hundreds of different titles.

The image of *Spiritual Midwifery* cozily nestled up to *Which Tests for My Unborn Baby?* on the bookstore shelf hints at the extent to which reproduction itself has come to be construed in terms of consumption. Women who pursue a "wholistic" approach to pregnancy and childbirth might be regarded, in terms of the feminist argument by analogy to production, as "workers in revolt"; I suggest, however, that we must (also) recognize them as consumers in action. The ideological opposition between "wholistic" and "technocratic" models of pregnancy and childbirth plays itself out against the backdrop of a consumer culture and a class structure that remain fundamentally unchallenged.[7] The feminist religious studies scholar Pamela Klassen, in her ethnographic study of women who opted for home births for religious reasons, notes:

> While home birth may often be understood as a challenge to the dominant economic system, just as frequently it requires a substantial

outlay of money, approximately $750 to $3000. Even though many direct-entry midwives use a sliding scale to set their fees, home birth is generally not an option for those who cannot afford this expense. Not all certified nurse-midwives who attend home births choose to or are able to accept Medicaid reimbursement, and many direct-entry midwives, due to their unlicensed status, cannot interact with state or private health insurance even if they choose to. The economics of birth in the United States—like the economics of all kinds of health care—are affected by the structure of the insurance system, no matter what mode of birth is chosen. (2001:104)

When a woman plans and contracts for a particular kind of prenatal care, for a particular kind of birth, she is (to the extent that such a thing is possible) engaging to purchase a particular kind of pregnancy experience. Women who choose a "high-tech" approach and those who choose a "natural" approach may find each other's decisions incomprehensible, unenlightened, or simply silly, but the differences that separate them are perhaps ultimately less significant than the commonalities—namely, that a woman demonstrates her powers and her talents as a consumer, and engages in the construction of her identity, by the manner in which she consumes her pregnancy and birth.

In this context, as part of the consumption of pregnancy as a commodified experience, women's demand for ultrasound is perhaps more comprehensible. Middle-class women from many different positions along the ideological spectrum have come to regard ultrasound as an important standard feature of the larger package deal, if not always for the same reasons. As a glitzy high-tech medical procedure, ultrasound may seem to be evidence that one is receiving the best of modern medical attention, with the "reassurance" that this seems to promise:

I was an infertility patient, so I was having ultrasound like every other day while I was taking infertility treatments, and then when I got pregnant I had [an ultrasound exam] every week, for about the first eight weeks. . . . Then there was this lull . . . until I had amnio which was at fourteen weeks. So there was about six weeks where I didn't have any ultrasounds at all. . . . I can't imagine waiting until the sixth month, or even the fourth month, I just can't. You [see the

ultrasound and you] know he's there, and he's safe, and it was kind
of odd to go even those six or eight weeks between my last infertility ultrasound and the amnio one. (Libby, a thirty-five-year-old
white lawyer)

Given that usually no problems are detected, however, the ultrasound
exam also seems to promise an emotionally gratifying moment of "reassurance" and "bonding" that has itself come to be regarded by many as a
not-to-be-missed part of the experience of pregnancy.

I feel a lot happier now since I know the heart is okay. . . . Every time
I get ultrasound it relaxes me, it's reassuring. (Amy, a twenty-five-
year-old African American college student)

[My husband] was just very anxious about the whole thing, just
wondering whether he could handle it. And it wasn't until the ultrasound, when he saw it moving, and he *completely* changed his attitude about the pregnancy—I was so *happy*! I didn't care *why* we were
there! (Jane, a thirty-five-year-old white psychologist)

Nor is it only middle-class women who demand ultrasound. Among
the women I spoke with in the course of my research were "clinic" patients
(i.e., poor women relying upon publicly subsidized programs and clinics
for prenatal care, as opposed to "private" patients who have private medical insurance) who sought out ultrasound both because it is understood
to be a standard of good medical care and because they, too, wanted to partake of the pleasures it may offer. Again, recall the words of Charlotte, in
chapter 3: "I felt cheated. I wanted to see that it was normal, and also,
I didn't want to miss out on that experience."

Consuming the Fetus

I have suggested a number of different ways in which I believe reproduction has become constructed not only in terms of production, but also as a
matter of consumption. Women engage in consumption of baby clothes
and other mass-produced goods on behalf of the fetus during pregnancy;
consumption (especially of food) to a considerable extent constitutes
the experience of pregnancy, especially in its early stages; and women

approach prenatal medical care and education as the consumption of a commodified pregnancy experience. At this point, let us return to the most obvious, but also the most distinctly unsettling implication of this argument—namely, the suggestion that women "consume" their fetuses. What might it mean to say that the fetus is a commodity? In what sense does one consume such a commodity?

Much of the theoretical literature on commodities turns upon the distinction between use-value and exchange-value—commodities are items that are produced not in order to be used directly, but rather in order to be exchanged for money (which may then be used to purchase other commodities) in a capitalist market. In an important departure from this traditional definition, Appadurai proposes that we understand the commodity not as something that belongs to a certain class of objects (those produced for exchange), but rather as something that occupies, even temporarily, the "commodity situation—the situation in which its exchangeability is its socially relevant feature" (Appadurai 1986:13). In the case of the fetus, however, both of these approaches seem somewhat inadequate.

First of all, regarding the fetus, exchange cannot be neatly separated from or opposed to consumption. Ultrasound (along with other prenatal diagnostic technologies) objectifies the fetus in ways that not only make possible certain sorts of exchanges, but also make the fetus available for the pregnant woman herself to possess and enjoy in new ways. An ultrasound examination produces visual imagery and medically authorized information about the fetus—its size, sex, appearance, heart rate, position, activities, and so forth—which endow it with a sort of objectified existence. In this form, the fetus may be "consumed" by a pregnant woman, who may take considerable pleasure in being able not only to feel its presence within her body, but also to see it, name it, show it around to others, and construct for it the rudiments of a personal and social identity (a point to which we shall return in a moment). At the same time, the fetus as objectified in this form may in certain contexts be said to have an "exchange value." For example, a fetus that displays a particularly rare and interesting anomaly may have considerable value within the obstetrician's professional world, leading to publications and research presentations and other professional rewards. The pregnant woman carrying that same fetus, on the other hand, would be compelled first either to accept or reject the equivalence being made between the fetus within her and the fetus as externalized through ultrasound diagnosis and imagery, and then to weigh the value of this fetus against the possible futures (or the possible future fetuses) for which it might be exchanged.[8]

In cases where no problems are detected, the fetus may be said to have other sorts of exchange values, in the context of a pregnant woman's social world. The image itself and other bits of information gleaned from the ultrasound examination are exchanged with others and valued as tangible evidence of the presence of the fetus as a new "person" to be incorporated into networks of family and kin. The vast majority of women I spoke with planned to show the ultrasound "picture" they were given during the examination to the baby's father, and/or their older children and their own parents or other family members. A good number said they planned to show it to friends, coworkers, or "anyone who will let me." A few couples told me that they had faxed their ultrasound images to family members living in other parts of the country, or planned to do so. Sometimes, control over the image and its circulation was contested (with varying degrees of seriousness). For example, one young couple, clearly excited about the impending birth of their first child and delighted at seeing the image on the ultrasound screen, got into a good-natured argument when I asked LaToya what she would do with the "picture" that the sonographer had given her.

ANDRE: *I'm* gonna keep it!

LATOYA [laughing]: I know, he's not gonna let anyone have it. 'Cause *I* can't even see it, he keeps taking it away!

JANELLE [to Andre]: Okay, so what are *you* gonna do with it?

ANDRE: Oh, I'm gonna show it off, you know. I don't know if this can be framed or not, but I'm gonna take it to work. I'll explain it to them, you know, how this is his spine right here, and that's his stomach, his head, he has a big head like mine.

Clearly, just as exchange is entangled with consumption in the case of the fetus, so too is commoditization inextricably bound up with personification. The visual image of the fetus on the screen, the take-home Polaroid snapshot, the diagnosis, the medically certified knowledge that it is a boy or a girl, the narrative descriptions provided by the sonographer in the course of the ultrasound exam—all contribute to the process by which a pregnant woman and the people around her construct for her fetus a more specific social identity. Lisa Meryn Mitchell, drawing upon ethnographic fieldwork conducted in an ultrasound clinic in Montreal, has detailed the ways in which

> [s]onographers' accounts of the fetal image . . . situate the fetus in a world of other selves. In particular, sonographers personalize their accounts of the image for parents, comparing parental and fetal behaviour and appearance, employing kinship terms to describe the image, creating a voice to enable the fetus to talk to parents, and encouraging them to reply. . . . [T]he fetus emerges as a social being, a social actor with a distinctive identity—"the baby"—enmeshed in a social network of kin. (2001:136)

In the course of my research, I regularly observed how, during an examination, visible physical features or movements of the fetus were translated into terms that created a personality and a social identity for it. For example, consider an exam performed by Sondra, a sonographer who occasionally filled in at the clinic, on Audrey, a young African American woman pregnant with her first child:

AUDREY: Are you gonna be able to tell me what it is today?

SONDRA: Maybe. If the baby lets us, put it that way. . . . Look, there's the legs, you see how they're stretching out?

AUDREY: Yeah! Look at that, looks like he's clowning. . . .

SONDRA: Now I can't see for sure, but it looks like it might be a girl. . . . That's the heart. . . . That's the jawbone. See all the little teeth that's in there? . . . Here, here's a picture for you . . . and here's another one.

AUDREY: I'll show these to my Mama, she'll say, "I can't see what it is! What is it?" [To the pictures]: You are too active! I think you are a boy. Are you a boy? I wanna know so I can go buy clothes!

The "baby" is constructed in this exchange as someone with the power to provide or deny the information its mother wants, someone who "clowns around"; and because it is "active," Audrey thinks it must be a boy, despite Sondra's informed guess that it's probably a girl. Through obstetrical ultrasound as it is practiced in the United States, then, the fetus is commoditized *and* personified, "produced" as an object for exchange *and* for consumption. To adopt the terminology proposed by Igor Kopytoff (1986), ultrasound commoditizes the fetus (i.e., makes it exchangeable) in the same movement that it also singularizes it (i.e., endows it with a singular social identity).

Yet the commoditization and the singularization of the fetus around and through obstetrical ultrasound take place in ways structured by the intersecting ideologies of motherhood, medicine, race, and class. Some of the sonographers I observed at work seemed to dispense "nonmedical" extras (showing the baby, giving a picture, informing of fetal sex) most readily only to women whom they perceived as *already* having demonstrated a certain seriousness about the "medical" aspects of the procedure (prenatal diagnosis), and who more generally were seen as taking a responsible attitude toward their health and their pregnancy. Not surprisingly, perhaps, some also displayed cultural attitudes widely shared in this country (and deeply entrenched in public policy and social theory alike), in regarding the pregnancies of young, poor, unmarried African American women in their care as symptomatic of their failure to be "serious" and "responsible" about reproduction—and regarding these young women as therefore less deserving of such "extras" than mature, middle-class, married (often white) women.

For example, after one examination, I stepped into the hall for a moment with the sonographer, Linda, while the patient, a seventeen-year-old African American woman named Talia who was seven months into her first pregnancy, rearranged her clothes. As we stood in the hallway Linda complained to me, "I can't stand the people that just want to get a picture!" Confused, I asked: "I thought she was here because she had had chicken pox?" (chicken pox contracted during pregnancy can lead to serious subsequent health problems for an affected fetus). Linda replied: "Yeah, the doctor has *his* reasons for ordering it, but . . . certain types of people, all they care about is getting a picture and knowing what sex it is. They say, 'Oh, my girlfriend's having a boy, I wanna know what I'm having,' like it's a big contest or something." When I followed Linda back in, Talia asked, "Can I get a picture?" Linda answered breezily, "I'm sorry, I didn't take an extra one! All the pictures I have I need for the file." It was hard not to interpret her response as punitive.

Or, to take another example, Rasheeda, a young African American woman from the Woodlawn neighborhood of Chicago, eighteen years old and six months pregnant with her first child, came to her ultrasound examination accompanied by one of her girlfriends. There was some confusion at the start of the exam, because she had apparently not brought with her certain forms from her doctor that she was expected to provide. Rasheeda's examination proceeded:

CAMILLA: Do you want to know the sex of the baby?

RASHEEDA: Yeah.

FRIEND: It's a male!

R [to F, with some irritation]: . . . Girl!

C: Look at your baby. . . . That's the baby's head, there's the spine, there's the baby's heart. Do you want to know? Are you sure you want to know?

F: It's a boy! I can tell, it *looks* like a boy!

R: What is it?

C: You're going to have to wait until the baby is born.

After the examination was finished, I followed Camilla out into the hall while Rasheeda got dressed. I asked her, "So you really couldn't see what it was?" She responded: "I could tell, but then she started on about it being a boy, I got annoyed. I decided not to tell her, she can wait until the baby is born. It annoys me, they don't appreciate it. I let her come in, she doesn't have her papers or anything, she probably never got them." Here, again, it was difficult to avoid the conclusion that the sonographer was deliberately withholding pleasurable elements of the ultrasound exam, for punitive reasons. The way in which Camilla thus conflated Rasheeda with her friend (she herself had, after all, said nothing about the baby being a boy) might be seen as hinting at the way in which both of them were, in Camilla's mind, conflated with a broader category of women, "certain types of people," who care altogether too much about "extras" such as knowledge of fetal sex, and don't take the medical aspects of ultrasound seriously, just as they don't take pregnancy itself (or sexual activity) seriously enough. There are, in other words, conventions of discourse at work in the practice of ultrasound that both presume and produce a "pathological" pregnant subject, in tandem with a "normal" pregnant subject formed in the image of bourgeois ideals of the kind of reproduction that is considered good (mature, married, financially stable, planned pregnancy, early prenatal care attendance, etc). And, as pregnant women are thus "produced," so too are their fetuses; in social practice some fetuses are clearly treated as "more equal" than others.

What sonographers think and say and do does not, of course, by any means determine how their pregnant patients think or feel about and value their own pregnancies and fetuses. It nonetheless seems worth noting that if, as I have argued, obstetrical ultrasound as practiced in the United States both commoditizes and singularizes the fetus, it does so in ways that also communicate to already disempowered groups of women a view that their children are less valued as commodities and regarded less fully as persons.

Mixed Metaphors: The Hungry Consumer and the Pregnant Woman

To consider the fetus in terms of questions about commodification and consumption might seem an obvious enough move to make. Consumption practices are involved in the experience of pregnancy in a number of ways, as we have discussed above. Furthermore, popular debates about abortion and new reproductive technologies, like theoretical discussions of consumption and commodification, both tend to revolve around the question of how best to understand and adjudicate the relationship between "persons" and "things." However, applying notions of consumption and commodification to the topic of reproduction turns out to be somewhat tricky. I suggest that this difficulty emerges, at least in part, out of the way in which implicit metaphors operate in social theory (no less than in medical practice!). Specifically, body metaphors of eating and digesting food remain implicit in theories of consumption, which mix rather badly with the metaphorical associations of procreation, making it difficult (or at least quite counterintuitive) to bring theories of consumption to bear specifically upon reproduction.

The concept of consumption, now taken within social theory to refer to all kinds of uses of goods and services, still retains heavy traces of its older association with eating. Indeed, *Webster's* defines "consumer" as "one that consumes: as a: one that utilizes economic goods b: an organism requiring complex organic compounds for food which it obtains by preying on other organism or by eating particles of organic matter" (Merriam-Webster's 2006). This association between the consumption (i.e., purchase and use) of commodities and the consumption (i.e., ingestion) of food has deep historical roots. Sidney Mintz has traced an important part of this history in his account of the rise of sugar, arguing that the development of a taste for sucrose among the British poor was a crucial first step in their historical transformation into modern industrial workers and consumers (1985:180). As Marshall Sahlins has pointed out, this linkage has also left its mark upon the theoretical literature on consumption. Modern economic theory presumes a view of the individual as a creature driven by needs that are construed as bodily hungers:

> In the world's richest societies, the subjective experience of lack increases in proportion to the objective output of wealth. Encompassed in an international division of labor, individual needs were seemingly inexhaustible. Felt, moreover, as physiological pangs, as deprivations like hunger and thirst, these needs seem to come from within, as dispositions of the body. The bourgeois economy made a fetish of human needs in the sense that needs, which are always social in character and origin and in that way objective, had to be assumed as subjective experiences of pain. (1996:401)

Mintz and Sahlins are two among many anthropologists whose work has enriched discussions of consumption with a critical focus on the social and cultural dimensions of goods and commodities, their exchange and their use, and the "needs" they are taken to satisfy. A particularly vibrant literature has also emerged within anthropology that focuses specifically on the intersections between changing regimes of consumption and processes of commodification of bodies and persons, primarily in non-Western contexts.[9] Too often, however, consumption continues to be defined exclusively as the purchase and use of mass-produced material things. For example, Daniel Miller's (1998) influential ethnographic study of shopping in North London draws fascinating connections between consumption and kinship, especially the mother-child relationship, but proceeds from an understanding of consumption as having to do only with material things. Indeed, in a review article on the anthropology of consumption and commodities Miller states that "almost all of the cited literature . . . consists of studies in anthropology and material culture" (1995:144). Too much of the anthropological literature on consumption still preserves largely intact the image of a restless, hungry subject inhabiting a world of needed-and-desired objects external to himself.

Indeed, within Karl Marx's definition of the "very queer thing" that is the commodity, hunger already is inscribed as the paradigm for consumption: "A commodity is, in the first place, an object outside us, a thing that by its properties satisfies human wants of some sort or another. The nature of such wants, whether, for instance, they spring from the stomach or from fancy, makes no difference" (Tucker 1978:199). "Wants that spring from the stomach" stand here for real physical need (to the extent that any such unmediated needs might be said to exist), while other sorts of desires, "wants that spring from fancy," are refigured as a sort of mental or spiritual hunger. The consumer, then, is a metaphysically hungry individual, a person whose desires are oriented toward some "object outside," whether food or some other material object symbolically standing in its place.

All of this makes it rather difficult to conceptualize reproduction in terms of consumption. The consumer of social theory inhabits a body which, if not necessarily male (for women also eat and feel hunger), is at least not easily imagined as a specifically pregnant body. The fetus is, after all, emphatically *not* "an object outside us," and although it may nonetheless "satisfy human wants of some sort or another," it is difficult to imagine these wants as "springing from the stomach." How can the bearing of children be likened to the ingestion of food? The very suggestion seems to invoke that most frightening of all monsters, the mother who eats her own children. But if the awkwardness of looking at reproduction in terms of consumption serves thus to "wake up sleeping metaphors" (Martin 1990), then the attempt may perhaps bring to light unexamined aspects of the theoretical apparatus with which we approach the topic of consumption. Specifically, it raises questions about how the implicit metaphor of the hungry consumer may shape or hinder our critical understanding of ongoing transformations—at once technological, social, cultural, and political—in the meaning and practice of reproduction.

As I have shown, obstetrical ultrasound plays a part in constructing the fetus more and more as a commodity *at the same time and through the same means* that it is also constructed more and more as a person. The experience of pregnancy and indeed the fetus itself are, in a variety of ways, increasingly firmly embedded within U.S. consumer-capitalist society and culture, as commodities available for consumption like any others. But in the same motion, the fetus also increasingly is construed as a baby, a person, from the earliest moments. By the same token, pregnant women are positioned as "consumers" through the same processes that they are positioned as reproductive "laborers." The feminist argument by analogy to production cannot easily account for the ways that obstetrical ultrasound technology has come to figure in the experience of pregnancy in contemporary U.S. society. We must therefore consider reproduction in light of questions of commodification and consumption, even if doing so requires that we struggle against gendered body metaphors implicit within these theoretical constructs themselves. My aim is not to replace one analogy with another, much less to argue that consumption is liberating or free. Nor, indeed, do I concede that "producer" and "consumer" are the only possible subject positions from which to approach reproduction. Rather, my aim in this chapter has been to try to view things from another angle, to fill out the explanation—because I believe that, in order to effectively engage as feminists with ultrasound and the panoply of other technologies now brought to bear upon reproduction, we need to begin by recognizing that in this society, at this moment, pregnancy is both a labor of production and an "all-consuming" experience.

6

Entertaining Fetuses

Keepsake Ultrasound and
Crisis Pregnancy Centers

I mean, this stuff looks cool. Google and you'll see. By comparison,
seeing routine sonograms at your doctor's office is like watching
Disney's "Fantasia" on your great-aunt's rabbit-eared black-and-white
Magnavox. Still, part of me cannot help thinking: "Man, do we need
another way to a) fuel our culture's [and parents'] baby-mania and b)
separate doting moms-and-dads-to-be from their money?" There's
also this point. . . . Antiabortion activists think this stuff looks pretty
cool, too. Several Web sites I peeked at tout stills from these videos
(and in some cases, videos themselves) as "proof" that abortion is
wrong. . . . Neither this, nor the specter of danger, seems sufficient
reason to outlaw these outfits. It is, after all, a free 4-D country. But
given the choice, I think I'll stick with my great-aunt's TV.

—Lynne Harris 2006

One need not dig far to find confirmation of just how tightly interwoven
ultrasound, pregnancy, and consumption are in U.S. society today. With
the advent of new 3D and 4D ultrasound devices capable of generating
more visually appealing and "realistic" images, businesses have sprung up
that market ultrasound scanning directly to the public, offering women the
opportunity to view and acquire fetal ultrasound images on their own initiative and at their own expense, outside the purview of medical authority.

Quite independent of the special interest that I take in ultrasound,
I have several times chanced to come across glossy color advertisements

for such "keepsake" ultrasound businesses in the course of my ordinary life. One such ad turned up in a copy of the free *Northwest Parenting* magazine that I happened to pick up, another in the program for a children's theater production that I attended with my son, and another in a brochure I picked up at a local business called "Jump Planet, the Inflatable Party Center of the Universe!" to which my daughter had been invited for a friend's birthday party. Had I not come across the topic in these other ways, I might have read about it in *People* magazine, which in June 2004 featured an article that profiled one of the "chain stores" run by a franchise called Fetal Fotos, and reported on the controversies surrounding such businesses among ultrasound professionals (Schindehette and Finan 2004). Similar articles that address the rise of "keepsake" ultrasound enterprises have appeared in a number of local and national newspapers (see, e.g., Harris 2006; Hughes 2006; Lubell 2004; Ostrom 2006).

In this chapter I examine "entertainment" ultrasound businesses as a phenomenon that manifests, in a particularly striking manner, some of the ambiguities and simmering tensions that surround the practice of obstetrical ultrasound in this country. These businesses are controversial because they situate what most understand to be a *medical* technology and procedure squarely in the marketplace and outside the medical domain. In doing so, they are hardly unique. From "concierge medicine," to elective plastic surgery, to direct-to-consumer television ads for pharmaceuticals, to medical tourism, the commodification of medicine is more the rule than the exception. The "crisis of the uninsured" remains a perpetual crisis, year after year, because U.S. society is presently committed to solving health problems through marketplace solutions, however demonstrably these fail to meet the needs of the disadvantaged. Thus, pharmacies become the "doctors" to the poor, nurses compete with local doctors for "continuing care patients" in low-cost clinics located in Wal-Mart stores (Bowe 2007), and nearly a third of the population suffers from untreated tooth decay, even as dentists work fewer and fewer hours for higher and higher salaries serving those with means (Berenson 2007; Sered and Fernandopulle 2005). That obstetrical ultrasound too gets drawn into the marketplace is not particularly surprising. What is more interesting, because less obvious, is how all of this relates to the politics of reproduction. As this chapter shall show, the closer we look at the debates and practices surrounding "entertainment" ultrasound, the more clear it becomes how the problematic nexus of medicine and consumerism has, in very concrete ways, created the conditions of possibility for ultrasound technology to become involved in some of the peculiarly American cultural politics of abortion.

Troubling Medical Boundaries

As one might expect, given the discussion of policies regarding ultrasound in chapter 3, medical professional organizations have come out unanimously in expressing stern disapproval of ultrasound scanning for other than approved purposes. For example, the Society of Diagnostic Medical Sonography released the following statement in January 2002:

> Within the past few years . . . a small number of private businesses have opened for the sole purpose of providing expectant parents with images (including 3D) of the developing fetus on videocassette or other method of record. Because the service is provided for entertainment purposes only, it is considered non-diagnostic. . . . The Society of Diagnostic Medical Sonography recognizes the responsibility we have to the health care community and to patients. As Diagnostic Medical Sonographers, we are committed to act in the best interest of the patient and to maintain ethical standards to preserve and promote professionalism and our commitment to the use of ultrasound as a diagnostic procedure. Therefore, the SDMS does not condone the use of ultrasound solely for entertainment purposes. (SDMS 2004)

Similar statements in opposition to nondiagnostic ultrasound have been issued by the American College of Radiology, the American Registry of Diagnostic Medical Sonography, and the ECRI (formerly the Emergency Care Research Institute), as well as the AIUM, whose statement on this issue was discussed in chapter 3 (Pinkney 2005).

The FDA, which has regulatory oversight over ultrasound as a medical device, has reiterated its long-standing opposition to any use of ultrasound without a prescription, and warned:

> Persons who promote, sell or lease ultrasound equipment for making "keepsake" fetal videos should know that the FDA views this as

an unapproved use of a medical device. In addition, those who subject individuals to ultrasound exposure using a diagnostic ultrasound device (a prescription device) without a physician's order
may be in violation of state or local laws or regulations regarding
use of a prescription medical device. (Rados 2004)

The FDA's ability to enforce this admonition is limited, however, because it
can only regulate the sales of equipment, whereas state or local laws gov-
ern whether the operation of an ultrasound device requires permission. It
becomes a question of whether the state in which one is located is a prescription state or not:

> The licensing of health care providers is left to individual states. For
> the time being the companies do not need to be licensed, and the
> technicians do not need to be certified. But Dr. Daniel G. Schultz,
> director of the agency's Center for Devices and Radiological Health,
> said the agency was advising states about the potential health risks
> of elective ultrasounds and ensuring that machines were labeled for
> specific medical functions. "In the end it's up to the states," he said.
> (Lubell 2004)

Even in regulating sales, the FDA's enforcement ability appears quite weak.
Only one ultrasound manufacturer, SonoSite, has announced a policy of
making equipment sales only in conformance with these policies; "many
others continue to supply ultrasound scanners for keepsake or entertainment purposes" (Pinkney 2005; see also Abella 2005).

But it is not only unscrupulous practitioners and manufacturers who
engage in "keepsake" scanning. Even those within the medical professional community who have most strongly opposed "entertainment" ultrasound also have expressed support for *the same practices,* as long as these
take place in the context of an exam ordered for valid medical reasons. For
example, in an article strongly objecting to "keepsake" ultrasound, radiologist Beryl Benacerraf writes:

> It is certainly acceptable to print out and give patients keepsake
> images of their fetuses, such as 3D images, regular 2D images, or
> even a short videotape obtained during the course of an indicated
> scan, and most of us do this. On the other hand . . . it is unacceptable

to perform sonography for the sole purpose of obtaining a fetal photograph or videotape for entertainment. (2002:1065)

As was mentioned in chapter 3, the AIUM's 2005 statement on "keepsake ultrasound imaging" similarly approves and encourages practices amounting to keepsake scanning, in the context of a medical exam, so long as no additional fee is charged.

Frank Chervenak and Laurence McCullough (2005) published an opinion piece in a major journal of obstetrics in which they objected to "boutique" ultrasound and called for "the medicalization of fetal imaging." This drew a very angry and bitter letter to the editor of the journal from F. Rex Nielsen, an obstetrician who operates a keepsake ultrasound business. Responding to Nielsen's letter, Chervenak and McCullough clarify that "we did not object to offering 'keepsake' images, on the condition that they are provided in the context of a regular ultrasound examination, not something as casual as getting 'another look' at the fetus" (2006:1502). As shown in chapter 3, the hybrid cultural form of the obstetrical ultrasound exam makes it very difficult definitively to separate medical from nonmedical scanning.

Some of the same professional organizations that officially condemn nonmedical scanning also condone and even themselves organize scanning that is not medically indicated when it is part of an educational effort, for example at professional conferences. This point was raised by Jeanette Burlbaw, one of the two "keepsake" entrepreneurs I interviewed, who is herself a registered sonographer with twenty years of clinical experience before she opened her business in a Midwestern city in 2002:

> The AIUM provides the sound-bites concerning how the patient needs to be careful not to expose their baby to nonmedically indicated sonography. My question to them is how do they justify using the pregnant patient for hands-on scanning during AIUM sponsored educational activities? This is not a medically indicated exam. Is it safe if it benefits the medical community?

Similarly, scans that are not medically indicated are performed regularly under the auspices of ultrasound manufacturers, to test or demonstrate equipment, without incurring any official disapproval. Marilyn, the other "keepsake" ultrasound entrepreneur I interviewed, is a registered sonographer with years of experience working primarily in the ultrasound industry before she opened her business in a fast-growing West Coast suburb in 1996 (the first such business in the entire region). She had worked first for one manufacturer as an "application specialist"—someone whose job it is to train and educate customers on new ultrasound technology, work with sales staff to assist in product training and ongoing sales and marketing efforts, provide customer support through follow-up training, and gather customer feedback for a company's marketing and sales divisions. She then worked for two other manufacturers in their research and development divisions. On the basis of this experience, Marilyn raised the same question as Jeanette:

MARILYN: We did demonstrations, we did apps and demos and then we were involved in education. I also went around with the transvag [the special transducer designed for conducting transvaginal ultrasound scans], teaching people about how to do transvag. . . .

JANELLE: When you were doing that, say you want to demonstrate the equipment to someone who's thinking about buying it, and you need a person to demonstrate it on, where does that person come from?

MARILYN: You know, they had patients who would come, sent there from the physicians—it was the same thing! So that's why, you were talking about the laws and stuff, the FDA didn't want to get involved because if they did make laws about that then they couldn't do any more scanning like that, they couldn't do any more scanning at shows, they couldn't do any more of that, because—what's the difference? There *is* no difference.

Distinguishing medical from nonmedical scanning is further complicated by the fact that some clinics that specialize in diagnostic ultrasound have expanded their offerings to include separate nondiagnostic "entertainment" scans as well. For example, Elite Diagnostics, a freestanding ultrasound clinic in Cape Canaveral, Florida, explains on its website that

[a]longside diagnostic scans ordered by a physician and billed to insurance, Elite Diagnostics offers a "3D Reassurance Ultrasound" which a woman may schedule directly with the clinic and which must be paid out-of-pocket. . . . Why this scan is performed: We offer three-dimensional ultrasounds to provide a positive bonding experience for the mother, father and family members with the

unborn baby. We feel that realistic surface images provide a connection between parents and child that can be beneficial to the whole family. (ThreeDSono 2004)

By the same token, some businesses that primarily offer "entertainment" ultrasound also carry out diagnostic scans, mainly for patients who lack insurance coverage. Jeanette Burlbaw says:

I offer diagnostic service alongside nondiagnostic. I offer reassurance ultrasound . . . but I also do diagnostic scans, for people who don't have insurance or whose insurance company won't allow an additional exam. If that's your situation, being uninsured, then you go and present yourself to the people who you want to care for you, and you negotiate the price of care, that's just what you have to do. When I was at [the university where she had worked in clinical practice for many years before leaving to start up her own business] they would pay $500 to come to you and see no doctor. [This] was for those uninsured patients that had to pay fee for service and wanted to fulfill what the doctor ordered at twenty weeks . . . the traditional diagnostic exam. So I figured that I could offer diagnostic ultrasound more cheaply, they come to my suite, I measure, do it all here for $250, and give them all the 3D images, the doctor gets a report.

While Jeanette's keepsake ultrasound business may accommodate uninsured patients, not all do. Marilyn explained to me some of the reasons why she requires that anyone who comes to her provide evidence that she has a primary physician and that the physician approves of her decision to get a nondiagnostic scan:

MARILYN: I don't want someone to come to me that's had no prenatal care. It doesn't happen so much now, but when I started, people—they think because you do an ultrasound, that when you put a probe down, they immediately say, "Is everything okay?" Like it's a magic wand, that you just can see that everything is okay immediately. And it's not like that. So they'll think that if they come here, then the baby's okay, they don't necessarily need to go to a doctor. And that came up a few times.

JANELLE: Would this be people who don't have insurance or something?

MARILYN: Yeah. It happens sometimes when they switch doctors, I had a few low-income people that didn't really get the concept of medical care at all. One of them showed up with her cousin, and said, "This is my cousin, she doesn't like her doctor, will you be her doctor?" So [requiring approval from a physician] eliminates that. Also, if I find something wrong, then [the physician will] know who I am. So if I call them and say, "This is what I saw," they'll say, "Oh, okay." And they'll know it right away, because I have a little form that I fill out when I get verbals [approval/ referrals]. And I know who I'm supposed to contact.

Such comments remind us that the debate over which ultrasound scans are medically acceptable and which are merely consumer entertainment plays itself out against the backdrop of a society in which millions of people, including millions of pregnant women, have no insurance coverage and little if any access to good affordable health care, especially preventive care (Sered and Fernandopulle 2005). Not only are poor and uninsured women unable to partake in the pleasures of "entertainment" ultrasound, dubious as those may be, but they face real difficulty as well even gaining access to scans whose medical legitimacy might be unquestioned. Although Marilyn, like many people, tends to blame individual poor and uninsured women for their situation, one may argue reasonably that it is not they but the society in which they live—in which we live—that "doesn't really get the concept of medical care at all."

Practicing in the Margins

What Marilyn's and Jeanette's comments also reveal is that however stridently the voices of medical authority may condemn "keepsake" ultrasound, a considerable amount of interaction and cooperation takes place at the level of practice between physicians and sonographers who operate such businesses.

Both Marilyn and Jeanette get much of their clientele in the form of referrals from physicians. Marilyn, who is in fact quite committed to upholding the distinction between medically indicated and nondiagnostic scans, regards her own work performing "entertainment" scans as in fact helping to keep medical ultrasound more strictly medical:

This is one of the controversies with what I do, where do you draw the line between entertainment versus diagnostic? To me, I think it alleviates some of the pressure from the diagnostic scans, they don't feel they have to put on a show. And here, that's what I do. You know, I schedule an hour for each person, and they can bring as many people as they want. . . . I think the line between diagnostic and entertainment is important. I hear people complaining about that they feel very rushed [during a diagnostic ultrasound exam], because they only schedule fifteen minutes or twenty minutes, and they don't want to videotape . . . And I do understand why they don't want to videotape, because when I worked in a hospital I wouldn't have wanted to do it either. Because your main objective is to make sure the baby's healthy, and it's very distracting to have someone say "what's that, what's that, what's that. . . ." It's hard, it's very hard, to do both. And also to have multiple people in the room when you're doing diagnostic is really distracting, and that's something I think people don't understand.

Relationships of personal trust and the professional networks built up during years of working in the field within a particular region can help to build bridges between medical practitioners and keepsake ultrasound entrepreneurs, although this is not without its own complications. Jeanette recounts:

There are frustrations with working independently of a physician. Obstetrics as a profession is often very paternalistic, the doctor has more control than the patient realizes. One of the old physicians that I worked with, when I told him that I was starting up this business, he had some business sense and he asked me: "Who'd you align yourself with?" And I told him that I wasn't aligning myself with anybody. And he said, "Well, good luck, honey." Referral relationships are difficult, because there really is a lot of backscratching that goes on, and if you're outside of that network it's difficult. But on the other hand there are some physicians who do refer to me because their patients have told them what a great experience it was, or I've helped a patient of theirs. So many of these are really kind guys, and they know that their patients want it, and the obstetrician hears that the patients loved it, it benefits them.

Similarly, Marilyn says:

> The thing that surprised me when I started was I got phone calls
> from doctors. The doctors themselves called to thank me for opening
> the business, because the patients were seeing them for another
> ultrasound, and—I learned a lot about insurance companies—if
> a doctor will order on all their patients [a scan to assess fetal]
> size-versus-[gestational]-dates or something, and if Blue Shield or
> whoever insurance covers them, if they notice that then they audit
> them. And if they don't like what they see, then. . . . So they have to
> be really really careful. So the doctor's not willing to do it except for,
> you know, if there's a real problem.

According to Jeanette, her nondiagnostic ultrasound enterprise
sometimes supports physicians in ways more direct than simply by making
their clients happy as well, though they may later downplay or deny any
such connections. In the city where she lives, 3D ultrasound equipment
such as she uses was still quite rare in medical settings when she opened
her business:

> I had sent letters to all the physicians [in the area], saying: "If you
> have a patient with a known malformation who would benefit from a
> 3D scan, please send them to me and I will do it for free." So he did,
> he sent me this woman, and she later wrote me a letter thanking me
> for providing care for her in "a thoughtful non-clinical setting, it
> reduced my anxiety, and I was allowed to ask questions." The physi-
> cian thanked me and said it was the best thing he could have done for
> the patient. I called the same physician later to ask about referring to
> my office. He responded, "I'm not supporting photomat ultrasound!"

Skill and Caring in "Keepsake" Ultrasound

I was interested in this woman's description of Jeanette's practice as
"nonclinical," and asked Jeanette what she thought that meant, and whether
perhaps it had to do with the way the place was furnished and decorated:

> I don't know, I mean it's full of photography and stuff, but it's prob-
> ably more about the way we interact. My practice is in a strip-mall,

beside a BBQ joint, but there's also a family practice group's office, so it's sort of mixed-use. I've got wicker chairs with cream-colored cushions, two floral chairs that I wanted to get out of my house, my diplomas etc. framed by the desk. Hanging over the desk I've got a Swedish mobile of storks, that's probably the most fanciful thing. And I've got a bookcase promoting the work of my patients—my photographer friend has some of her photographs on display. I have lots of chairs, and I have a big monitor so that nobody has to crane around to see—that really is no big whoop-de-do thing, every physician could do this if they wanted to. But I think the "nonclinical" reference comes from speaking with her on a personal level, sitting by her to show her appropriate references, etc.

Indeed, both Jeanette and Marilyn comment that the ability to spend plenty of time talking with each of the women who comes to them is what they enjoy most about the work, and it is also what brings customers in the door. Jeanette says:

Because I'm not dependent on insurance, I'm allowed to give the patient what they want. I'm allowed to be kind, to give them time, to give them stuff, just allowed to treat the patients as people. You're gonna want to hear that the reason I do this is because I love babies, and it's not. I love my patients. . . . [Sometimes] if they've had a scan already, but the sonographer was mean or rude or abrupt, then they'll come to me because they want to have a better experience.

I tell these sonographers, if you don't want to support this [non-diagnostic ultrasound], then be nicer to your patients. Or just go ahead and keep right on being rude and unpleasant, because you're generating a whole lot of business for me!

Indeed, the women I spoke with who had sought out keepsake ultrasounds gave just such reasons. Carolyn described seeking out Marilyn's keepsake ultrasound business because of her disappointment with the time spent and explanations provided during the diagnostic ultrasound she had already had during this, her third, pregnancy:

They were really busy, I don't think I'd ever seen them that busy, and I had to wait for half an hour, and my bladder was full, and when I got in there they just were really quiet and they weren't going to have a break with me and my husband. . . . And that's one thing that was really important to me, I wanted Aaron, the two-year-old, I wanted him to see the pictures of the baby. Because he was excited. And they . . . I mean, I know they have to do their job and—I'm assuming they were in a hurry, the technician just wasn't talkative at all, and I was trying to explain things to Aaron. And I know that they're doing their job and everything but, I was trying to say like "there's a foot! that's a foot!" and I was asking her, "Is that a foot?" Because I still am not really good at it, you'd think that I'd just know by now, but . . . I was trying to show Aaron everything and she just wasn't talking very much.

In chapter 2, technological skill and a gendered conception of caring were shown to be tightly conjoined in how sonographers understand and describe their work. While both Jeanette and Marilyn emphasize the attention and care they are able to provide women by working outside of the constraints of the medical setting, both also assert that the level of training, skill, and professionalism they bring to this work as sonographers is what distinguishes their practices from "photomat ultrasound." Jeanette's last comment continues: "At one of these conferences I actually stood up at the microphone and said, 'Please do not demean those of us who give of our time and emotions.' And the whole place went silent, you could have heard a pin drop."

Jeanette refers to the people who come to her as "patients," and the scan as an "exam," and says that each "reassurance" ultrasound scan (her preferred term) in fact contains all the elements of a full diagnostic exam:

First I sit down with them and I explain some things. I explain the safety issues, and I also explain that I do look at *anatomy*, and if I find anything that seems to be wrong, then this is what I'll do. . . . Then they get interested very quickly, because I show them everything, I show the entire baby to the parents—cardiac structures, stomach, kidneys, bladder, etc. They always want to see the spine, that's one thing they always want to see, and the heart. And they want reassurance about the sex—no one ever trusts the first person that diagnoses the sex. And I have a great ability, with my equipment, to show an explicit image of the spine and the ribs, so I always show them that . . . I don't measure. But I do look at intracranial anatomy, I look at the heart, I do all the same views.

Because of their training and experience as sonographers, both Jeanette and Marilyn occasionally detected previously unsuspected problems with the fetus. Faced with such an occurrence, both of them report that they spoke about it directly with the woman and then referred her to her own physician, sending him copies of the images they had produced. Jeanette says:

> I would love to change attitudes about keepsake ultrasound in the medical community, get them to see that it's not a bad thing to have a second set of eyes looking at this baby, as long as the person is skilled and trained. There are those who have spoken out very strongly against "entertainment ultrasound," putting out there all this negative stuff. How "I don't want to be fetal photographer." Whereas I think that this is all misplaced, I think the emphasis should be to keep this technology in the hands of those who are skilled.

It is certainly true that not all proprietors of keepsake ultrasound enterprises possess the kind of training and experience that Jeanette and Marilyn bring to their work. Jeanette says that she receives inquiries regularly from people wanting to open keepsake businesses of their own who have no training at all:

> Initially I got a lot of weird calls and e-mails from people wanting to set up their own businesses who have no skills, no training in ultrasound. I heard from a secretary in Texas who wanted to do this. My favorite one was this woman in Oklahoma who had a lot of experience with computers and she paid a sonographer $3,000 to teach her how to use ultrasound to make pretty pictures. I communicated with her through e-mail and asked, "But you don't know anything about fetal anatomy and physiology. What if there's something terribly wrong and you miss it because you don't know?" And she said, "That's not my problem, that's your problem."

Nor was this likely an isolated incident. A recent news account makes clear just how little and questionable is the training received by some of the people who offer keepsake ultrasounds under the "brand name" of the large national franchise Womb With a View:

> Owner Maria Ruby opened up the Elmwood Park shop last year and has another in Lake Hopatcong that has been in business for about two years. Ruby had her own 3-D ultrasound at a Womb With a View franchise when she was pregnant and was "blown away."
>
> "It's an awesome thing," Ruby said. "I used to be a health-care lawyer, and I quit my job and bought my business." The service is popular; Ruby said she has 30 to 40 clients each week at each location. . . .
>
> As for training, Ruby said she studied at other Womb With a View locations with franchise owners for about three months, practicing on fluid-filled decoys before moving on to real moms-to-be. (Hughes 2006)

This kind of scenario is exactly what concerns many in the medical community.

> Doctors are . . . worried about the training of keepsake operators and the upkeep of equipment, said Joshua A. Copel, president-elect of the American Institute of Ultrasound in Medicine.
>
> "The equipment today is capable of putting out much higher energy levels than in the past," said Copel, who is also a professor of obstetrics, gynecology and reproductive sciences at Yale University. "Most equipment in an obstetrical setting defaults to a low enough emission. . . . But we don't know the training of these people doing the ultrasounds."
>
> Ruby, owner of the Womb With a View, bristled at the notion that her service is for "entertainment" only: "This is a bonding experience you have with your baby—that's not just 'for fun,'" she said. (Hughes 2006)

Bonding Redux: From Keepsake Ultrasound to "Crisis Pregnancy Clinics"

Some clinics specializing in diagnostic ultrasound that have expanded their "entertainment" ultrasound operations have argued that their activities and services are in some sense medical and thus not in violation of FDA and other guidelines, on the grounds that ultrasound promotes maternal bonding. Fetal Fotos, which operates a national franchise chain of keepsake ultrasound businesses, has posted on its Web site a "frequently asked questions" page, which until recently featured a statement, since removed, that responded to such criticisms and concerns. That statement explained that even though the ultrasound scans that Fetal Fotos offers are explicitly billed as nondiagnostic, Fetal Fotos—unlike other operations that use ultrasound for nonmedical reasons—serves a "larger wellness purpose." How so? Because, as they explained, the real purpose of the scans is not the images but the maternal bonding that the images help achieve:

> The objection to keepsake videos is not that a video is provided, but that the video is the sole purpose of the sonogram, which is unacceptable. The video is not the purpose of our service. What we offer is a bonding experience using this technology and the skills we have developed. . . . We do provide the best prenatal images available in the country, but for us, this is a tool to serve a larger wellness purpose. That we record these sessions serves to further involve extended family in investing them in this pregnancy as well as hopefully returning the parents to that experience when they watch it to continue that bonding effect, even after delivery. (Fetal Fotos 2004)

Indeed, even though they may hold very different views on the importance of training, virtually all advocates for "keepsake" ultrasound make similar arguments about the importance of bonding. Jeanette Burlbaw (2004) has published an article about nondiagnostic ultrasound in the *Journal of Diagnostic Medical Sonography* in which she argued that such scanning is justified on the grounds that it enhances maternal bonding. In support of this point she cites a recent statement by Stuart Campbell, whose 1982 study we considered in some detail in chapter 4.

In 2002, Professor Campbell addressed members of the International Society for Ultrasound in Obstetrics and Gynecology (of which he is also a founding member and past president) to speak about the advantages and limitations of the new 4D imaging devices. He admitted that 4D had little benefit over conventional ultrasound with regard to prenatal diagnosis, but asserted that its great advantage was its enhanced ability to facilitate parental bonding. The text of his address appeared as an article in the society's journal, *Ultrasound in Obstetrics and Gynecology* (of which he is also the founding editor and was, until recently, editor in chief). The passage that Jeanette quotes in her article runs thus:

> There is evidence from randomized studies that ultrasound examination enhances maternal-fetal bonding, at least in the short term, and there is some evidence of added value with 3D scanning. This therapeutic aspect of scanning for pleasure may at least help us to respond to the general disapproving attitude of official bodies to the practice of allowing parents to enjoy looking at their baby. In the long term, however, I believe our Society [International Society of Ultrasound in Obstetrics and Gynecology] will have to adjust to the demands of prospective parents for this service. (Campbell 2002)

Whether or not ultrasound "bonds" mothers and fathers to their fetuses, apparently it has had this effect on Campbell himself, who reported recently that his views on abortion have changed over the years, as his admiration for fetuses has grown in the course of his work with ultrasound:

> These feelings were compounded when I began 3D ultrasound studies of fetuses throughout pregnancy. I was astonished to see complex co-ordinated movements from as early as 12 weeks gestation. I have been called sentimental for indicating my distress at the thought of aborting these beautiful complex potential human beings. Perhaps this is so, but I believe it will be a sign of a civilised and humane society that it limits the gestational age at which normal fetuses are aborted. ("Viewpoints: Abortion," 2004)

While Campbell has devoted much energy to communicating with his fellow medical professionals, he has also worked to share what he sees as the wonders of fetal ultrasound with the broader public. Through his London clinic, Campbell offers a forty-minute "Complete Pregnancy Scan (2D/3D/4D/Doppler)" for £200 (Create Health Centre for Reproduction and Advanced Technology 2006). One British journalist recently published an account of her visit to Campbell's clinic for a "keepsake" scan (Lambert 2006).

In October 2004, Campbell published a lavishly illustrated hardback book written for and marketed to expectant parents, titled *Watch Me . . . Grow!: A Unique, 3-Dimensional, Week-by-Week Look at Baby's Behavior and Development in the Womb*. In his foreword, Campbell writes:

> It has for many years been recognized that prenatal bonding between a mother and her unborn child is hugely beneficial for the emotional and even physical wellbeing of both the child and the mother herself. Many years ago, my colleagues and I showed that the conventional 2-D scan was helpful in promoting bonding before birth but now, with the experience that I have gained over the years, I can say confidently that 3-D and 4-D is much superior in this regard. The reaction of parents to "seeing" their, as yet, unborn baby is extraordinary. The father, who frequently is a passive observer during a conventional scan, is now totally involved in the whole process. I have seen fathers kiss the screen or their partners' abdomens in an ecstasy of recognition and love for the new baby. In an age when we acknowledge that every unborn baby's life is precious, the role of this ultrasound technique in promoting bonding is indeed a new factor of great importance. (2004:5)

Campbell has also regularly fed the BBC News with images they have then featured in news articles. One of these, which ran in July 2004, showed 4D images that Professor Campbell had produced of fetuses seeming to make the motions of walking, breathing, and thumb sucking, announcing:

> The abortion debate has been reignited in the UK by revolutionary ultrasound scans showing pictures of a 12-week-old fetus seemingly walking in the womb. There have been calls for the legal time limit for abortions to be reduced from 24 to 12 weeks and Prime Minister Tony Blair has hinted that the law may be re-examined. We asked six commentators for their views on abortion and the possibility of a change in the law. ("Viewpoints: Abortion," 2004)

When the British Medical Association subsequently voted down a proposed reduction in the gestational age at which abortions would be allowed, Professor Campbell spoke to a reporter from Scotland's *Sunday Herald* newspaper about his disappointment with their decision, and about how gratified he is that his ultrasound images have entered into debates surrounding abortion. Campbell regards it as entirely appropriate that these images, with their powerful emotional appeal, should influence public opinion and policy regarding this issue:

> Of course it's emotive. . . . It's a natural human response to see something that looks and behaves like a child, and to be emotional and protective towards it, not rip it out of the uterus. It's good emotion, not bad. And what is scientific about the decision to terminate a pregnancy? Obviously it's an unfortunate occurrence, all too common, and we have to allow women to terminate unwanted children. That's part of the law, and I accept it—but only up to 18 weeks. In fact, when I show parents the images at that stage, they say, "Wow, it looks like a baby." It's a shock to them, and they are overwhelmed by it. (Baggini 2005)

Although Campbell practices in the U.K., his professional stature and his very active efforts to promote his views both within the medical profession and in public culture more broadly have earned him a secure place in U.S. controversies and discussions. Antiabortion activists in the United States, who already in the early 1980s grasped the antiabortion implications of the theory of ultrasound bonding, have, not surprisingly, enthusiastically embraced the new 3D and 4D equipment, and they welcome "entertainment" ultrasound as serving the antiabortion cause by promoting maternal bonding. For example, the author of an article in the conservative Catholic publication *Crisis Magazine* stated:

> New evidence suggests that ultrasound plays a key role in persuading women not to have abortions. Psychologists say the reason for this is maternal-fetal bonding. . . . Prenatal scientists have discovered that ultrasound triggers those feelings even in the first trimester—two to three months earlier than they had thought. And now that 3-D and 4-D ultrasound is going commercial . . . many think that maternal bonding will have an even greater effect on pregnant women. (Stricherz 2002)

Opponents of abortion have attempted to incorporate obstetrical ultrasound directly into antiabortion "counseling" activities. In this,

Shari Richard, whose efforts in this direction we touched upon in chapter 2, is far from alone. Not only pro-life sonographers, but the pro-life movement more generally have seized enthusiastically upon ultrasound, especially since the advent of 3D and 4D imaging and the rise of commercial "keepsake" enterprises. Some in Richard's home state of Michigan have sought to require that a woman be shown her own ultrasound image prior to obtaining an abortion:

> In 2005, a bill was introduced in Michigan that would call for women contemplating abortion to be given the option of viewing ultrasound images of their fetuses. . . . Those seeking an abortion must already be provided images of a fetus at the gestation age of their own fetus, 24 hours prior to an abortion. That can be done through the mail or via the Internet. [Rep. Dave] Robertson's bill would add a requirement that a woman be offered images of *her* own fetus. (Putnam 2005)

Similar legislation has been proposed or passed in many other states (Jonsson 2007).

Other antiabortion advocates have sought to get in on the ultrasound bonding action in a more direct manner, on the model of keepsake ultrasound enterprises. In recent years several major antiabortion organizations have mounted large campaigns to outfit "crisis pregnancy centers" with state-of-the-art 3D ultrasound equipment, and to offer pregnant women "counseling" and support intended to steer them away from abortion.

> Southern Baptist Convention and the evangelical organization Focus on the Family, have spent $20,000 to $30,000 apiece on ultrasound machines, and some of the clinics are vying for more expensive state-of-the art machines that show the fetus in three dimensions. Focus on the Family has budgeted $4.2 million in the current fiscal year for the machines and on training on how to use them.
>
> . . . The groups say donations have flowed steadily, from individuals, churches and businesses. The Psalm 139 Project, which is the Southern Baptist program, bought ultrasound machines last year

for two centers in Indiana and Texas. Focus on the Family, which covers 80 percent of ultrasound costs, helped 70 centers last year buy equipment and train staff and hopes to outfit at least 600 more by 2010. (Banerjee 2005; see also Gibbs 2007; Johnson 2005; Heartlink 2006)

The political scientist Joanne Boucher astutely observes that for an antiabortion entrepreneur such as Richard, whose company markets training manuals and courses to assist Crisis Pregnancy Centers wishing to use ultrasound, this campaign reflects

a curious mixture of the commercial and moral motive. Richard's depiction of herself in the video [*Ultrasound: A Window to the Womb*] as educator, scientist, and concerned citizen obfuscates the essential economic dimension of her project. . . . Perhaps it is hardly surprising that Richard suppresses this aspect of her endeavors, as it would appear that Richard is in the morally awkward position of engaging in an entrepreneurial venture—on behalf of the unborn. (2004b:18; see also Boucher 2004a)

Within the U.S. government, some conservative abortion opponents have sought ways of directing federal tax money toward Crisis Pregnancy Clinics (CPCs).

Because promoting abstinence before marriage is a part of the CPC mission, centers are eligible for federal abstinence-education grants, which in some cases have instantly doubled or tripled their budgets. In 2005, roughly 13% of Care Net affiliates [the largest pregnancy-center network] got state or federal money; their average budget was $155,000. (Gibbs 2007:26)

An investigative report prepared at the request of Rep. Henry Waxman (a Democrat from California) found that well over $30 million in federal support was disbursed to CPCs between 2001 and 2006 (U.S. House of Representatives Committee on Government Reform Minority Staff Special Investigations Division 2006). In 2002, Representative Cliff Stearns (a Republican from Florida) introduced "Informed Choice Act, H.R. 216," a bill that ultimately died in July 2005 but, had it passed, would have allocated up to $3 million in federal funding specifically to support the purchase of new ultrasound equipment for "crisis pregnancy centers" (Crary 2002).

The training undergone by the people who perform scans at "crisis pregnancy centers" is apparently as cursory and superficial as that of the least scrupulous "keepsake" entrepreneurs. A *Time* magazine reporter describes the training undergone by staff at a CPC clinic in Asheville, North Carolina, that Focus on the Family equipped with an ultrasound device in summer 2006:

> Nurse Wilson and her colleague Denise Bagby had two weeks of intensive training in "limited obstetrical ultrasound," practicing on pregnant women recruited from local doctors' offices and churches and by word of mouth. They learned how to confirm and date a pregnancy and measure a fetus—but not how to diagnose fetal abnormality. Two medical directors sign off on every report. "We're not giving medical care," Wood insists, although she stresses the value of early ultrasound in helping persuade women to quit smoking, eat better, get prenatal care and come to grips with what is happening inside their bodies. (Gibbs 2007:28)

While some, like Nurse Wood quoted in this passage, insist that they are *not* providing medical care, others who use ultrasound as part of their antiabortion efforts take a different approach. The National Institute of Family and Life Advocates, an antiabortion organization dedicated to providing assistance and support to "pregnancy help centers," seeks through The Life Choice (TLC) project to help such centers convert their operations into licensed medical clinics, so that they can legally offer ultrasound. The organization's Web site, addressing itself to people who run these bogus abortion clinics, says:

> Why should your center consider medical clinic conversion? Simply put, centers that convert to medical clinic status experience: 1) *an increase* in the total number of clients seen on an annual basis; 2) *an increase* in the number of abortion-minded clients seen; and 3) *a dramatic increase* in the percentage of clients choosing life! The offering of medical services, such as ultrasound, is particularly

effective in empowering your clients to choose life. Ultrasound opens "a window to the womb" to a mother in a crisis pregnancy. Ultrasound introduces this mother to her unborn child and enables her to bond with her baby. (NIFLA 2006)

The organization's "frequently asked questions" page highlights, yet again, how tenuous the boundaries of the medical domain can be. The advice offered there includes the following:

The provision of ultrasound services is the practice of medicine. Ultrasound is a diagnostic procedure which must be supervised and directed by a licensed physician experienced in ultrasound. Hence, before your center provides such services it must be operating to provide medical services. This means you must either be licensed as a medical clinic or have a licensed physician who serves as your Medical Director and oversees and is responsible for the provision of ultrasound services.

. . . Only a few states . . . have detailed and complicated licensing requirements for a center to be acknowledged as a "clinic." In these states the regulations must be complied with and state inspection is required. However, the vast majority of states do not have such regulations. In a state which is not regulated the only legal requirement is to have a physician (MD) who is licensed to practice medicine in the state serve as the Medical Director of the clinic and supervise all of the medical services being offered. The legality of the center providing medical services flows from the legality of this physician to practice medicine under his or her medical license.

. . . By "converting to a medical clinic" a center is not changing its mission. Rather, it is enhancing your mission by attracting, reaching and serving at risk women with the professional medical services they really need. (NIFLA 2006)

Only in America

In the fall of 2005, actor Tom Cruise caused a major tumult in the world of people who work with ultrasound when he took the idea of keepsake ultrasound another step. In the course of a television interview for Barbara Walters's annual show on "the year's most fascinating people," Cruise announced that he had bought an ultrasound device for his pregnant girl-friend Katie Holmes to use at their home (Kritz 2005). Medical profession-als were up in arms. My e-mail inbox was filled with furious messages.

In fact, Cruise's purchase of an ultrasound device for home use is less radically novel than might appear at first. Amazon.com offers a number of different ultrasound and Doppler devices for sale, and the Amazon Web site also offers a link to the Web site for a company called Dynamic Doppler that offers Doppler ultrasound devices for rent (Dynamic Doppler 2006). A quick internet search turned up a number of other companies, with names such as Belly Beats and Heart Beats at Home, that specialize in rentals of Doppler devices (Belly Beats 2006; Heart Beats at Home 2006). Indeed, rental Doppler comes in at number six on BabyCenter's "reader's choice" list of "seven pregnancy products you can't live without" (BabyCenter 2006b).

Ruminating on the AIUM's warning that keepsake ultrasound exposes fetuses unnecessarily to possibly harmful levels of energy, Jeanette Burlbaw asked what seems a quite reasonable question:

> If you're concerned about exposure, what about the rental of obstet-ric Dopplers? I had one patient who had rented a Doppler, and she told me that she would use that and listen to the heartbeat every day. She said, "Sometimes it takes me 20 minutes to find it." I told her, "You know that Doppler is ultrasound. You have exposed your baby to a *lot* of ultrasound."

Even if Cruise was not the first to bring ultrasound equipment into his home, his high-profile announcement moved legislators in California to introduce a bill that would limit sales of these devices to licensed medical professionals. As a news article on the matter reports:

> 3DBabyVu spokesman Mark Hayward said the company would not be affected by the proposed law because it is considered a satel-lite of a licensed radiologist's office. [Meanwhile], opponents say the bill is really an attempt by abortion advocates to prevent anti-abortion pregnancy clinics from using the equipment to discourage abortions. But Albert Lee, a spokesman for the Bay Area clinic First

Resort, a pregnancy crisis center that does not perform abortions and does not refer women to clinics that do, said his clinic would not be affected by the bill because it is licensed to administer ultrasounds. (Geiger 2006)

All official protestations to the contrary, medical uses of ultrasound simply cannot be separated definitively from the politics of abortion, for the same reason that they cannot be separated definitively from consumer culture. All are melded together in the hybrid practice of ultrasound, across a range of settings, and in the notion of ultrasound bonding that recurs with such perennial tenacity.

Keepsake ultrasound businesses do exist outside the United States as well. Also in the Netherlands, for example, "ultrasound-for-fun clinics" have become common, according to the media studies scholar José Van Dijck (2005:111). In urban Vietnam, too, "both public and private clinics often use ultrasound images to advertise their services, displaying large photos of fetuses at the clinic entrance. At a cost equivalent to $1.30–$2.00 for a 2-D scan, $5.00–$6.00 for a 3-D scan, and $13.00–$20.00 for a 4-D scan, sonographies are affordable for most urban women" (Gammeltoft 2007). As the medical anthropologist Tine Gammeltoft rightly notes, however, the contexts within which such enterprises operate matter a great deal. One must attend to the "'local moral worlds where pregnancies are lived and children born," or else

> the social processes that mediate the relationships between personal experience and discursive constructions of risk and pleasure tend to remain obscured, as the specific local contexts through which personal experience is generated are left relatively unexamined. Yet [it is within] such local moral settings and the "micro-level politics of social relationships" they entail . . . that the specific meanings and urgencies of a "good pregnancy outcome," a "normal baby," or an "at-risk pregnancy" are generated. (2007:135–136)

I would not expect the analysis offered here to apply in its entirety to keepsake ultrasound as practiced in other local contexts. The U.S. keepsake clinics discussed in this chapter are profoundly shaped by the specific configuration of technology, consumption, and abortion politics found here.

How ultrasound technology has taken shape in this country has every-thing to do with the fact that health care in the United States is largely privatized, commodified, and self-regulated by medical professional organizations. What we might call, with apologies to Luce Irigaray, "this health care system which is not one" routinely excludes millions of women, men, and children from access to basic medical care of all kinds, while at the same time sustaining a very large and highly profitable market for all kinds of pharmaceuticals and procedures whose medical necessity is highly questionable (Elliott 2003). These conditions have allowed for the emergence of both the keepsake businesses where ultrasound is put to the task of making fetuses entertain pregnant women, and the crisis preg-nancy centers that seek to make pregnant women entertain new under-standings of their fetuses.

7

Afterword

I have kept the copy of *Harper's* magazine containing the Volvo advertisement that initially drew me to this topic; it has yellowed a bit over the years. Looking at it now, it occurs to me that the ultrasound device that produced the sonogram featured in there must have been consigned long ago to the junkyard or the storage closet, or sold on the secondhand equipment market, replaced by a newer generation of equipment, itself soon replaced in turn. By the time you read these words, yet other new devices will have been developed, with new features and capabilities holding out new promises and leading to new applications and procedures. If the fetus whose image was featured in that long-ago Volvo ad was carried to term and born, and if the person it became is still alive today, he or she will have grown into a young adult by now. I have no way of knowing who that fetus might have become, and I would guess that whoever it is probably knows nothing about that brief moment of prenatal stardom. Perhaps he or she is someone who watches television advertisements, or works with medical technology, or eats Carl's Jr. hamburgers, or is pregnant, or drives a Volvo, or shops for baby clothes, or studies anthropology, or is named "George." Whoever he or she might be, that person's life is clearly entangled with the public life of the fetal sonogram—but so too is my life, and yours.

In the preceding chapters, I have sought to reframe obstetrical ultrasound, situating this newly routinized technology of reproduction within its full sociocultural context. In chapter 2 I showed how sonographers' gendered formation of professional selves gave rise to particular ways of

practicing the ultrasound examination that set the stage for fetal sonogram imagery to move, as it has, beyond the clinical setting into public culture and abortion politics. Chapter 3 explored the tension between
"reassurance" and "bonding" as "psychological benefits" that ultrasound is
supposed to offer, which I argued points toward a deeper tension between
the personification of the fetus and its commodification, both processes in
which ultrasound plays a significant role. The fourth chapter critically
examined the theory of ultrasound bonding, revealing both the paucity of
scientific backing for it, and the very real effects that it has nonetheless
exerted on policies, practices, and expectations regarding ultrasound.
Chapter 5 considered how the central importance of commodification and
consumption to reproduction, documented in this study, stands to com-
plicate and enrich existing feminist analyses, which have tended to
foreground questions of production. The sixth chapter examined nondiagnostic "entertainment" ultrasound and the controversies that surround it,
showing how upon closer examination medical applications prove to be
quite inextricably entangled both with consumption and with the politics
of reproduction.

Throughout, my aim has been to show how ultrasound has entered
into medical practice, everyday life, and public culture in the United States,
in the process becoming implicated in complex and contradictory ways in
the politics and practices of reproduction. In that respect, this is both a
study of the social and cultural dimensions of ultrasound technology, and
a study of American society and culture as revealed by a focus on ultrasound. It is also an extended argument for the value and the promise of
ethnographic research as a project of situating systems of thought in relation to systems of social action, and attending to the relationship between
ideas and practices. Tracing ultrasound through social life in this manner
reveals some surprising connections—between, for example, the professional struggles of sonographers; the embrace of pregnancy-related consumption; and the persuasive strategies of antiabortion activists.

One important goal of this book is to provide the basis for an expanded
sense of how and why and for whom something as seemingly ordinary and
innocuous as obstetrical ultrasound might matter. Relatively privileged
U.S. women who embrace ultrasound as an enjoyable moment of consuming pregnancy and the fetus inhabit the same world as many others

whose lives are affected very differently by current configurations of technology and social life that this study documents. As we have seen, these include sonographers who bring to their work with ultrasound their own particular set of perspectives, concerns, and commitments. But they also include many others who suffer or find their lives constrained in particular ways. They include, for example, people with disabilities who find their lives devalued and threatened by the unreflected assumptions about "lives not worth living" (Proctor 1995) that are implicit in the rush to prenatal diagnosis and selective abortion (Asch 2005; Rapp 1999). They include women who respond to patriarchal pressures to bear sons by using ultrasound to selectively abort female fetuses (Jha et al. 2006; Marquand 2004; Silliman 2003; Wertz and Fletcher 1989). They include women in the developing countries of the global South, whose embrace of ultrasound during pregnancy takes shape amid circumstances very different from those that prevail in the United States (Gammeltoft 2007). They include women in the United States who have irregular or inadequate access to health care (Sered and Fernandopulle 2005). They include women whose encounter with fetal ultrasound is part of an effort to coerce them to behave in particular ways—by physicians who want to make them comply with instructions, or by antiabortion advocates who want to make them decide against an abortion. They include women here and elsewhere in the world who suffer, and in some cases even die, as a result of restrictions on reproductive health care imposed by people who find antiabortion deployments of the public fetus compelling ("Access Denied" 2007). They include women and men here and elsewhere in the world who work to assemble the components of today's ultrasound devices. And, finally, they include women, men, children, and health care professionals whose lives and work are affected by the patterns of resource allocation that devote so much money, time, and human talent to prenatal diagnostic technology, and so little to many other pressing needs.

In all of these ways, the public life of the fetal sonogram is deeply involved with the processes through which the edges of the public sphere, the market, and the state come to extend into people's bodies—into women's bodies more and in different ways than into the bodies of men, and into the bodies of poor and racialized women more and in different ways than into the bodies of other women.

Because ultrasound technology is part of social life, to really change this configuration will require meaningful social change from the ground up. If only there actually *were* a little bald man hiding behind the curtain and secretly controlling everything, in Wizard of Oz fashion, we could simply expose him, scold him, and make him carry us off in his balloon to wherever we wish to go. Instead, what we have found behind the curtain, so to speak, is the whole vast complex edifice of U.S. consumer-capitalism within which health care, including ultrasound and other medical technologies, is embedded. As this study has shown, the public life of the fetal sonogram has not arisen in a necessary and natural manner out of the capabilities of diagnostic ultrasound devices, just as those devices themselves did not simply emerge in a manner fated and determined. Rather, ultrasound technology itself, and the public life of the fetal sonogram, are the outcome of long histories of political, economic, professional, and social struggle, some aspects of which have been explored in these pages. Those histories are ongoing, of course, and being nothing more (and nothing less!) than patterns of collective social action, the direction they take in the future can change.

The hopeful aspect of all this, of course, and the one that ethnographic research is uniquely well suited to document, is simply that ordinary people have real insights into the world they—we—inhabit. Ordinary women in all their diversity, as producers and as consumers of fetal sonograms, have thoughtful things to say about the social, political and technological transformations through which they are living, and about how their own experiences and actions are both shaped by them and shape them in turn. In this book, I have sought to collect, present, reflect upon, and analyze their insights, and synthesize them with my own. The process of researching the public life of the fetal sonogram, seizing upon a fleeting moment of dissonance in an encounter with public culture and taking that as an entry point to explore many aspects of social life, has for me been a great privilege and a gift, a work whose delight lies in its seriousness. As I suggested in chapter I, reclaiming both technology and women's bodies as fully social requires that we craft for them new contexts, both intellectually and politically. This study has sought to create a new context of understanding by documenting how ultrasound technology and the fetal bodies it images are animated by the particular constellation of ideas, practices, and institutions within which both are embedded. The political work of creating new contexts, by mobilizing people to transform the social world that has created this configuration of bodies and technologies, lies before us still. I hope that the perspectives offered here may help make "common sense" into "good sense," and help others ask new kinds of questions and arrive—not only individually, but collectively—at new ways of engaging with technology, consumption, and reproduction, as part of broader efforts to create a more just social world. In that case, the public life of the fetal sonogram will have accomplished at least one very good deed.

NOTES

CHAPTER 1   INTRODUCTION

1. A small portion of this chapter overlaps with my review article on "Surfacing the Body Interior" (Taylor 2005). Reprinted by permission of the *Annual Review of Anthropology*.

CHAPTER 2   SONOGRAPHERS AND THE MAKING OF
THE PUBLIC FETUS

1. A version of this chapter was previously published as a chapter in the volume *Consuming Motherhood* (Taylor 2004b). Reprinted by permission of Rutgers University Press.

2. See Layne (1999, 2000) for a complementary discussion of how the concept of the fetish may apply to women's attachment to material objects associated with a desired but lost fetus, in cases of pregnancy loss.

3. As of late October 2000, the American Registry of Diagnostic Medical Sonographers (ARDMS) counted 39,339 registrants all told; 30,258 registrants with the status of passed for ob/gyn; 25,699 female registrants with the status of passed for ob/gyn; and 4,559 male registrants with the status of passed for ob/gyn (Gwen Henderson, Director of Registrant Services of ARDMS, personal communication).

4. Yoxen ends his historical account of ultrasound on this note, with a call for research along these lines; his own account, however, ends earlier.

5. Jean Lea Spitz, personal communication.

6. "Sonographer" is the preferred and appropriate term for people working in this capacity today. Since this term was not invented until 1980, however, I use the term "ultrasound technician" to describe people working with ultrasound to produce diagnostic information before that time.

7. See Blizzard (2007) for a parallel account of how a novel and controversial procedure gets "built," a process that involves creating a social context in which a new procedure makes sense and convincing others that they should support specific developments.

8. Thanks to Jean Lea Spitz for alerting me to this development.

9. See note 3 above.

10. This is a private organization named for Arthur S. DeMoss who, as founder of the National Liberty Life Insurance Co., helped pioneer the art of selling low-cost insurance by direct mail. When he died in 1979, National Liberty, which employed Art Linkletter as its spokesman, had 1.5 million policyholders, $500 million in assets, and was listed on the New York Stock Exchange. Since DeMoss's death, his wife has run the foundation, and does not grant interviews. Nor do his children, who are all active in foundation work and other evangelical Christian causes. The DeMoss Foundation is a major financial backer of a number of right-wing organizations and causes, but its primary activity is the advertisement and distribution, free of charge, of the book *Power for Living* (van Biema 1999).

11. For a detailed critical reading of Richard's videotape "Ultrasound: Window to the Womb," with reference to exactly the sort of questions considered here, see Boucher (2004b).

12. Allen Worrall, who operates an ob/gyn ultrasound clinic in Alaska, comments that "since 1991 I have recorded all my ultrasounds (ob and gyn) on SVHS video as my official documentation of the exam. I just started my 355th ST-120 tape. I can do this because I do my own scans and do not have to watch the video after the exam unless I want to. In the conventional sonographer/radiologist setup I doubt if many practices use video for the documentation, because it would take the radiologist too long to review the case." (Joseph A Worrall, MD RDMS, personal communication).

13. "Digital image processing" means that the ultrasound image is processed electronically at every stage of production. By eliminating the need to work with films, digital processing streamlines performance (it is no longer necessary to interrupt examinations in order to develop films) provides much higher image quality, and facilitates computerized storage and communication of images. This also opens new possibilities for teleradiology—transmission of digital images via telephone or Internet connections means that an ultrasound examination being performed at one site may be simultaneously observed or reviewed by a physician at a site elsewhere in the hospital (or indeed elsewhere in the world).

14. Joan P. Baker, as noted earlier, has long been at the forefront of organizing sonographers in the United States. Since retiring from teaching, she has gone on to found a company called Sound Ergonomics that consults with ultrasound device manufacturers, employers, and others on how to reduce sonographers' work-related injuries. See the company's Web site at http://www.soundergonomics.com/.

CHAPTER 3   OBSTETRICAL ULTRASOUND BETWEEN MEDICAL
PRACTICE AND PUBLIC CULTURE

1. An earlier version of this chapter (Taylor 1998) previously appeared in the volume *Reproducing Reproduction: Kinship, Power, and Technological Innovation*, ed. Sarah

Franklin and Helena Ragone. Reprinted by permission of the University of Pennsylvania Press.

2. While these figures would seem to suggest a decline from 78.8 percent in 1987 to 67 percent in 2003, the two studies employ very different methods, such that we must exercise some caution in how we read the results together. Moore et al. (1990) focused their study specifically on the use of diagnostic ultrasound, X-ray, and electronic fetal monitoring during pregnancy, and relied upon the National Maternal and Infant Health Survey to collect information from prenatal care providers, hospitals, and mothers. Martin et al. (2005) report on ultrasound and other obstetric procedures as part of a global study of trends regarding birth, based on birth certificates of the 4.09 million births recorded in the United States in 2003. This enormous sample includes many underserved mothers whom the 1990 study might have missed. Furthermore, as the 2003 study's first author Joyce Martin explains (personal communication), it is widely recognized that ultrasound usage is underreported on birth certificate data, and actual usage is likely much higher.

3. Such modifications in a woman's behavior might be expected to improve her own physical health as well, of course, but I have not seen this point made in the context of discussions of ultrasound's "psychological benefits" in the medical literature.

4. This description appears in Fleishman (1995). It is perhaps worth noting that "maternal anxiety" has been considered adequate medical grounds for ordering an ultrasound scan in Denmark since at least as early as 1988 (Sjögren 1988, cited in Wertz and Fletcher 1989).

5. Rothman (1993) coined the term "tentative pregnancy" to describe how prenatal diagnostic testing has altered the experience of pregnancy, for women who now find themselves awaiting the results of such testing before fully embracing and committing to the pregnancy. For an unparalleled exploration of women's experiences of and perspectives on amniocentesis, see Rapp (1999, 1995, 1993).

6. Linda Layne's monumental ethnographic study of pregnancy loss in the United States (1992, 2003, 2004) includes considerable discussion of the ways that ultrasound figures into that experience, both as the means by which fetal death is discovered in many cases of pregnancy loss, and as the source of fetal imagery valued and used in many ways by parents grieving such a loss.

7. The increasing pace of sonographers' scanning workload in most clinics has in recent years become the focus of considerable attention and discussion, as it has resulted in increased rates of injury among sonographers. See chapter 2, note 14.

8. Sandelowski (1994) discusses the way in which this arrangement turns the sonographer herself into a sort of spectacle, as patients and those accompanying them attempt to read from the sonographer's facial expressions the information that she is not authorized to deliver to them. As well as challenging the hierarchy that separates the sonographer as medical professional from the

patient, this convention also highlights the hierarchy that separates the sonographer from the "sonologist" or supervising physician, who alone has the authority to make diagnoses. In fact, it often happens that the physician whose signature is required on each examination, and who receives a fee for reviewing the images, is less competent in ultrasound than the sonographer working under him or her.

9. However, the notion of what may count as "natural" is very flexible (see, for example, MacDonald 2007; Wertz and Wertz 1989), and women embracing natural and feminist approaches to childbirth do not necessarily reject or escape dynamics of consumption and commodification (see Klassen 2004; Davis-Floyd 2004).

10. On pregnancy experienced as a quest for scientific knowledge, see especially Davis-Floyd (2003) and Davis-Floyd and Sargent (1997).

CHAPTER 4   LOVE MACHINE: THE THEORY OF ULTRASOUND BONDING

1. In the interest of readability, I will henceforth refrain from placing quotation marks around the word "bonding" each time it appears, but they remain there in spirit: the whole purpose of this chapter is to defamiliarize the term and interrogate the range of its meanings and the contexts in which it is deployed. Feel free to wiggle your fingers in the air, quotation-mark style, every time you come across the word, if doing so helps you resist its powerful naturalizing magic.

CHAPTER 5   PRENATAL DIAGNOSIS, PREGNANCY, AND CONSUMPTION

1. An earlier version of this chapter appeared as Taylor (2000). Reprinted by permission of the publisher, *Feminist Studies,* Inc. For a discussion of how consumption relates to motherhood more generally, both at the level of ideas and at the level of social practice, please see Taylor (2004a).

2. Rayna Rapp (1999) presents a very powerful account of what she refers to as a "chosen loss." See also Layne (2003) for discussion of this as one among many forms of pregnancy loss.

3. Interestingly, ultrasound equipment itself comes in at #6 on the "reader's choice" list of "seven pregnancy products you can't live without." As will be discussed in chapter 6, Doppler equipment is readily available for rental by women who wish to use it at home to hear fetal heartbeats (BabyCenter 2006b).

4. We might note that this convention itself is relatively recent, dating back only to the 1940s (Paoletti and Kregloh 1989, cited in Cook 1995).

5. For a discussion of ultrasound as "something surefire," see Sandelowski (1993:126)

6. I am grateful to Rayna Rapp for this point.

7. For discussion of how such ironies are negotiated by midwives and others committed to providing feminist and alternative care to pregnant and birthing women, see Klassen (2004) and Davis-Floyd (2004).

8. See Layne (2003, 2004) and Landsman (2004) for powerful critiques of this manner of framing the issues from the point of view of women whose children die or are disabled.

9. Comaroff (1997) is exemplary and indexes much of this literature.

BIBLIOGRAPHY

Abella, H. A. 2005. "AIUM Toughens Policy on Keepsake Ultrasound: Scrutiny of 3D Fetus Images Has Moved from Malls to Accredited Practitioners as Well as Vendors." *Diagnostic Imaging* 18:2711.

"Access Denied: U.S. Restrictions on International Family Planning." http://www. globalgagrule.org. Accessed 11/19/07.

Adrian, S. 2006. *Nye Skabelsesberetninger om Æg, Sæd, og Embryoner: Et Etnografisk Studie af Skabelser på Sædbanker og fertilitetsklinikker.* Linköping Studies in Arts and Science No. 370. Linköping, Sweden: Linköpings Universitet.

Ambassador Speakers Bureau & Literary Agency. 2006. "Shari Richard's Biography." http://www.ambassadoragency.com/client_profile.cfm/cid/108. Accessed 8/23/06.

American College of Obstetricians and Gynecologists (ACOG). 2004. "Ultrasonography in Pregnancy." *ACOG Practice Bulletin* 58:1449–1458.

American Institute of Ultrasound in Medicine (AIUM). 2005. "Keepsake Ultrasound Imaging." http://www.aium.org/publications/statements/_statementSelected. asp?statement=31. Accessed 10/6/06.

———. 2003. "AIUM Practice Guideline for the Performance of an Antepartum Obstetric Ultrasound Examination." Laurel, Md.: American Institute of Ultrasound in Medicine. *http://www.aium.org/publications/clinical/obstetrical.pdf. Accessed 10/4/06.*

Anagnost, A. 2004. "Maternal Labor in a Transnational Circuit." In *Consuming Motherhood*, ed. J. S. Taylor, L. L. Layne, and D. F. Wozniak, 139–167. New Brunswick, N.J.: Rutgers University Press.

Appadurai, A. 1996. *Modernity at Large: Cultural Dimensions of Globalization.* Minneapolis: University of Minnesota Press.

———. 1986. "Introduction: Commodities and the Politics of Value." In *The Social Life of Things: Commodities in Cultural Perspective,* ed. A. Appadurai, 3–63. Cambridge: Cambridge University Press.

Arney, W. R. 1982. *Power and the Profession of Obstetrics.* Chicago: University of Chicago Press.

Asch, A., and D. Wasserman. 2005. "Where Is the Sin in Synecdoche? Prenatal Testing and the Parent-Child Relationship." In *Quality of Life and Human*

Difference: Genetic Testing, Health Care, and Disability, ed. D. Wasserman, J. Bickenbach, and R. Wachbroit, 172–216. Cambridge: Cambridge University Press.

BabyCenter. 2006a. http://store.babycenter.com/checklists/?stage=. Accessed 10/6/06.

———. 2006b. http://www.babycenter.com/refcap/pregnancy/pregnancygear/1194829.html. Accessed 10/8/06.

Baggini, J. 2005. "Time Is of the Essence." *Sunday Herald*. http://www.sundayherald.com/50544. Accessed 10/6/06.

Baker, J. P. 1995. *Society of Diagnostic Medical Sonographers Focus on the Future: The History of SDMS's First 25 years*. Philadelphia: Lippincott-Raven Publishers.

Baker, M. L., and G. V. Dalrymple. 1978. "Biological Effects of Diagnostic Ultrasound: A Review." *Radiology* 126:479–483.

Banerjee, N. 2005. "Church Groups Turn to Sonogram to Turn Women from Abortions." *New York Times*, February 2, A1.

Barad, K. 2003. "Posthumanist Performativity: Toward an Understanding of How Matter Comes to Matter." *Signs: Journal of Women in Culture and Society* 28(3):801–831.

———. 1998. "Getting Real: Technoscientific Practices and the Materialization of Reality." *differences: A Journal of Feminist Cultural Studies* 10(2):87–126.

Bashour, H., R. Hafez, and A. Abdulsalaam. 2005. "Syrian Women's Perceptions and Experiences of Ultrasound Screening in Pregnancy: Implications for Antenatal Policy." *Reproductive Health Matters* 13(25):147–154.

Baum, L. F. 2003 [1900]. *The Wonderful Wizard of Oz*. Ann Arbor, Mich.: For Your Knowledge.

Belly Beats. 2006. http://www.bellybeats.com/. Accessed 10/9/06.

Benacerraf, B. 2002. "Three-Dimensional Fetal Sonography: Use and Misuse." *Journal of Ultrasound in Medicine* 21:1063–1067.

Berenson, A. 2007. "Boom Times for Dentists, but Not for Teeth." *New York Times*, October 11. http://www.nytimes.com/2007/10/11/business/11decay.html.

Blizzard, D. 2007. *Looking Within: A Sociocultural Examination of Fetoscopy*. Cambridge, Mass.: MIT Press.

Blume, S. 1992. *Insight and Industry: On the Dynamics of Technological Change in Medicine*. Cambridge, Mass.: The MIT Press.

Boucher, J. 2004a. "The Politics of Abortion and the Commodification of the Fetus." *Studies in Political Economy* 73:69–88.

———. 2004b. "Ultrasound: A Window to the Womb? Obstetric Ultrasound and the Abortion Rights Debate." *Journal of Medical Humanities* 25(1):7–19.

Bowe, C. 2007. "Wal-Mart Health Clinics Divide U.S. Medics." *Financial Times*, May 23. http://www.ft.com/cms/s/0/5b301a64-093c-11dc-a349-000b5df10621.html?nclick_check=1. Accessed 11/18/07.

Boyer, D. 2006. "Gender and the Solvency of Professionalism: Eastern German Journalism before and after 1989." *East European Politics & Societies* 20:152–179.

Braidotti, R. 1994. *Nomadic Subjects: Embodiment and Sexual Difference in Contemporary Feminist Theory.* New York: Columbia University Press.

Briggs, C., and C. Mantini-Briggs. 2003. *Stories in the Time of Cholera: Racial Profiling during a Medical Nightmare.* Berkeley: University of California Press.

Burlbaw, J. 2004. "Obstetric Sonography: That's Entertainment?" *Journal of Diagnostic Medical Sonography* 20:444–448.

Butler, J. 1993. *Bodies That Matter: On the Discursive Limits of "Sex."* New York: Routledge.

Campbell, S. 2004. *Watch Me . . . Grow! A Unique, 3-Dimensional, Week-by-Week Look at Baby's Behavior and Development in the Womb.* New York: St. Martin's Press.

———. 2002. "4D or Not 4D: That Is the Question." *Ultrasound in Obstetrics and Gynecology* 19:1–4.

Campbell, S., A. E. Reading, D. N. Cox, C. M. Sledmere, R. Mooney, P. Chudleigh, J. Beedle, and H. Ruddick. 1982. "Ultrasound Scanning in Pregnancy: The Short-Term Psychological Effects of Early Real-Time Scans." *Journal of Psychosomatic Obstetrics and Gynecology* 1(2):57–60.

Casper, M. J. 1998. *The Making of the Unborn Patient: A Social Anatomy of Fetal Surgery.* New Brunswick, N.J.: Rutgers University Press.

Casper, M. J., and L. M. Morgan. 2004. "Constructing Fetal Citizens." *Anthropology Newsletter* 45(9):17–18.

Caviness, V. S., and P. E. Grant. 2006. "Our Unborn Children at Risk?" *Proceedings of the National Academy of Sciences of the United States of America* 103(34):12661–12662.

Chervenak, F. A., and L. B. McCullough. 2006. "Reply." *American Journal of Obstetrics and Gynecology* 194(5):1501–1502.

———. 2005. "An Ethical Critique of Boutique Fetal Imaging: A Case for the Medicalization of Fetal Imaging." *American Journal of Obstetrics and Gynecology* 192(1):31–33.

Chin, E. 2001. *Purchasing Power: Black Kids and American Consumer Culture.* Minneapolis: University of Minnesota Press.

Chung, W. 2007. "The Relation of Son Preference and Religion to Induced Abortion: The Case of South Korea." *Journal of Biosocial Science* 39:707–719.

Clarke, A. J. 2004. "Maternity and Materiality: Becoming a Mother in Consumer Culture." In *Consuming Motherhood,* ed. J. S. Taylor, L. L. Layne and D. F. Wozniak, 55–71. New Brunswick, N.J.: Rutgers University Press.

Comaroff, J. 1997. "Consuming Passions: Child Abuse, Fetishism, and 'The New World Order.'" *Culture* 17(1–2):7–19.

Comaroff, J., and J. L. Comaroff. 1993. "Introduction." In *Modernity and Its Malcontents: Ritual and Power in Postcolonial Africa*, ed. J. Comaroff and J. L. Comaroff, xi–xxxvii. Chicago: University of Chicago Press.

———. 1990. "Goodly Beasts and Beastly Goods: Cattle and Commodities in a South African Context." *American Ethnologist* 17:196–216.

Comprehensive Genetics. 2006. http://www.comgenetics.com/. Accessed 8/8/06.

Cook, D. T. 2004. *The Commodification of Childhood: The Children's Clothing Industry and the Rise of the Child Consumer*. Durham, N.C.: Duke University Press.

———. 1995. "The Mother as Consumer: Insights from the Children's Wear Industry, 1917–1929," *Sociological Quarterly* 36(3):505–522.

Coste, P. 1989. "An Historical Examination of the Strategic Issues Which Influenced Technologically Entrepreneurial Firms Serving the Medical Diagnostic Ultrasound Market." Ph.D. dissertation, Claremont College Graduate School, Claremont, Calif.

Craig, M. 1993. "Pro-Life/Pro-Choice: A New Dilemma for Sonographers." *Journal of Diagnostic Medical Sonography* 9(3):152–158.

Crary, D. 2002. "Activists Tout Ultrasound to Discourage Abortions." *Seattle Times*, February 2, A6.

Create Health Centre for Reproduction and Advanced Technology. 2006. http://www.createhealth.org/dimensional.html. Accessed 10/8/06.

Daniels, C. R. 1999. "Fathers, Mothers, and Fetal Harm: Rethinking Gender Difference and Reproductive Responsibility." In *Fetal Subjects, Feminist Positions*, ed. L. M. Morgan and M. W. Michaels, 83–98. Philadelphia: University of Pennsylvania Press.

———. 1993. *At Women's Expense: State Power and the Politics of Fetal Rights*. Cambridge, Mass.: Harvard University Press.

Davis-Floyd, R. E. 2004. "Consuming Childbirth: The Qualified Commodification of Midwifery Care." In *Consuming Motherhood*, ed. J. S. Taylor, L. L. Layne and D. F. Wozniak, 211–248. New Brunswick, N.J.: Rutgers University Press.

———. 2003. *Birth as an American Rite of Passage*. Berkeley: University of California Press.

Davis-Floyd, R. E., and J. Dumit, eds. 1998. *Cyborg Babies: From Techno-Sex to Techno-Tots*. New York: Routledge.

Davis-Floyd, R. E., and C. F. Sargent. 1997. *Childbirth and Authoritative Knowledge: Cross-Cultural Perspectives*. Berkeley: University of California Press.

de Crespigy, L., and R. Dredge. 1991. *Which Tests for My Unborn Baby? A Guide to Prenatal Diagnosis*. Melbourne: Oxford University Press Australia.

DeVault, M. 1999. "Whose Science of Food and Health? Narratives of Profession and Activism from Public-Health Nutrition." In *Revisioning Women, Health and*

Healing: Feminist, Cultural, and Technoscience Perspectives, ed. A. E. Clarke and V. L. Olesen, 166–183. New York: Routledge.

Downey, D. B., A. Fenster, and J. C. Williams. 2000. "Clinical Utility of Three-Dimensional US." *Radiographics* 20:559–571.

Doyle, E. T. 1992. "Window on the Womb." *RT Image* 5(30):4–6.

Dreger, A. D., ed. 1999. *Intersex in the Age of Ethics.* Hagerstown, Md.: University Publishing Group.

Duden, B. 1993. *Disembodying Women: Perspectives on Pregnancy and the Unborn.* Trans. Lee Hoinacki. Cambridge, Mass.: Harvard University Press.

Dumit, J. 2004. *Picturing Personhood: Brain Scans and Biomedical Identity.* Princeton, N.J.: Princeton University Press.

Durbin, S. A. 1997. "Words Spoken in a Dimly Lit Room." *Journal of Diagnostic Medical Sonography* 13:175–178.

Dynamic Doppler. 2006. http://www.dynamicdoppler.com/ProductCart/pc/mainIndex .asp. Accessed 10/9/06.

Eisenberg, A., H. E. Murkoff, and S. E. Hathaway. 1986. *What to Eat When You're Expecting.* New York: Workman Publishing.

Elite Diagnostics. 2006. http://www.elitediagnostics.com/index2.html. Accessed 10/6/06.

Elliott, C. 2003. *Better Than Well: American Medicine Meets the American Dream.* New York: W. W. Norton.

Eurenius, K., O. Axelsson, I. Gällstedt-Fransson, and P.-O. Sjöden. 1997. "Perception of Information, Expectations and Experiences among Women and Their Partners Attending a Second-Trimester Routine Ultrasound Scan." *Ultrasound in Obstetrics and Gynecology* 9:86–90.

Evans, M. I., M. I. Kaufman, A. J. Urban, D. W. Britt, and J. C. Fletcher. 2004. "Fetal Reduction from Twins to a Singleton: A Reasonable Consideration?" *Obstetrics and Gynecology* 104(6):1423–1424.

Eyer, D. K. 1992. *Mother-Infant Bonding: A Scientific Fiction.* New Haven, Conn.: Yale University Press.

Farmer, P. 2003. *Pathologies of Power: Health, Human Rights, and the New War on the Poor.* Berkeley: University of California Press.

———. 1999. *Infections and Inequalities: The Modern Plagues.* Berkeley: University of California Press.

Fausto-Sterling, A. 2000. *Sexing the Body: Gender Politics and the Construction of Sexuality.* New York: Basic Books.

Fetal Fotos. 2004. http://www.fetalfotosusa.com/media.html. Accessed 7/30/04.

Filly, R. A. 2000. "Obstetric Sonography: The Best Way to Terrify a Pregnant Woman." *Journal of Ultrasound in Medicine* 19:1–5.

Filly, R. A., and J. P. Crane. 2002. "Routine Obstetric Sonography." *Journal of Ultrasound in Medicine* 21:713–718.

Fleishman, S. 1995. "Too Young to Be Movie Stars? FDA Warns Firms Making 'Keepsake' Sonogram Videos." *Washington Post*, February 13, D5.

Fletcher, J. C., and M. I. Evans. 1983. "Maternal Bonding in Early Fetal Ultrasound Examinations." *New England Journal of Medicine* 308(7):392–393.

Forgacs, D., ed. 2000. *The Antonio Gramsci Reader: Selected Writings 1916–1935.* New York: New York University Press.

Forsythe, D. E. 1996. "New Bottles, Old Wine: Hidden Cultural Assumptions in a Computerized Explanation System for Migraine Sufferers." *Medical Anthropology Quarterly* 10(4):551–574.

Fraiberg, S. 1977. *Every Child's Birthright: In Defense of Mothering.* New York: Basic Books.

Franklin, S., and M. Lock, eds. 2003. *Remaking Life and Death: Toward an Anthropology of the Biosciences.* Albuquerque, N.M.: SAR Press.

Freidson, E. 1970. *Profession of Medicine: A Study in the Sociology of Applied Knowledge.* New York: Dodd, Mead.

Gabbe, S. G. 1994. "Routine versus Indicated Scans." In *Diagnostic Ultrasound Applied to Obstetrics and Gynecology*, ed. R. E. Sabbagha, 67–8. Philadelphia: J. B. Lippincott.

Gammeltoft, T. 2007. "Sonography and Sociality: Obstetrical Ultrasound Imaging in Urban Vietnam." *Medical Anthropology Quarterly* 21(2):133–153.

Geiger, K. 2006. "Measure Would Keep Ultrasound Machines from Parents' Homes." *San Francisco Chronicle*, September 8, B6.

Georges, E. 1996. "Fetal Ultrasound Imaging and the Production of Authoritative Knowledge in Greece." *Medical Anthropology Quarterly* 10(2):157–175.

Gerber, E. G. 2002. "Deconstructing Pregnancy: RU486, Seeing 'Eggs,' and the Ambiguity of Very Early Conceptions." *Medical Anthropology Quarterly* 16(1):92–108.

Getz, L., and A. L. Kirkengen. 2003. "Ultrasound Screening in Pregnancy: Advancing Technology, Soft Markers for Fetal Chromosomal Aberrations, and Unacknowledged Ethical Dilemmas." *Social Science and Medicine* 56:2045–2057.

Gibbs, N. 2007. "1 Woman at a Time (The Grassroots Abortion War)." *Time*, February 26, 22–31.

Ginsburg, F. 1989. *Contested Lives: The Abortion Debate in an American Community.* Berkeley: University of California Press.

Ginsburg, F., and R. Rapp. 1999. "Fetal Reflections: Confessions of Two Feminist Anthropologists as Mutual Informants." In *Fetal Subjects, Feminist Positions,* ed. L. M. Morgan and M. W. Michaels, 279–295. Philadelphia: University of Pennsylvania Press.

———, eds. 1995. *Conceiving the New World Order: The Global Politics of Reproduction.* Berkeley: University of California Press.

Goldberg, B., and B. A. Kimmelman. 1988. *Medical Diagnostic Ultrasound: A Retrospective on Its 40th Anniversary.* Rochester, N.Y.: Eastman Kodak.

Goodman, A., D. Heath, and M. S. Lindee, eds. 2003. *Genetic Nature/Culture: Anthropology and Science beyond the Two-Culture Divide.* Berkeley: University of California Press.

Greene, G. J. 2001. *The Woman Who Knew Too Much: Alice Stewart and the Secrets of Radiation.* Ann Arbor, Mich.: University of Michigan Press.

Haraway, D. 1998. *Modest_Witness@Second_Millenium.FemaleMan©_Meets_OncoMouse™.* New York: Routledge.

Harris, L. 2006. "Your Baby In Utero: The Movie." *Salon.com,* June 28.

Heart Beats at Home. 2006. http://www.heartbeatsathome.com. Accessed 10/9/06.

Heartlink. 2006. http://www.heartlink.org/oup/a000000093.cfm. Accessed 10/8/06.

Heath, D. 1998. "Locating Genetic Knowledge: Picturing Marfan Syndrome and Its Traveling Constituencies." *Science, Technology & Human Values* 23(1):71–97.

Hesketh, T., and Xing Z. W. 2006. "Abnormal Sex Ratios in Human Populations: Causes and Consequences." *Proceedings of the National Academy of Sciences of the United States of America* 103(36):13271–13275.

Huet, M.-H. 1993. *Monstrous Imagination.* Cambridge, Mass.: Harvard University Press.

Hughes, J. V. 2006. " 'Keepsake' Ultrasound Boom: As Fetal-Photo Companies Grow in Popularity, Medical Professionals Question Their Legitimacy." *The Record* [Bergen County, N.J.], March 14, F1.

Intersex Society of North America. 2006. http://isna.org. Accessed 8/7/06.

Ivry, T. 2006. "At the Back Stage of Prenatal Care: Japanese Ob-Gyns Negotiating Prenatal Diagnosis." *Medical Anthropology Quarterly* 20(4):441–468.

Jain, S. S. 1998. "Mysterious Delicacies and Ambiguous Agents: Lennart Nilsson in *National Geographic.*" *Configurations* 6(3):373–394.

Jha, P., R. Kumar, P. Vasa, N. Dhingra, D. Thiruchelvam, and R. Moineddin. 2006. "Low Male-to-Female Sex Ratio of Children Born in India: National Survey of 1.1 Million Households." *The Lancet* 367:211–218.

Johnson, M. C. 2005. "Unplanned Pregnancy: Center Offers Ultrasounds to Women Considering Abortion." *Press Enterprise* [Riverside, Calif.], April 14, B1.

Jolly, H. 1978. "The Importance of 'Bonding' for Newborn Baby, Mother and Father." *Nursing Mirror* 147(9):19–21.

Jonsson, P. 2007. "Ultrasounds: Abortion Deterrent?" *Christian Science Monitor,* May 15, 3.

Jordan, Brigitte. 1978. *Birth in Four Cultures: A Cross-Cultural Investigation of Childbirth in Yucatan, Holland, Sweden, and the United States.* Prospect Heights, Ill.: Waveland Press.

Kahn, J. 2004. "How a Drug Becomes 'Ethnic': Law, Commerce, and the Production of Racial Categories in Medicine." *Yale Journal of Health Policy, Law, and Ethics* 4(1):1–46.

———. 2003. "Getting the Numbers Right: Statistical Mischief and Racial Profiling in Heart Failure Research." *Perspectives in Biology and Medicine* 46(4):473–483.

Kahn, S. M. 2000. *Reproducing Jews: A Cultural Account of Assisted Reproduction in Israel.* Durham, N.C.: Duke University Press.

Kevles, B. H. 1997. *Naked to the Bone: Medical Imaging in the Twentieth Century.* New Brunswick, N.J.: Rutgers University Press.

Klassen, P. E. 2004. "Mothers between God and Mammon: Feminist Interpretations of Childbirth." In *Consuming Motherhood,* ed. J. S. Taylor, L. L. Layne, and D. F. Wozniak, 249–268. New Brunswick, N.J.: Rutgers University Press.

———. 2001. *Blessed Events: Religion and Home Birth in America.* Princeton, N.J.: Princeton University Press.

Knoppers, B. M., S. Bordet, and R. M. Isasi. 2006. "Preimplantation Genetic Diagnosis: An Overview of Socio-Ethical and Legal Considerations." *Annual Review of Genomics and Human Genetics* 7:201–221.

Kopytoff, I. 1986.."The Cultural Biography of Things: Commoditization as a Process." In *The Social Life of Things: Commodities in Cultural Perspective,* ed. A. Appadurai, 64–91. Cambridge: Cambridge University Press.

Krieger, N., ed. 2005. *Embodying Inequality: Epidemiologic Perspectives.* Amityville, N.Y.: Baywood Publishing.

Kritz, F. 2005. "Doctors Not Fans of Tom Cruise's Baby Gift: Sonogram Machines Aren't Meant for Living Rooms, Experts Say." MSNBC.com, December 6. http://www.msnbc.msn.com/id/10309963. Accessed 10/8/06.

Lambert, V. 2006. "Is This a Souvenir Too Far?" Telegraph.co.uk. http://www.telegraph.co.uk/arts/main.jhtml?xml=/arts/2006/08/10/bafoetus10.xml. Accessed 10/8/06.

Lancaster, R. 2003. *The Trouble with Nature: Sex and Science in Popular Culture.* Berkeley: University of California Press.

Landecker, H. 2007. *Culturing Life: How Cells Became Technologies.* Cambridge, Mass.: Harvard University Press.

———. 2003. "On Beginning and Ending with Apoptosis: Cell Death and Biomedicine." In *Remaking Life and Death: Toward an Anthropology of the Biosciences,* ed. S. Franklin and M. Lock, 23–59. Albuquerque: School of American Research Press.

Landsman, G. 2004. "'Too Bad You Got a Lemon': Peter Singer, Mothers of Children with Disabilities, and the Critique of Consumer Culture." In *Consuming*

Motherhood, ed. J. S. Taylor, L. L. Layne, and D. F. Wozniak, 100–121. New Brunswick, N.J.: Rutgers University Press.

Layne, L. 2004. "Making Memories: Trauma, Choice, and Consumer Culture in the Case of Pregnancy Loss." In *Consuming Motherhood,* ed. J. S. Taylor, L. L. Layne, and D. F. Wozniak, 122–138. New Brunswick, N.J.: Rutgers University Press.

———. 2003. *Motherhood Lost: A Feminist Account of Pregnancy Loss in America.* New York: Routledge.

———. 2000. "Baby Things as Fetishes? Memorial Goods, Simulacra, and the 'Realness' Problem of Pregnancy Loss." In *Ideologies and Technologies of Motherhood: Race, Class, Sexuality, Nationalism,* ed. H. Ragoné and F. W. Twine, 111–138. New York: Routledge.

———. 1999. "'I Remember the Day I Shopped for Your Layette': Consumer Goods, Fetuses, and Feminism in the Context of Pregnancy Loss." In *Fetal Subjects, Feminist Positions,* ed. L. M. Morgan and M. Michaels, 251–278. Philadelphia: University of Pennsylvania Press.

———. 1992. "Of Fetuses and Angels: Fragmentation and Integration in Narratives of Pregnancy Loss." Special issue of *Knowledge and Society,* ed. D. Hess and L. Layne, 9:29–58. Hartford, Conn.: JAI Press.

Layne, L., ed. 1998. *Transformative Motherhood: On Giving and Getting in a Consumer Culture.* New York: New York University Press.

Levins, H. 2005. "Talking Fetus Hawks Hamburgers for Carl's Jr.—And Other Current TV Commercials of Note." *Advertising Age,* April 11. Published online at AdAge.com.

Lubell, S. 2004. "The Womb as Photo Studio." *New York Times,* September 23, G1.

Luker, K. 1984. *Abortion and the Politics of Motherhood.* Berkeley: University of California Press.

Lutz, C. A. 1990. "Engendered Emotion: Gender, Power, and the Rhetoric of Emotional Control in American Discourse." In *Language and the Politics of Emotion,* ed. C. A. Lutz and L. Abu-Lughod, 69–91. Cambridge: Cambridge University Press.

Lykke, N., and M. Bryld. 2002. "Fra Rambo-sperm til Æggedroninger: To Versioner af Videnskabsfotografen Lennart Nilssons Film om det Menneskelige Forplantning." *Kvinder, Køn, og Forskning* [Denmark] 3.

MacDonald, M. 2007. *At Work in the Field of Birth: Midwifery Narratives of Nature, Tradition, and Home.* Nashville, Tenn.: Vanderbilt University Press.

Magnavita, N., L. Bevilacqua, P. Mirk, A. Fileni, and N. Castellino. 1999. "Work-Related Musculoskeletal Complaints in Sonologists." *Journal of Occupational and Environmental Medicine* 41(11):981–988.

Marcus, G. E. 1995. "Ethnography in/of the World System: The Emergence of Multi-Sited Ethnography." *Annual Review of Anthropology* 24:95–117.

Markens, S., C. Browner, and N. Press. 1997. "Feeding the Fetus: On Interrogating the Notion of Maternal-Fetal Conflict." *Feminist Studies* 23(2):351–372.

Marquand, R. 2004. "China Faces Future as Land of Boys." *Christian Science Monitor,* September 3. http://www.csmonitor.com/2004/0903/p01s03-woap.html. Accessed 8/22/06.

Martin, E. 1880. *Histoire des monstres depuis l'antiquité jusqu'à nos jours.* Paris: Reinwald.

Martin, E. 1998. "Anthropology and the Cultural Study of Science." *Science, Technology & Human Values* 23(1):24–44.

———. 1990. "The Egg and the Sperm: How Science Has Constructed a Romance Based on Stereotypical Male-Female Roles." *Signs: Journal of Women in Culture and Society* 16(3):485–501.

———. 1987. *The Woman in the Body: A Cultural Analysis of Reproduction.* Boston: Beacon Press.

Martin, J. A., B. E. Hamilton, P. D. Sutton, S. J. Ventura, F. Menacker, and M. L. Munson. 2005. "Births: Final Data for 2003." *National Vital Statistics Reports* 54(2). Hyattsville, Md.: National Center for Health Statistics.

Martin, J. A. 2006. Personal communication, 8/24/06.

Marx, L. 1997. "Technology: The Emergence of a Hazardous Concept." *Social Research* 64(3): 965–988.

Marx, L., and M. R. Smith. 1994. "Introduction." In *Does Technology Drive History? The Dilemma of Technological Determinism,* ed. M. R. Smith and L. Marx. Cambridge: MIT Press.

Mazzoni, C. 2002. *Maternal Impressions: Pregnancy and Childbirth in Literature and Theory.* Ithaca, N.Y.: Cornell University Press.

Merriam-Webster's Online. 2006. *http://www.m-w.com/dictionary.* Accessed 10/6/06.

Michaels, M. W. 1999. "Fetal Galaxies: Some Questions about What We See." In *Fetal Subjects, Feminist Positions,* ed. L. M. Morgan and M. W. Michaels, 113–132. Philadelphia: University of Pennsylvania Press.

Miller, B. 2001. "Female-Selective Abortion in Asia: Patterns, Policies, and Debates." *American Anthropologist* 103(4):1083–1095.

Miller, D. 2004. "How Infants Grow Mothers in North London." In *Consuming Motherhood,* ed. J. S. Taylor, L. L. Layne, and D. F. Wozniak, 31–51. New Brunswick, N.J.: Rutgers University Press.

———. 1998. *A Theory of Shopping.* Ithaca, N.Y.: Cornell University Press.

———. 1995. "Consumption and Commodities." *Annual Reviews in Anthropology* 24:141–161.

Mintz, S. 1985. *Sweetness and Power: The Place of Sugar in Modern History.* New York: Penguin.

Mitchell, L. M. 2001. *Baby's First Picture: Ultrasound and the Politics of Fetal Imaging.* Toronto: University of Toronto Press.

——. 1993. "Making Babies: Routine Ultrasound Imaging and the Cultural Construction of the Fetus in Montreal, Canada." Ph.D. dissertation, Case Western Reserve University, Cleveland, Ohio.

Mitchell, L. M., and E. Georges. 1997. "Cross-Cultural Cyborgs: Greek and Canadian Women's Discourses on Fetal Ultrasound." *Feminist Studies* 23(2):373–401.

Mitchell, W. J. T. 1986. *Iconology: Image, Text, Ideology.* Chicago: University of Chicago Press.

Mol, A. 2002. *The Body Multiple: Ontology in Medical Practice.* Durham, N.C.: Duke University Press.

Moore, R. M., Jr., L. L. Jeng, R. G. Kaczmarek, and P. J. Placek. 1990. "Use of Diagnostic Imaging Procedures and Fetal Monitoring Devices in the Care of Pregnant Women." *Public Health Reports* 105(5):471–475.

Morgan, L. M. In press, *Embryo Genesis: How a Handful of Scientists Shaped an American Origin Story.* Berkeley: University of California Press.

——. 2003. "Embryo Tales." In *Remaking Life and Death: Toward an Anthropology of the Biosciences,* ed. S. Franklin and M. Lock, 261–291. Albuquerque, N.M.: SAR Press.

——. 2000. "Magic and a Little Bit of Science: Technoscience, Ethnoscience, and the Social Construction of the Fetus." In *Bodies of Technology: Women's Involvement with Reproductive Medicine,* ed. A. R. Saetnan, N. Oudshoorn, and M. Kirejczyk, 355–367. Columbus: Ohio State University Press.

Morgan, L. M., and M. W. Michaels, eds. 1998. *Fetal Subjects, Feminist Positions.* Philadelphia: University of Pennsylvania Press.

Nathanson, B. N. 1984. *The Silent Scream.* Anaheim, Calif.: American Portrait Films.

National Institute of Family & Life Advocates (NIFLA). 2006. *http://www.nifla.org/tlc.asp.* Accessed 10/8/2006.

Navarro, V., ed. 2004. *The Political and Social Contexts of Health.* Amityville, N.Y.: Baywood Publishing.

New England Journal of Medicine. 2006. "Author Center." http://authors.nejm.org/Misc/Articles.asp#other. Accessed 10/6/06.

Newman, K. 1996. *Fetal Positions: Individualism, Science, Visuality.* Stanford, Calif.: Stanford University Press.

News Wave. 1994. "FDA Investigates Fetal Sonogram Video Businesses." *News Wave* 15(4).

Nilsson, L. 1966. *A Child Is Born: The Drama of Life before Birth in Unprecedented Photographs: A Practical Guide for the Expectant Mother.* Photos: L. Nilsson. Text: A. Ingelman-Sundberg [and] C. Wirsén. [Translated by B. Wirsén, C. Wirsén, and A. MacMillan.] New York: Delacorte Press.

Oakley, A. 1993. *Essays on Women, Medicine and Health.* Edinburgh, U.K.: Edinburgh University Press.

———. 1984. *The Captured Womb: A History of the Medical Care of Pregnant Women.* London: Basil Blackwell.

Oaks, L. 2001. *Smoking and Pregnancy: The Politics of Fetal Protection.* New Brunswick, N.J.: Rutgers University Press.

Ostrom, C. M. 2006. "'Keepsake' Ultrasounds: Should a Medical Device Be Used for Fun?" *Seattle Times,* June 25, M1.

Oxford English Dictionary. 2007. Oxford University Press. http://dictionary.oed.com. Accessed 6/13/2007.

Paoletti, J. B., and C. L. Kregloh. 1989. "The Children's Department." In *Men and Women: Dressing the Part,* ed. C. B. Kidwell and V. Steele, 22–41. Washington, D.C.: Smithsonian Institution Press.

Paxson, H. 2004. *Making Modern Mothers: Ethics and Family Planning in Urban Greece.* Berkeley: University of California Press.

Petchesky, R. P. 1987. "Foetal Images: The Power of Visual Images in the Politics of Reproduction." In *Reproductive Technologies: Gender, Motherhood, and Medicine,* ed. M. Stanworth, 57–80. Minneapolis: University of Minnesota Press.

Pickering, A. 1995. *The Mangle of Practice: Time, Agency, and Science.* Chicago: University of Chicago Press.

Pietz, W. 1987. "The Problem of the Fetish, II." *Res* 13:23–46.

———. 1985. "The Problem of the Fetish, I." *Res* 9:5–17.

Pinkney, N. 2005. "'Keepsake' Ultrasound Raises Medical Hackles: Entrepreneurs Pursue Parents, but Physicians Cite Potential Risks of Unnecessary Scanning." *Diagnostic Imaging* 27(1):57–61.

Pinto-Correia, C. 1997. *The Ovary of Eve: Egg, Sperm, and Preformation.* Chicago: University of Chicago Press.

Pitkin, R. M. 1991. "Screening and Detection of Congenital Malformations." *American Journal of Obstetrics and Gynecology* 164(4):1045–1048.

Proctor, R. 1995. "The Destruction of 'Lives Not Worth Living.'" In *Deviant Bodies: Critical Perspectives on Difference in Science and Popular Culture,* ed. J. Terry and J. Urla, 170–196. Bloomington: Indiana University Press.

"The PR Quagmire." 2005. *MedGadget: Internet Journal of Emerging Medical Technologies,* November 30. http://www.medgadget.com/archives/2005/11/the_pr_quagmire.html. Accessed 10/8/06.

Putnam, J. 2005. "Bill Calls for Ultrasound Photo of Fetus before Abortion." *Booth Newspapers* [Michigan], Lansing Bureau, May 4. Published online at http://www.mlive.com.

Rabinow, P., and T. Dan-Cohen. 2005. *A Machine to Make a Future: Biotech Chronicles.* Princeton, N.J.: Princeton University Press.

Rados, C. 2004. "FDA Cautions against Ultrasound 'Keepsake' Images." *FDA Consumer Magazine* 38(1):12–16.

Rapp, R. 1999. *Testing Women, Testing the Fetus: The Social Impact of Amniocentesis in America.* New York: Routledge.

———. 1995. "Heredity, or: Revising the Facts of Life." In *Naturalizing Power,* ed. Sylvia Yanagisako, 69–86. New York: Routledge.

———. 1993. "Accounting for Amniocentesis." In *Knowledge, Power, and Practice: The Anthropology of Medicine and Everyday Life,* ed. S. Lindenbaum and M. Lock, 55–76. Berkeley: University of California Press.

Rhodes, L. A. 2002. "Psychopathy and the Face of Control in Supermax." *Ethnography* 3(4):442–466.

Richard, S. 2007. "George's Story." http://unborn.com/george-text.htm. Accessed 11/09/07.

Rivera, P. V. 2002. "Sonography Grows in Stature: New Technology Brings New Career Field." *Seattle Times,* February 24, HI.

Roberts, D. 1997. *Killing the Black Body: Race, Reproduction, and the Meaning of Liberty.* New York: Vintage.

Rothman, B. K. 2000. *Recreating Motherhood: Ideology and Technology in a Patriarchal Society.* New Brunswick, N.J.: Rutgers University Press.

———. 1993. *The Tentative Pregnancy: Prenatal Diagnosis and the Future of Motherhood.* New York: Viking.

Saetnan, A. R. 2000. "Thirteen Women's Narratives of Pregnancy, Ultrasound and Self." In *Bodies of Technology: Women's Involvement with Reproductive Medicine,* ed. A. R. Saetnan, N. Oudshoorn, and M. Kirejczyk, 331–354. Columbus: Ohio State University Press.

———. 1996. "Ultrasonic Discourse: Contested Meanings of Gender and Technology in the Norwegian Ultrasound Screening Debate." *European Journal of Women's Studies* 3(I):55–75.

Sahlins, M. 2000. "Colors and Cultures." In *Culture in Practice: Selected Essays.* New York: Zone Books.

———. 1996. "The Sadness of Sweetness: The Native Anthropology of Western Cosmology." *Current Anthropology* 37(3):395–428.

Sandelowski, M. 1994. "Separate, but Less Unequal: Fetal Ultrasonography and the Transformation of Expectant Mother/Fatherhood." *Gender & Society* 8(2):230–245.

———. 1993. *With Child in Mind: Studies of the Personal Encounter with Infertility* Philadelphia: University of Pennsylvania Press.

Scheper-Hughes, N. 1992. *Death without Weeping: The Violence of Everyday Life in Brazil.* Berkeley: University of California Press.

———. 1985. "Culture, Scarcity, and Maternal Thinking: Maternal Detachment and Infant Survival in a Brazilian Shantytown." *Ethos* 13(4):291–317.

Scheper-Hughes, N., and L. Wacquant, eds. 2002. *Commodifying Bodies.* London: Sage.

Schindehette, S., and E. Finan. 2004. "Ultrasound, Ultrasafe? While Photographic Unborn Babies Is a Booming Business, Some Experts Are Questioning the Dangers." *People* 61(23):III.

Schmid, R. E. 2006. "Ultrasound Scans Can Affect Brain Development." *Seattle Times,* August 8, page?.

Schmidt, L. E. 1995. *Consumer Rites: The Buying and Selling of American Holidays.* Princeton, N.J.: Princeton University Press.

Sen, A. 2003. "Missing Women—Revisited." *British Medical Journal* 327:1297–1298.

Sered, S. S., and R. Fernandopulle. 2005. *Uninsured in America: Life and Death in the Land of Opportunity.* Berkeley: University of California Press.

Sharp, L. A. 2006. *Strange Harvest: Organ Transplants, Denatured Bodies, and the Transformed Self.* Berkeley: University of California Press.

———. 2001. "Commodified Kin: Death, Mourning, and Competing Claims on the Bodies of Organ Donors in the United States." *American Anthropologist* 103(1):112–133.

———. 2000. "The Commodification of the Body and Its Parts." *Annual Reviews in Anthropology* 29(1):287–328.

Silliman, J. 2003. "Science, Politics, and Reproductive Rights: The Case of Ultrasound Technology." *Different Takes* 18. Hampshire College Population and Development Program. http://popdev.hampshire.edu/projects/dt/pdfs/DifferenTakes_18.pdf.

Sjögren, B. 1988. "Parental Attitudes to Prenatal Information about the Sex of the Fetus." *Acta Obstetrica Gynecologia Scandinavia* 67:43–46.

Slater, L. 2004. *Opening Skinner's Box: Great Psychological Experiments of the Twentieth Century.* New York: W. W. Norton.

Smith, M. R., and L. Marx. 1994. "Introduction." In *Does Technology Drive History? The Dilemma of Technological Determinism,* ed. M. R. Smith and L. Marx, 2–35. Cambridge, Mass.: MIT Press.

Society of Diagnostic Medical Sonography (SDMS). 2004. "SDMS Position Statement: Non-Diagnostic Use of Ultrasound." http://www.sdms.org/positions/nondiagnostic.asp. Accessed 10/06/06.

Sorgen, C. 2006. "Bonding with Baby before Birth." WebMD Feature Archive. http://my.webmd.com/content/Article/57/66217.htm?pagenumber=1. Accessed 8/7/06.

Spyer, P. 1997. "Introduction." In *Border Fetishisms: Material Objects in Unstable Spaces,* ed. P. Spyer, I–II. New York and London: Routledge.

Stabile, C. A. 1999. "The Traffic in Fetuses." In *Fetal Subjects, Feminist Positions,* ed. L. M. Morgan and M. W. Michaels, 133–158. Philadelphia: University of Pennsylvania Press.

———. 1994. *Feminism and the Technological Fix.* Manchester, U.K.: Manchester University Press.

Stafford, B. M. 1993. *Body Criticism: Imaging the Unseen in Enlightenment Art and Medicine.* Cambridge, Mass.: MIT Press.

Stricherz, M. 2002. "Bonding with Baby: Why Ultrasound Is Turning Women against Abortion." *Crisis: Politics, Culture & the Church,* December 2.

Sullivan, A. 2000. "What's So Bad about Hate?" In *Best American Essays, 2000,* ed. Alan Lightman. Series ed. Robert Atwan. Boston: Houghton Mifflin.

Taussig, K. S. forthcoming. *Ordinary Genomes.* Durham, N.C.: Duke University Press.

Taussig, K. S., R. Rapp, and D. Heath. 2003. "Flexible Eugenics: Technologies of the Self in the Age of Genomics." In *Genetic Nature/Culture: Anthropology and Science beyond the Two-Culture Divide,* ed. A. H. Goodman, D. Heath, and M. S. Lindee, 58–76. Berkeley: University of California Press.

Taylor, J. S. 2005. "Surfacing the Body Interior." *Annual Review of Anthropology* 34:741–756.

———. 2004a. "Introduction." In *Consuming Motherhood,* ed. J. S. Taylor, L. L. Layne, and D. F. Wozniak, 1–16. New Brunswick, N.J.: Rutgers University Press.

———. 2004b. "A Fetish Is Born: Sonographers and the Making of the Public Fetus." In *Consuming Motherhood,* ed. J. S. Taylor, L. L. Layne, and D. F. Wozniak, 187–210. New Brunswick, N.J.: Rutgers University Press.

———. 2000. "Of Sonograms and Baby Prams: Prenatal Diagnosis, Pregnancy, and Consumption." *Feminist Studies* 26(2):391–418.

———. 1999. "Mediating Reproduction: An Ethnography of Obstetrical Ultrasound." Ph.D. dissertation, University of Chicago.

———. 1998. "Image of Contradiction: Obstetrical Ultrasound in American Culture." In *Reproducing Reproduction: Kinship, Power, and Technological Innovation,* ed. S. Franklin and H. Ragoné, 15–45. Philadelphia: University of Pennsylvania Press.

———. 1992. "The Public Fetus and the Family Car: From Abortion Politics to a Volvo Advertisement." *Public Culture* 4(2):167–183

Taylor, J. S., L. L. Layne, and D. F. Wozniak, eds. 2004. *Consuming Motherhood.* New Brunswick, N.J.: Rutgers University Press.

ThreeDSono. http://www.threedsono.com/article4.html. Accessed 8/13/04.

Tucker, R. C., ed. 1978. *The Marx-Engels Reader.* New York: W. W. Norton.

Turner, V. 1967. *The Forest of Symbols: Aspects of Ndembu Ritual.* Ithaca, N.Y.: Cornell University Press.

U.S. Department of Health and Human Services, National Institutes of Health, Office of Medical Applications of Research. 1984. "Diagnostic Ultrasound Imaging in Pregnancy." *National Institutes of Health Consensus Development Conference Consensus,* Statement 5(1).

U.S. Department of Labor, Bureau of Labor Statistics. 2002. "Health Technologists, Technicians, and Healthcare Support Occupations." Bulletin 2540–9. http://www.bls.gov/oco/reprints/ocor009.pdf.

U.S. House of Representatives Committee on Government Reform Minority Staff Special Investigations Division. 2006. *False and Misleading Health Information Provided by Federally Funded Pregnancy Resource Centers.* http://oversight.house.gov/documents/20060717101140–30092.pdf.

van Biema, D. 1999. "Who Are Those Guys?" *Time,* August 9, 52–53.

Van Dijck, J. 2005. *The Transparent Body: A Cultural Analysis of Medical Imaging.* Seattle: University of Washington Press.

van Kammen, J. 2003. "Who Represents the Users? Critical Encounters between Women's Health Advocates and Scientists in Contraceptive R&D." In *How Users Matter: The Co-Construction of Users and Technologies,* ed. N. Oudshoorn and T. Pinch, 151–171. Cambridge, Mass: MIT Press.

"Viewpoints: Abortion." 2004, July 29. BBC News U.K. Edition.

Watts, K. 2003. "Kristi's Baby: First Photos from Inside the Womb." *The 700 Club,* July 1. http://www.cbn.com/700club/features/kristi_baby.aspx. Accessed 10/6/06.

Wertz, D. C., and J. C. Fletcher. 1989. "Fatal Knowledge? Prenatal Diagnosis and Sex Selection." *Hastings Center Report* 19(3):21–27.

Wertz, D. C., and R. W. Wertz. 1989. *Lying-In: A History of Childbirth in America.* New Haven, Conn.: Yale University Press.

West, C. 1994. "Hill Sentenced to Life in Prison on Federal Charge." Reuters News Service, December 2.

Winner, L. 1986. *The Whale and the Reactor: A Search for Limits in an Age of High Technology.* Chicago: University of Chicago Press.

"Womb View Boost for Expectant Parents." 2001. BBC News http://news.bbc.co.uk/2/hi/health/1424021.stm. Accessed 10/6/06.

Wozniak, D. F. 2004. " 'What Will I Do With All the Toys Now?': Consumption and the Signification of Kinship in U.S. Fostering Relationships." In *Consuming Motherhood,* ed. J. S. Taylor, L. L. Layne, and D. F. Wozniak, 72–99. New Brunswick, N.J.: Rutgers University Press.

Yoxen, Ed. 1987. "Seeing with Sound: A Study of the Development of Medical Images." In *The Social Construction of Technological Systems: New Directions in the Sociology and History of Technology,* ed. W. E. Bijker, T. P. Hughes, and T. Pinch, 281–303. Cambridge, Mass.: MIT Press.

INDEX

abortion: and cost-benefit assessments, 63–64, 119–120; dread of, 62–64; fetal reduction in multiple pregnancies, 94; legislation requiring women to view sonograms before, 94, 162; regret after, 49; selective, after prenatal diagnosis, 5, 9, 62–65, 91–92, 119–120, 171, 178n2; selective, after sex determination, 10, 30, 122–123, 171; ultrasound as dissuading women from, 4, 42–51, 89–95, 160–161; ultrasound influencing public policy on, 160–161; ultrasound preparatory to, 4, 44–45, 49–50, 54; women's reasons for considering, 88, 90–92

abortion clinics, 52; bogus (*see* Crisis Pregnancy Centers)

abortion politics, 1, 76, 140; and commodification of medicine, 146; ethnographic research on 18, 127. *See also* antiabortion activists and organizations; Crisis Pregnancy Centers; feminists; pro-choice; pro-life; reproductive freedom and rights

abstinence-education grants, 163

ACLU Reproductive Freedom Project, 130

adoption, 97

ADR, 34–36

Adrian, S., 16

advertisements, 64, 125; antiabortion, 14, 42–49; AT&T, 107–111; Carl's Jr. Hamburgers, 128–129; Volvo cars, 1–3, 169

ALARA ("as low [exposure] as reasonably achievable"), 58

Amazon.com, 166

American College of Obstetricians and Gynecologists (ACOG), 55, 68, 74

American College of Radiology, 146

American Institute of Ultrasound in Medicine (AIUM), 55, 73–74, 83, 146, 157, 166

American Medical Association (AMA), 37

American Registry of Diagnostic Medical Sonography, 31, 37, 146, 175n3

amniocentesis, 54, 56, 91, 133

anthropology, 3, 6, 20. *See also* ethnographic research

antiabortion activists and organizations: advertisements, 14, 42–49; Care Net, 163; DeMoss Foundation, 42–49, 176n10; Focus on the Family, 162–163; P. Hill, 52, 76; Informed Choice Act, 163; and keepsake ultrasound, 161–168; The Life Choice (TLC) Project, 164; media and publications, 82–83, 160–161; National Institute of Family and Life Advocates (NIFLA), 164–165; National Right to Life Committee, 44; professional identity of, 50; The Psalm 139 Project, 162; reproductive history of, 50; S. Richard, 44–50, 162–163, 176n11; Southern Baptist Convention, 162–163; use of fetal imagery, 3, 28; use of ultrasound, 4, 24, 42–52, 64, 76–115, 144, 170. *See also* abortion politics; Crisis Pregnancy Centers; pro-life

Appadurai, A., 126, 135

Arney, W. R., 96–100

AT&T advertisement, 107–111

attachment, *see* bonding

BabyCenter, 124, 166

baby shower, 126

Bagby, D., 164

Baker, J. P., 31–34, 37–38, 176n14

Barrett, J., 52

BBC News, 160

"behavioral benefits" of ultrasound, 60–61, 86–88, 164, 171. *See also* bonding; psychological benefits of ultrasound; reassurance; *see under* ultrasound examination

Belly Beats, 166

Benacerraf, B., 147

197

ABOUT THE AUTHOR

JANELLE S. TAYLOR is associate professor of anthropology at the University of Washington. She co-edited the 2004 collection *Consuming Motherhood* (Rutgers University Press), and has written on other topics including "surrogate decision makers" in end-of-life care, and "cultural competence" in medical education.